Words of praise for *Bamboozled*

"Angela McGlowan is definitely a forceful voice in communities of color. *Bamboozled* is exhaustively researched, deftly-written, and chock-full of personal interviews with political leaders from both sides of the aisle. A must read to get the other side's point of view."
—*The Afro-American*

"Some may not agree with Angela McGlowan's political perspective; but there's no denying she's a rising star in the conservative movement. *Bamboozled* is a hard hitting and sobering look into uncharted territory. She is someone that we'll be keeping our eye on."
—Judge Joe Brown

"Read this book and see in living color that one can be black and Republican and still be an informed and dedicated member of our race, committed to building instead of acting out."
—John McWhorter, author, *Winning the Race*

D1281732

BAMBOOZLED

BAMBOOZLED

How Americans Are Being Exploited
by the Lies of the Liberal Agenda

ANGELA McGLOWAN

THOMAS NELSON
Since 1798

NASHVILLE   DALLAS   MEXICO CITY   RIO DE JANEIRO   BEIJING

© 2007 by Angela McGlowan

All rights reserved. No portion of this book may be reproduced, stored in a retrieval system, or transmitted in any form or by any means—electronic, mechanical, photocopy, recording, scanning, or other—except for brief quotations in critical reviews or articles, without the prior written permission of the publisher.

Published in Nashville, Tennessee, by Thomas Nelson. Thomas Nelson is a registered trademark of Thomas Nelson, Inc.

Thomas Nelson, Inc. titles may be purchased in bulk for educational, business, fundraising, or sales promotional use. For information, please e-mail SpecialMarkets@thomasnelson.com.

Library of Congress Cataloging-in-Publication data on file with the Library of Congress.

ISBN: 978-1-59555-090-3 (HC)
ISBN: 978-1-59555-336-2 (TP)

Printed in the United States of America

09 10 11 — 6 5 4 3 2 1

In loving memory of my father, Reverend James Thomas McGlowan, an educator, a builder, a man who inspired all who knew him: a man who refused to be bamboozled.

Don't be afraid to see what you see.

—Ronald Reagan

Oh, I say and I say it again, ya been had!

Ya been took!

Ya been hoodwinked!

Bamboozled!

—Malcolm X

TABLE OF CONTENTS

CONTENTS

THE LIBERAL DILEMMA: BAMBOOZLE OR BUST?

You think the Republican National Committee
could get this many people of color in a single room?
Only if they had the hotel staff in here.

—Democratic National Chairman Howard Dean
  speaking words of white liberal condescension

Forget about red states versus blue states. Forget about all the other cleverly tagged groups bandied about on the Sunday talk shows: the Blue Dog Democrats versus the progressives, the value voting Republicans versus the fiscal conservatives. Forget about the free traders, the isolationists, the independents, the newly popular populists. Forget about all of them and focus on this: three constituencies alone hold the power to control the political playing field in the 2008 presidential campaign—and the political future of this country for decades to come.

These critical groups are women, Latinos, and blacks. For years, liberals thought they had a lock on the votes of all three. Through a combination of spin, scare tactics, and deception, liberals have manipulated millions of these Americans controlling their minds and taking their votes for granted.

But the liberal grip is finally loosening. New technologies and greater access to information have begun exposing a half-century's worth of liberal fallacies. Women, Latinos, and blacks are beginning to find the facts and see the light—and liberals, Democrats, and the American political landscape are about to undergo a major sea change.

If liberals know anything, if there is anything of which they are certain, surely it is this: when Americans aren't completely bamboozled, liberals lose—big time. Consider, for example, the 2004 presidential election and the pivotal battleground state of Ohio. In 2000, 9 percent of black voters cast ballots for then governor George W. Bush. In 2004, that number grew to 16 percent, a modest increase of just seven percentage points. This slight improvement hardly represented a major shift of black public opinion, and yet it all but cinched the state of Ohio for President Bush and gave him another four years in the White House.

So what changed? Why did this band of black Ohioans break with past voting behavior? Answer: these voters woke up and realized that they had been conned into supporting a political party whose liberal agenda stood in direct conflict with many of their most deeply held core values. This group of courageous black voters rejected liberals' time-worn "smear and fear" tactics. Put another way, these blacks realized they'd been bamboozled.

We've been bamboozled and we didn't even know it. These brave Ohioans left the plantation protesting with their votes. They refused to stand by and let the liberal neo-slavemaster have his way as he did for centuries during a time when our race was raped, lynched, and pillaged. Oh a change is gonna come! A change is coming!

One man who knows a lot about Ohio is Ken Blackwell, 2006

Republican gubernatorial candidate and the first black elected to a statewide executive office as state treasurer in 1994 and later secretary of state in 1998. I asked Secretary Blackwell how President Bush had increased his support among black Ohioans:

> There was a real responsiveness by a growing set of the black community in Ohio to many of the elements in the president's agenda. His initiative to expand home ownership, his initiative to expand community-based health clinics, his initiative and defense of traditional marriage as a union between one man and a one woman, all of a sudden he was speaking to those folks who had shared his agenda, shared his interests, and, I think, shared his basket of values across economic, social, and cultural lines. There is a tendency by political operatives to think of blacks in monolithic terms. They think that we are not capable of individual thought, but that we are all saddled to groupthink. So they miss the point that there are many blacks that believe that government must protect innocent life, that government and public policy must defend and protect the institution of marriage.[1]

The Ohio experience demonstrates what liberals have long known—that even tiny flashes of ideological emancipation can grind the liberal locomotive to a halt—or cause a train wreck. Liberals must either bamboozle blacks or go bust. A former elected Democrat and United States senator, Zell Miller, explains, "The magic formula for the Democratic nominee to win against a Republican has been to get 40 percent of the white vote and 90 percent of the black vote. Increasingly, it has been easier to get the latter. But the margin of black votes for liberal policies is likely to change soon. And it has to change only a fraction to make a huge difference."[2]

When women and people of color flee this plantation, liberal power fizzles. For this reason, the foot soldiers of liberalism remain tireless in their efforts to saddle us with dependency-inducing policies; policies that mire us in poverty, squelch enterprise, and snuff out self-reliance and individual initiative. Better to keep Americans fearful, distracted, and angry at the conservative "white" establishment. Liberals figure it is better to convince women, Latinos, and blacks that Republicans are racist, sexist oppressors of minorities. The mainstream liberal media wants us to believe that the only minorities in the Republican Party are tokens, sell-outs, "Oreos," and "Uncle Toms." They claim that those who vote Republican are out of touch with reality. Not because liberals hate minorities; most don't. Rather, liberals know that any ebb in support for liberal policies could trigger seismic electoral shifts. So, liberals make a Machiavellian decision to manipulate minorities to keep their agenda on track.

How have they pulled it off? How have they successfully conned so many Americans to blindly support the liberal agenda? If there is one question that baffles conservatives and terrifies liberals it is this: "Why in the *world* would any American vote for the ultra-liberal agenda?" Especially minorities! Yet statistics demonstrate that 90 percent of black voters vote the straight Democratic ticket and a majority of Latinos do as well.

It's a smart question, and this high level of voter loyalty is really ironic, especially in the case of blacks whose ancestors were literally put in chains by Democrats. But even when focusing on women and Latinos, the true record of Democrats is almost as abysmal. The truth is that from its Ku Klux Klan past and antisuffrage sentiments to its liberal exploitative present, the liberal agenda has been, over time, a wrecking ball that destroys self-empowerment and individual advancement. But herein lies the problem: most Americans don't know what they don't know.

This party's murderous history of oppression, lynching, and intimidation has been hidden so well for so long that the mere mention of it seems conspiratorial rather than factual.

So, for example, when we visit the history section of the Democratic National Committee (DNC) website, we will overlook the fact that there is no mention of the Democratic Party's stance on slavery, or much of anything it did prior to 1960 for black Americans except for President Harry S Truman's efforts to integrate the military. And this from a party that never misses a chance to breathlessly assert its credentials as the "pro-equality" and "pro-civil rights" party.

By contrast, the Republican National Committee's (RNC) website history section recounts the great battles the party waged to end slavery and its struggle to win battle after battle for civil rights for all Americans.³ But the Democratic Party remains curiously silent on these matters. *Strange*, a young Democrat surfing her party's website might think to herself, *but I'm sure it's just a DNC oversight. And besides, I don't have time to give it much thought. I'm running out the door to attend one of the biggest party events of the year, the annual Jefferson-Jackson Dinner.* Jackson, as in Andrew Jackson—the co-founder of the Democrat Party and a virulent racist.⁴ And Jefferson, as in Thomas Jefferson, a widowed Southern slave owner, who reputedly fathered many of his own slaves.⁵ The irony would be funny if it weren't so sad. And so the hypocrisy goes unchallenged.

But surely you must be mistaken; I thought those evil conservative Republicans were the ones who historically held our people down? That's what liberals *need* us to believe. How else are liberals going to dupe overwhelming numbers of women and minorities into voting for liberal policies each and every time they enter the voting booth? How else are liberals going to make whites feel guilty for the past sins of murderous racists who were Democrats? Again, the irony would be comical if the consequences weren't so devastating. The reason this strategy works is that many Americans—black and white—live in a haze of historical amnesia. That doesn't mean they're bad people. It means they've been *bamboozled.*

Astute students of history know the facts: they know which political party produced the first black U.S. senator, Hiram Revels; they haven't forgotten which political party won passage of the Thirteenth Amendment, Fourteenth Amendment, Fifteenth Amendment, and the Civil Rights Act of 1957; they know who authored and introduced the Civil Rights Act of 1960. They know which party thwarted attempts to filibuster and kill the Civil Rights Act of 1964 and which party has the audacity to have a former "Grand Kleagle" of the Ku Klux Klan (KKK) roaming the floors of the United States Senate still *today.* They know all about senator Robert Byrd, whose party elected him to serve eight years as its Senate majority leader. These history buffs also know which party backed the women's suffrage movement from the beginning and which party gave America its first female Supreme Court Justice. They also know which party originally created the idea of affirmative action. Yes, citizens who know the facts of history know all of these things. They know that it wasn't the Democrats. They know that President Kennedy opposed the "March on Washington" and was even embarrassed by the sight of the large gathering of blacks on the Mall.[6] They know that the only former Klansman Democrat in the United States Senate voted against both of the only blacks nominated to the United States Supreme Court.[7]

But what about those Americans who don't know their history?

I'm delighted that Democrats in the 1960s joined with Republicans who, once again, were busy doing the heavy lifting they've done throughout American history of ensuring passage of yet another series of civil rights bills. How Democrats managed to snatch the civil rights moniker from the party of Lincoln is one of the greatest heists in history. And the fact is that Democrats portray themselves as the leaders of women's rights and history ignores the fact that Woodrow Wilson only reluctantly signed onto the Nineteenth Amendment granting women's suffrage. And he only did so after a Republican senator from Tennessee provided the final vote for passage.[8]

Today FDR ranks as one of America's greatest presidents, but history reveals that the four-term president did little for blacks directly, despite wife Eleanor's efforts to promote federal anti-lynching legislation. FDR was unwilling to risk losing World War II or sacrifice his New Deal agenda by forcing his Southern Democratic senators to accept racial justice in America. Harry Truman, FDR's successor, finally integrated the military after World War II had been won and yet, as we will see, Truman was unwilling to push through federal civil rights bills.

From the dawn of the twentieth century it was the Democrats (primarily those from the South, but aided and abetted by their northern enablers) who were on the wrong side of racial and gender justice. History reveals that it was men like Everett Dirksen and Dwight Eisenhower who strongly supported racial equality even in the face of filibusters and other roadblocks put forward by Democrats. After the Supreme Court upheld Louisiana's "separate but equal" policy in 1896, Democrats were emboldened, believing they now had the Constitution on their side.[9] In fact, the lion's share of America's civil rights battle would never have had to be waged had it not been necessary to reverse the Democrats' policies.

Conservatives don't feel the need to proclaim their commitment to "equality for all" for this simple reason: the Republican Party, from its founding, has been the party for equality. When you've been in "the business" for 150 years, you hardly feel promoting your own record is necessary. Liberals, on the other hand, are understandably wracked with guilt. As liberal author Paul Waldman only half-jokingly concedes, "Many liberals are congenitally gloomy folk."[10] Well, of course they are! How can they not be? Look at the legacy to which they've hitched themselves! Someone asked me about this recently. They wanted to know why I thought so many liberals seem so unhappy and negative. "Don't be so hard on our liberal friends," I said. "After all, if your ideology required you to vote for a political party with a racist history like theirs, you would be gloomy too!"

Fair enough, says the Democrat, but aren't the sins of Democrats all in the past? Aren't liberal leaders today different? What about all the amazing achievements liberal Democrats have won for women and minorities?

Once again: you've been bamboozled.

Post-Jim Crow, the poor and disadvantaged have been used and exploited by Democrats to advance an abysmal policy agenda that has produced catastrophic results. Generational welfare dependency, a near-fatherless generation, soaring criminal delinquency, rampant drug addiction, and disastrous educational results are all legacies of the liberal establishment. The Great Society that liberals promised has turned out to be the "Great Travesty."

For decades, liberals have masterminded the exploitation of the downtrodden, often in the name of helping them. To achieve their broader aims to change American society, liberals have successfully bamboozled minorities. Why should women, blacks, and Latinos be loyal to a party that has been so disloyal to them? The answer to this question is simple. They shouldn't; but as long as they remain ignorant of the true goals of liberals, liberals will stay in power. And since power corrupts, over time the oppressors have become absolutely corrupted!

Liberalism is a political philosophy that believes that traditions and dogmas often restrict freedom and individual autonomy, and that the resources of big government should be marshaled to engineer equality in society without regard to whether individual property rights are protected. In contrast, conservatism is a political philosophy that generally favors free markets, traditional values, and a strong national defense. On issues ranging from school prayer, the war on terror, and tax relief for small businesses, conservatives can be counted on to promote policies that reflect their philosophy.

None of this is to say that conservatives are blameless for the limited number of minorities in the Republican Party. We must ask: why aren't there more women and people of color in the party?

Unfortunately, clumsy communications, a reluctance to challenge the shameless tactics of liberal leaders, and a lack of appreciation for grassroots politics go a long way toward explaining why the Left has successfully exploited minorities in America for so long. But even if conservatives weren't clumsy or reluctant to challenge the tactics of the Left, the Left would still continue to engage in its tactics. Why? Because the truth is that without blacks, Latinos, and women, liberals aren't politically viable. And thus, they have to continue the same old, tired, race-baiting scare tactics.

The Grand Old Party is not, nor has it ever been, perfect. There have been times when the GOP has fumbled the mission of its founding. But if the cause of liberty and equality were to be measured over time on a balanced scale, with the efforts of Republicans on one side and the efforts of Democrats on the other, the Republican side would easily tip the scales. Fighting for freedom and equality has always been an overwhelmingly Republican project. Furthermore, on issues that relate most to the poor and people of color, such as school choice, welfare reform, empowerment zones, expanding businesses, home ownership, the sanctity of marriage, and the right to life, conservative prescriptions are best. As former RNC chairman Ken Mehlman and incoming chairman Mel Martinez demonstrate, the GOP is increasingly showing a willingness to fight aggressively for every vote.

And a fight will be needed, because liberals have begun looking elsewhere to new and emerging populations to exploit. The battle in the twenty-first century will be waged over the Latino vote. Latinos, who are the fastest growing demographic group in America, have liberals and conservatives vying for their votes. Latinos' conservative values, support for family, faith, and work make them natural supporters for the Republican Party. But liberals believe that they can overcome these conservative traits. And to keep their agenda intact, they have to.

It's actually pretty easy to see why liberals view Central and South American illegal aliens as a group ripe for exploitation. These aliens are often poor, uneducated, discontented with their economic plight, decent, and unfamiliar with American history—and liberals believe that they can be manipulated easily.

Liberals see in the waves of illegal immigrants that breach our nation's borders the raw human material with which they can repair, renovate, and expand the now-rickety big government welfare state that liberals built in the 1960s. Latinos are now being bamboozled the same way women and blacks have been for the last forty years. Cynically, in order to thrive, liberalism needs a new host from which to drain support. Latinos are now the prime targets.

The targeting starts immediately upon their arrival. Instead of being called illegal aliens, liberals insist on labeling them "undocumented workers" and welcoming them into America with open arms. Undocumented workers? They aren't employees who have lost their papers they are people who have entered the country illegally, and therefore, they are working here illegally.

In March 2006, millions of Americans were shocked when they turned on their televisions and saw hundreds of thousands of protestors supporting illegal immigration. Many of these protestors were themselves illegal aliens. They brazenly waved Mexican flags as they protested the "oppressive" and "racist" America. The U.S. Senate's "liberal lion," Ted Kennedy, decided to pounce. The Kennedy clan, along with Lyndon Baines Johnson, had long ago written the book on how to bamboozle minorities, especially blacks. It would only take minor modifications to use the same playbook to bamboozle Latinos.

As BBC reporter Nick Bryant has written, "The Kennedy administration taught Washington an ugly political lesson: that politicians could win black support through grand, symbolic gestures, which obviated the need for truly substantive reforms."[11] Thus, in an effort to conflate Dr. Martin Luther King Jr.'s civil rights legacy with Mexicans breaking into the country, Ted Kennedy telegraphed the liberal playbook for the decade to come, saying: "More than four decades ago, near this place, Martin Luther King called on the nation to let freedom ring. It is time for Americans to lift their voices now, in pride for our immigrant past and in pride for our immigrant future."

The third group upon which the liberal exploitation program depends is women. Myrna Blyth, the former editor-in-chief of *Ladies' Home Journal*, says that "there is a liberal tilt in the media aimed especially at women." This liberal targeting, says Blyth, means that "stories in the media are masterfully spun for a woman's audience to tug fiercely at our emotions."[12] This goes a long way toward explaining why liberals' often hysterical rants are rooted in emotion-laden appeals designed to pluck our more sensitive, nurturing heartstrings. Thus the tired old mantra that conservatives are mean-spirited white male troglodytes is unlikely to cease anytime soon.

For those women who've been hurt or disappointed by men in their lives, liberals package and market their emotional appeals in a sterner, more jaded form—it's called feminism. Bamboozling these women means filling their heads with alarmist rhetoric that validates their negative male preconceptions: *Men are all misogynists! Marriage is a manmade institution designed to oppress women! Men earn more than you do! Aborting your baby is empowering!* This is the mantra spewed by radical feminists. The majority of women and people of color, of course, are often unaware of the actions of these radicals on the left.

Sadly, many young women follow this dangerous propaganda. Girls growing up in fatherless homes where they are starved for positive, healthy, male attention are vulnerable, especially if their mothers bought the feminist lie from a movement that portrayed fathers as little more than wallets, and otherwise worthless. These girls nurse hollow hearts, voids only a father can fill. And that's where liberals rush in. "Sister, have no fear!" feminists say. "Liberalism is here!" "A little girl needs a father like a fish needs a bicycle!"

Wrong.

A little girl needs a father who will be there, a dad who will take the time to love her, to build her up and make her strong in the knowledge that she is special, protected, and loved. The truth is that strong marriages, especially those between men and women of faith, ultimately are politically disastrous for the liberal agenda. And that's why, as this book will reveal, liberals have at best turned a blind eye toward the erosion of the institution of the family and at worst have cheered its destruction.

My inspiration in writing this book is my father. For most of his life, my father, the Reverend James Thomas McGlowan, lived in Oxford, Mississippi, the place where I was born and reared. He and Mother were married for twenty-five years before he passed away when I was a child. Father was a remarkable and beautiful man. Mother likes to say that Father's determination and ambition were the result of having to take care of her and my four siblings. But in truth, I think his vision and drive had been there all along.

In the twentieth century Deep South, my father was a rarity. James Thomas McGlowan was a professor; a United Methodist minister in the Mississippi Delta with an undergraduate degree, and two master's degrees; and a doctoral candidate who was writing a manuscript focusing on literary titan William Faulkner's belief in empowerment in the black community. My father was selected by the William Faulkner Foundation and received his second master's degree at Hampton University under the auspices of this organization. Yes, I'd say my father was something of an anomaly. But what was truly rare, what set him apart, was his deep appreciation for education and history and their many lessons. He taught us that you have to know your past before you can chart your future, and that the only person who can ever control your destiny is you. Father was passionate about our certainty of our own future, by consistently stating, "Any man who knows where he is going, the world will step aside and let him pass on to a great destiny. Keep moving towards your goal, meditate on the road ahead, and success will crown your efforts." Father articulated self-reliance, self-sufficiency, and independent responsibility at every opportunity. I can still hear his voice reciting one of his favorite Henry Wadsworth Longfellow quotations:

> *The heights by great men reached and kept,*
> *Were not obtained by sudden flight.*
> *But they, while their companions slept,*
> *Were toiling upward in the night.*

My father lived those words. And maybe that's why throughout his life he supported both Democrats and Republicans, based on the issues that would create not a better black America but a better

America. "Republican" was not considered a dirty word in our house. (I told you he was rare.) In fact, Mother and Father both had great affection for Jimmy Carter, Gerald Ford, and Ronald Reagan. I can remember Father and me watching Ronald Reagan speaking in 1981, a year before my father's death. I saw my father look at Reagan with admiration. I asked, "I thought that you liked Carter?" He said, "Angeletta, they are both great men." My father admired the fact that a peanut farmer and a Hollywood actor could both become the most powerful man in the world. He envisioned the development of our political process as our forefathers intended. My parents always stressed, "So many of us were never taught the true history of either political party. We need to learn to educate ourselves on how we got where we are."

My parents' relentless focus on the importance of education meant that from the start my siblings and I were challenged to take accelerated academic courses and pursue college degrees. I was blessed with two parents whose vision for their children included a serious focus on education. Excellence and hard work were expected and nurtured. Education, we were taught, was the key to achieving our dreams and goals. "We're not black Americans," Mother and Father used to tell us, "we're Americans who happen to be black." Our identity and potential, they stressed, had nothing to do with skin pigment but rather prayer and perseverance.

Even before he met and married my mother, my father's vision and passion for education led him to create and open the first secondary education school for blacks in Hernando, Mississippi, during segregation. He also believed in the arts and created the first black high school band in that same town where he met my mother. During the days of segregation, many black children whose parents wanted them to get a high school education were left to find black churches with in-house schools, often taught by well-meaning but unqualified instructors. Father felt that wasn't good enough; blacks deserved better, a sentiment also expressed by Mildred D. Taylor:

> *Roll of Thunder Hear My Cry*
> *Over the Water By and By*
> *Old Man Coming Down the Line*
> *Whip in His Hand to Beat Me Down*
> *But Ain't Gonna Let Him Turn Me Around*
> —MILDRED D. TAYLOR

My great father, during his short life on this earth, enhanced the school system for blacks in both Taylor and Batesville, Mississippi. He also organized the first black high school football team in Shannon, Mississippi. And because of his prior successes, Professor James Thomas McGlowan was asked to help integrate the school system in Lafayette County, Mississippi. He was also assistant to the warden at Parchman Prison. There he helped change the lives and treatment of prisoners, especially the black prisoners on death row, some of whom were accused of crimes dating back to the days of segregationist rule by racist Democrats in the state of Mississippi.

When I entered junior high school, Father died of cancer, but his legacy lives on. The knowledge that my father expected me to live out his dream of education propelled me forward. I went to the University of Mississippi, and I graduated with a bachelor's degree in public administration with a concentration in criminal justice. During my college years, I became politically active in the state of Mississippi. I worked with Jimmy Carter's Habitat for Humanity and Nancy Reagan's "Just Say No" Program; I was an advocate for cancer research and an opponent of the University of Mississippi's Rebel flag. During this time, I aligned myself with the Democrats. It seemed logical.

After graduation I moved to Washington, D.C. My first job was as a clerk for Judge Joe Brown, now of *Judge Joe Brown* TV fame. I conducted research on the civil rights movement and the history of lynching in the Commonwealth of Virginia. Later, I competed in the Miss USA pageant as Miss District of Columbia. Shortly after that, I made the decision that would shape the next decade of my life. I decided to enter public service.

My platform was to promote abstinence and higher education, to encourage young people to be responsible and to recognize the power of hard work. I also wanted to promote education and the notion that welfare mothers should get a General Education Diploma. Naively, I thought this was a message that would energize many liberals. After all, this was the message that Father and Mother taught my siblings and me based on W.E.B. Dubois's notion of the "talented tenth." Between the five of us, my siblings and I hold several degrees including M.D., Ph.D., and Ed.D. I would not have thought promoting empowerment would be controversial.

I started knocking on doors and meeting with the liberal leaders of Capitol Hill. Immediately, I received a crash course in how the game is *really* played in Washington. These "leaders" weren't interested in self-empowerment and self-reliance. They preached a gospel of victimhood, alienation, and anger at "The Man" and "The System." Like many idealistic young people, I thought Democrats were the party of "the little guy," especially for women and people of color. I quickly learned the people shouting the loudest against my solutions were the liberals. It seemed that they and their policies were the real obstacles blocking the path toward advancement. Up close and behind closed doors, these wannabe "leaders" were hustlers, charismatic shakedown artists, and bamboozlers whose power depended on the ideological and economic enslavement of women, blacks, and Latinos. The more I tried to find a sympathetic ear for my views, the more clearly I saw, and the more disappointed and disgusted I became.

These liberals were not interested in ending the "hopelessness and despair" of welfare, and moving poor people into the workforce, or challenging them to accept personal responsibility for their choices and behavior, or even encouraging that segment of society to live the values of family and faith. They were political race and poverty brokers, "think tank pimps." Their objective was to feed an irrational and unfounded anger toward evil, racist, sexist Republicans and conservatives in order to deliver to the Democratic Party machine the critical votes it must win to remain politically viable—and nothing else. For this impressive feat—and it is impressive even if unbelievably exploitative—the Democrats reward the race and poverty brokers with money, political influence, and a seat at the table.

"For what is a man profited, if he shall gain the whole world and lose his soul or what shall a man give in exchange for his soul?"
MATTHEW 16:26 (KING JAMES VERSION)

Then I met, of all the people in the world, Senator Bob Dole and Jack Kemp, former Secretary of Housing and Urban Development. Senator Dole and Secretary Kemp inspired me to explore more about the Republican Party. Here I was, this young, naïve, optimistic young lady from Mississippi, talking to two of the most powerful and influential leaders in the country, and we were agreeing on, well, just about everything.

Shortly thereafter, I became director of the Better America Foundation, an organization for which Senator Bob Dole was the honorary chairman. One day, Jack Kemp and I got into a discussion about fiscal policy, job creation, and building enterprise through small business ownership. His empowerment zone proposal intrigued me. Jack Kemp soon became Senator Dole's vice presidential running mate. And I knew then and there that Bob Dole genuinely meant all of the things he had told me about improving our country.

I have worked in Washington, D.C., for more than a decade in a variety of capacities, all of them involving public service. I have served as a policy advisor, a publicist, and a government affairs and corporate diversity development expert. I learned through personal experience that the true liberal agenda is an agenda that is antithetical to almost everything I stand for. For this reason, my intellectual and ideological transformation wasn't difficult. I had been an individualist, self-reliant, social, and fiscal conservative as long as I could remember. What I lacked was the rest of the story. So I set out on a journey to research and rediscover the Democrats' hidden history of oppression, a history about which the majority of Americans— black and white, conservative and liberal—remain unaware.

Armed with my new knowledge, I then started advocating programs designed to elevate individuals of all races and backgrounds. Here again, I saw that liberalism—even when espoused by well-intentioned individuals—was an ideological millstone hung around the necks of hardworking Americans. In almost every policy area I worked and specialized, I saw liberalism accomplishing the exact opposite of what it claimed it would. Liberals gave us "da hood" or "los barrios" and called it compassion. Instead of demanding high quality public schools, liberals gave us an education cartel controlled by powerful unions who cared more about their paychecks and benefits than academic performance. Instead of building safer communities, liberals coddled the gangsters and drug pushers who terrorized our neighborhoods. Instead of promoting abstinence, liberals cheered on a sexual revolution that spawned a nearly fatherless generation. Instead of supporting people of faith, liberals all too often mocked them. Instead of standing with the majority of folks who mourn the "choice" to abort a baby, liberals made abortion a sacrament.

This book, then, is both an argument against the exploitation agenda of the Left and a call to arms for conservatives. The book's structure embodies the two reasons I am proud to be a conservative Republican. I begin by uncovering the devastating consequences liberal policies have wrought for all Americans. Part 2 then pulls back the curtain of lies that shroud the Democratic Party's disgraceful history of past oppression and present exploitation. This part of the book will shock most Americans and will likely stir up strong emotions, questions, and reactions. This is healthy and good. Eyes that have been shut for decades often take time to adjust to the light. I challenge readers to be honest in asking themselves how much they truly know about the history of the Democrats and modern liberalism. If the answer is "not much," I strongly urge that they embark on their own journey of discovery. I'm still on mine.

From our country's founding, the arc of history has been defined by a steely sense of self-reliance, individual initiative, and an unyielding desire by Americans to live in a free society marked by equality and liberty. That liberals would sacrifice that proud tradition on the altar of political expediency is loathsome. Still, I remain optimistic. The future looks bright. Whether the party of Lincoln can welcome blacks and women home to the party that fought for their freedom remains to be seen. Yet one thing is certain: record numbers are waking up from their ideological slumber. More women and people of color are running for office as Republicans. More ministers of all races are speaking from the pulpit urging their parishioners to vote "conscience, not color." Preachers are rising up against the liberal gospel of cultural and moral relativism. Some prominent leaders—

black, Latino, and female alike—are courageously challenging liberal lies. The signs suggest that there is a conservative renaissance in the offing. It won't come quickly, easily, or painlessly. That's okay. What's important is that we begin debunking the myths and lies liberals have foisted on us for decades. What's important is that we challenge and expose, at every turn, point for point, how the liberal agenda has and continues to exploit blacks, Latinos, and women. We've been the stooges of Democrats—the electoral mules tugging the liberal agenda forward for far too long, and to our own detriment.

This book was written after years of research—interviews with experts, scholars, political leaders, and authors from both the Republican and Democratic Parties. It is about the liberal agenda's exploitative present, its allegiance to a party with a murderous past, and how knowledge of both can emancipate women and people of color to produce a bamboozle-free future.

No more. The bamboozlement must come to an end. We must achieve emancipation from exploitation. Now seems just as good a time as any.

PART 1

LIBERAL SCHEMES ALREADY IN PROGRESS

1

ACCOUNTABILITY: UNCLE SAM ISN'T YOUR "BABY DADDY"

Why What's Good for Families Is Bad for Liberals

We can't destroy the inequities between men and women until we destroy marriage.

—Robin Morgan, author and editor of *Ms. Magazine*

Now-a-days it [sic] *like a badge of honor to be a baby mama.*

—Fantasia Barrino, *American Idol* winner

Mark your calendar: September 29 is "Marry Your Baby Daddy Day."

On September 29, Brooklyn author and journalist Maryann Reid decided to host a contest to pay for ten "lucky" unwed black couples with children to get married. Reid held the contest to promote her not-so-subtly titled novel, *Marry Your Baby Daddy*. But the young black author says she also wanted to cast light on the staggering number of black Americans whose vocabularies no longer include "husband" and "wife" but instead the ubiquitous rap-fueled terms "baby daddy" and "baby mama."[1]

Reid may be onto something. Pop culture can sometimes provide clues to shifts in social norms, and that's certainly the case as it relates to unwed motherhood. *American Idol* winner Fantasia Barrino sparked a national debate when she released her autobiographical anthem "Baby Mamas," which boldly declared: "Now-a-days it [sic] like a badge of honor to be a baby mama." After hearing the lyric, *Washington Post* metro columnist Donna Britt wrote that she couldn't get it out of her head. "A badge of honor?" wrote Britt. "I remember when it was more like a badge of shame—and a pretty effective deterrent." The columnist was careful to add that she wasn't endorsing "the oft-crushing stigmatization of that era."[2] Yet the tribute to "baby mamas," she said, was a sign of a significant shift in the culture.

Indeed, it was. More and more rap songs now feature "baby mama" in the title or in the lyrics, including that loving ode to motherhood, "Baby Mama Must Die!" The slang term has become so popular among black Americans that it became fodder for a comedy movie starring black comedian Eddie Griffin. The title: *My Baby's Daddy*. But Kenneth B. Johnson, a senior fellow for the Seymour Institute for Advanced Christian Studies, sees nothing funny about the nearly 70 percent out-of-wedlock birthrate that the National Center for Health Statistics reports plagues today's black children, a figure over double that for whites. As a result, black children are also exponentially more likely to grow up poor. High illegitimacy rates have become so pervasive, says Johnson, that he frequently sees black teenagers "who've never seen a wedding."[3]

Other black conservative leaders, like Maryland's former lieutenant governor Michael Steele, the first black elected statewide official in Maryland history, says that skyrocketing black illegitimacy rates represent a body blow to the black American community. "Within the black community there has emerged a kind of disconnect from the value system that anchored it," Steele told me. "In fighting slavery, fighting segregation, fighting all of those things that would tear the family apart, that's when we were our strongest. In slavery, no matter how many times they took a mother away from a child, that bond could not be broken. The family found a way to strengthen itself from that horrible experience. . . . Strength in family is the ultimate strength of the black community. The strength of the black community is the family."[4]

Liberals scoff at those like former lt. governor Steele who champion the traditional two-parent family structure and the values that come with it as optimal. Instead, they contend that the dissolution of the traditional family, the explosion of "baby mamas," and multigenerational poverty are widespread phenomena. After all, they argue, Murphy Brown was the first prominent 'baby mama,' and she was white, rich, and happy. Single motherhood is universal; poverty can be cyclical and common to all races, not just blacks.

But the facts don't bear this out. "Not so," says Kay S. Hymowitz, a research fellow at the Manhattan Institute. "It is a largely low-income—and disproportionately black—phenomenon. Entrenched multigenerational poverty is largely black; and it is intricately intertwined with the collapse of the nuclear family in the inner city. The truth is that we are now a two-family nation, separate and unequal—one thriving and intact, and the other struggling, broken, and far too often African-American."[5]

Most Americans recognize that over the last forty years there has been a breakdown of the traditional family. And over the last few years that breakdown has accelerated. Just ask Thomas B. Edsall, former *Washington Post* political reporter. In his 2006 book, *Building Red America*, Edsall notes that almost 70 percent of black children and one-third of all children are born to unmarried mothers. He then launches into this jaw-dropping passage: "To social conservatives, these developments have signaled an irretrievable and tragic loss. Their reaction has fueled, on the right, a powerful traditionalist movement and a groundswell of support for the Republican Party. To modernists, these developments constitute, at worst, the unfortunate costs of progress, and at best—and this is very much the view on the political left as of the Democratic Party loyalists—they constitute the triumph over unconscionable obstacles to the liberation of the self-realization of much of the human race."[6]

Rather than lament this state of affairs, many liberals see this as a positive. This isn't the mainstream view—but it is the view of modern Democrats as Edsall reveals in his book. Most Americans do not believe that marriage is an instrument of oppression, an institution whose time has come and gone. They definitely don't believe that the destruction of the traditional family is in any way a "triumph." Nor do they feel that one-third of all births occurring out of wedlock are "unfortunate costs of progress."

Currently, one out-of-wedlock birth occurs every thirty-five seconds in America. The pathologies of broken homes have wreaked havoc on children and young mothers—black and white, rich and poor.

And rather than work to ameliorate this phenomenon, liberals in Washington are practically cheering it on. The truth is that many liberals have long been antifamily and antimarriage. In the late '50s and early '60s, when liberal social planners were busy building the modern welfare state that would someday trap and destroy poor and minority families and squelch opportunity, radical feminists were getting their start, too. Heritage Fellows Patrick F. Fagan, Robert E. Rector, and Lauren R. Noyes retraced radical feminists' antimarriage agenda from the late 1960s forward. What they uncovered would shock and alarm most Americans. Fortunately for their exploitation agenda, liberals have done such a bang-up job of bamboozling minorities that most Americans are unaware of the radical ideology pushed by many liberals. Here then, in their own words, is a taste of the feminists' antimarriage, antifamily rhetoric over four decades:[7]

1969   "The institution of marriage is the chief vehicle for the perpetuation of the oppression of women."
    —University of Chicago sociology professor Marlene Dixon

1970   "The family is . . . directly connected to—is even the cause of—the ills of the larger society."
    —Shulamith Firestone, author of The Dialectic of Sex

1983   "Like prostitution, marriage is an institution that is extremely oppressive and dangerous to women."
    —Feminist author Andrea Dworkin

1992   "The family is the primary site of female subjection, which is achieved largely through sexuality."
    —Marilyn French, author of the landmark social criticism, The War Against Women, *which liberal Gloria Steinem lauded: "If you could read only one book about what's wrong with this country,* THE WAR AGAINST WOMEN *is it."*

2001   "I think promoting marriage as a goal in and of itself is misguided . . . Marrying women off to get them out of poverty is not only backward, it is insulting to women.
    —N.O.W. president Kim Gandy

This proxy war against men in general and marriage in particular has, over time, chipped away at the way many women view men and the institution of marriage. I interviewed the popular television personality and real-life judge, the Honorable Joe Brown, about his impressions on this subject. He says that this is a trend he's observed as a judge:

> If I took your typical female parent who has a boy between four and seven, which is when human character is formed, and asked them what they thought of the merits of involving a man in the upbringing of that child, they would say something that would culminate in an utterance of, "What good is a man for? I don't see why you need one involved." And someone would Amen it and go, "I hear you, honey; what you need a man for?! They ain't good for nothing!" And I would say how are you going to raise your boy children if you don't know what they are supposed to be good for when they are grown?[8]

While some alarmists recognize the devastating effects that the breakdown in the American family has had on the black community, these consequences are beginning to be seen in the mainstream community as well.

How did it get this way? How did this happen? What accounts for a near-fatherless generation where marriage is rare and baby daddies are commonplace? And how did black children become disproportionately more likely to grow up in poverty than white children? Are things getting better or worse?

The liberal line is that poverty is caused by a vicious brew of "institutional" racism—conservative policies promoted by racist Republicans—combined with high incarceration rates of black males. In the fashion typical of bamboozlers, these liberals have it exactly backwards. Conservative policy prescriptions aren't the cause of underachievement for minorities and the poor, they're the cure. And furthermore, Republicans advocate policies that recognize the innate value of all humans, as opposed to the liberal policies that demean the poor and disadvantaged by encouraging victimhood.

Still, answering the above questions means focusing on two wrecking balls liberals have slammed against families for over forty years: 1) an aversion, and in some cases outright hostility, toward encouraging and promoting two-parent families as the best vehicle for positive child rearing and economic uplift, and 2) the expansion of welfare and government giveaways as a surrogate father, essentially making Uncle Sam a "baby daddy."

Consider that in 1960, only 5.3 percent of all children in America were born out of wedlock; by 2004, that figure had rocketed up to 35.7 percent.

Minnesota radical feminists Nancy Lehmann and Helen Fullinger say, "Male society sold us the idea of marriage . . . Now we know it is the institution that has failed us and we must work to destroy it."

That feminists today remain an integral and influential component of the Democratic Party is hardly surprising. To their credit, a handful of more moderate feminists follow the late Betty Friedan's ideology and have distanced themselves from the virulently anti-family thrust of the feminist movement. Likewise, aware of the political public relations consequences of an antimarriage, anti-family agenda, shrewd Democrats like former president Bill Clinton and former vice president Al Gore have been careful to sprinkle their public statements with token nods to marriage and family. But few leaders in the party dare to seriously challenge feminist orthodoxies and their power and influence within the party. After all, why would they? Feminist groups, such as N.O.W. and Emily's List, rake in huge sums of cash for candidates running as Democrats and related causes.

But feminists didn't single-handedly cause the lurch into the near-fatherless generation—what Judge Brown calls "a nonexistent family" and "more of a breeding unit than a family" in America.[9]

Indeed, for those familiar with the data on illegitimacy rates over the past four decades, the current cultural quagmire is hardly surprising. Because they are a majority, whites account for the highest total number of out-of-wedlock births. But the out-of-wedlock birthrate varies widely between whites, Latinos, and blacks, breaking down 28 percent for whites, 45 percent for Latinos, and 68 percent for blacks.

Ever since the late senator Daniel Patrick Moynihan published his now famous—which liberals might refer to as infamous—1965 report, "The Negro Family: The Case for National Action," liberals have demonized as "judgmental" and "callous" anyone who emphasized the virtues of two-parent families, traditional marriage, and personal responsibility. During a National Press Club event, Reverend Eugene Rivers III, president of the Seymour Institute, noted that when Moynihan sounded the alarm about the consequences of high black illegitimacy rates over forty years ago, he was "condemned and pilloried as misinformed, malevolent and even racist."[10]

The black illegitimacy rate Moynihan referred to was 25 percent then. Today, if the illegitimacy rate among blacks could be lowered to 25 percent, it would be considered a monumental achievement. Yet as soon as Moynihan drew attention to the issue, feminists and liberal civil rights leaders pounced. Why was Moynihan attacked when his intentions were noble? The answer, of course, is that highlighting the devastating pathologies associated with high out-of-wedlock communities threatened to shift public debate to calls for increased personal responsibility, greater parental monitoring of teen sexual behavior, limiting liberal media glorifications of promiscuity, and, most damningly, encouraging advocacy for strong two-parent families.

Not only do liberals reject these approaches, but if these approaches were to be adopted, it would be devastating for the causes they support. If individuals took greater personal responsibility for their own choices and behavior, the need for big government solutions would dissipate. Worse, if women (especially black women) got married, Uncle Sam would no longer need to play baby daddy, and a larger number of politicians and bureaucrats would be out of a job.

And there's the rub.

The exploitation agenda advocated by liberals is modeled after the dependency-inducing design of the drug dealer's business model: "We'll supply the first hit for free, and after that, you'll need us forever in order to survive." In order for the liberal scheme to succeed, all attempts at self-empowerment or individual initiative are to be met with fierce resistance and social sanction.

Anyone who tries to flee the liberal plantation must be publicly ostracized and humiliated. But perhaps the main reason Democrats will never pursue an aggressive pro-marriage, pro-traditional two-parent family agenda is that broken homes and out-of-wedlock birthing mothers are an electoral goldmine for the Democrats' liberal agenda. Just ask John Kerry's pollster, Mark Mellman, a Democrat pollster who's been shoveling donkey data for a quarter century. Following Kerry's 2004 presidential defeat, Mellman reported that his candidate won unmarried voters by 18 points, compared to a Bush margin of 15 points among married couples. This resulted in a marriage gap of 33 points. As Mellman confessed, "Never-married women are one of the most Democratic segments in the population . . . 63 percent of them identify as Democrats and our data suggest about two-thirds voted for Kerry."

Divorce is also a big winner for liberals. Mellman says that a ten-year longitudinal study "found that every single Democratic woman in the sample who got divorced between 1973 and 1982 remained a Democrat, whereas women who were not Democrats in the early wave, but got divorced between the two surveys, were 20 percent more likely to become Democrats. Men whose divorces made them poorer also tended to become Democrats."[11]

And according to Mellman, those disillusioned with the institution of marriage altogether hold great promise for liberals. "Never married are least likely to attend church, much more likely than average to support abortion rights and favor gay marriage," writes Mellman. But wait. It gets even better. "Nonmarriage is on the rise. Divorce, later marriage, increased life expectancy, and other forces have led to a decline of more than 25 percent since 1970 in the proportion of Americans who are married," the Democratic pollster explains. Mellman's giddy conclusion: "Mobilizing culturally progressive or economically hard-pressed singles should be a key priority for Democrats."[12]

The only thing worse for liberals than married couples are *Christian* married couples with children. When that's the case, says Bill Clinton's former pollster, Stanley Greenberg, liberals are *really* in trouble. Greenberg somewhat derisively labels white protestants who are evangelical, Pentecostal, fundamentalist, or charismatic as "the Faithful." This voting bloc, according to Greenberg, strongly opposes the liberal agenda:

> The Faithful comprise nearly one in five Americans, 17 percent . . . white evangelicals vote for the Republicans, as if it were an article of their faith. More than 70 percent of the Faithful align with the Republican Party, giving the Republicans nearly a 50-point margin (72 percent, compared to the few 'lost souls,' the 23 percent who align with the Democrats) . . .[13]

So what does all this mean for the exploitation agenda promoted by the Left? It means that when people get married, stay married, achieve financial independence, or if they are white protestant

Christians, they overwhelmingly reject the Democrats' liberal agenda. This is a serious threat to the liberal powerbase. Because "the Faithful" represent so many voters, liberals are constrained in the statistical slices of the electoral pie available for their taking. And that's why Democrats must continue to bamboozle blacks, Latinos, and women in order to remain politically viable.

"Compassion," when promoted by liberals, is all too often a verbal smoke screen to mask the fact that the erosion of the two-parent family has its roots in the liberal social policies that require zero personal responsibility. This verbal smoke screen frequently is used to demonize those who dare to raise flags of alarm whenever illegitimacy rates climb. The fact is that these policies pull the rug of self-reliance out from underneath women and inner-city blacks and leave them trapped in a cycle of dependency. In the "if it feels good do it" era of the sexual revolution, these messages and policies combined to accelerate the "tangle of pathologies" that Moynihan warned would choke black achievement. But in a mediated age of "I feel your pain" emotionalism, liberals were well-positioned to mount their assault on individual achievement. Black children, of course, bore the burdens of liberalism most severely.

When black illegitimacy rates began soaring, with single black mothers increasingly becoming the rule rather than the exception, it was easier for liberals to advocate the expansion of the welfare state as a way to fill the gaps. Only a few noticed that it also had the effect of keeping this same group locked into voting for the Democrats.

The bamboozlers' mantra became: "We liberals are here to help you. Don't let those evil conservatives judge you. You're the victim! You shouldn't have to work. Your standard of living isn't your responsibility. It's ours. You don't need to marry your baby daddy. Uncle Sam *is* your baby daddy, and will be as long as you keep voting for us."

This stands in sharp contrast to the view of conservatives. "We believe in empowering the individual," says former lt. governor Michael Steele, "and giving the individual the opportunity to empower themselves."[14] What conservatives understand is that what government gives you, it can take from you. And what liberal welfare policies took from black Americans is beyond compare.

And so it was Republican George W. Bush who had to intervene to change this state of affairs. President Bush announced a Marriage and Healthy Families Fatherhood Initiative. The proposed program goal is to increase healthy marriage by providing individuals and couples with:

- Accurate information on the value of marriage in the lives of men, women, and children;
- Marriage-skills education that will enable couples to reduce conflict and increase the happiness and longevity of their relationship; and
- Experimental reductions in the financial penalties against marriage that are currently contained in all federal welfare programs.

Proposed as part of welfare reform, the goal of the program was to aid in the reduction of dependence on other social services.

It has been a long-time tenet of modern liberalism that individuals are incapable of caring for themselves and must therefore rely on big government programs and bureaucracies in order to flourish. As a result, as more and more people recognize the benefits of self-reliance, the former victims find the consequences of liberal policies less attractive. But rather than yield to these changing circumstances and view them as success stories, quite often liberals try to force the victims to stay in their victimhood status.

Nowhere was this more apparent than the 1996 welfare reform debate, a legislative battle that produced one of the most successful anti-poverty policies in a generation. "The best thing for black people from 1992 to 2000 was welfare reform, which Clinton had to be forced into by Republicans," says John McWhorter. "We don't think about that; we just think about whether somebody feels our pain."[15] That was clearly the case with America's welfare policy in 1995. In the name of liberal "compassion," poor families were lured into a tranquilizing cycle of dependency that squelched self-reliance and individual initiative.

"The government declared war on poverty and poverty won."
—PRESIDENT RONALD REAGAN

By March 1994, welfare rolls had swelled to 14.2 million people including 5.1 million families. One in eight children in America was a welfare recipient. Welfare families spent, on average, thirteen years collecting welfare checks. "Welfare families" were typically headed by never-married mothers, whose children were three times more likely to go on welfare when they grew up than non-welfare children. Here again, soaring out-of-wedlock birthrates had conflated the already sizable challenges out-of-wedlock children face, which, according to U.S. Secretary of Health and Human Services Mike Leavitt, include lower academic performance; being twice as likely to use illegal drugs, drink alcohol, or smoke tobacco; being more likely to be physically abused or suffer physical or emotional neglect; and seven times more likely to live in poverty.[16]

This last dimension seems to have escaped most liberal policy planners. It hardly takes a rocket scientist to realize that two incomes are twice as much as one. In speaking with Fox News commentator and author Juan Williams, he noted that there is a simple four-step "magic formula" young people can follow to get out of poverty:

1. Finish high school and preferably college.
2. Take a job and hold it.
3. Marry after finishing school and while you have a job.
4. Delay marriage and having children until after one's twenty-first birthday.

Williams says that any man or woman who follows this path of personal responsibility can cut their chances of being poor by two-thirds.[17] These steps seem painfully obvious and easy to follow. But for children growing up with Uncle Sam playing the role of baby daddy, the cycle of dependency can seem appealing and even natural. That's true regardless of race, says former president of the Latino Coalition Robert de Posada, whom I interviewed:

> You saw your mother or your father every day going to work, so your expectations in your mind was, "When I grow up, I'm going to go to work." But if you have a system that you see the parents staying at home collecting a check, what do you expect that kid is going to do? He's going to expect the same, he's going to expect to be sitting at home, collecting a check from the government because "If my parents didn't work, I don't have to work."[18]

Both Williams' "anti-poverty pill" formula and de Posada's reflections on breaking the cycle of welfare dependency embody the kind of commonsense approach to welfare reform that Republicans proposed during the 1990s. The law, which would later be officially known as the Personal Responsibility and Work Opportunity Reconciliation Act, was designed to "end the dependence of needy parents on government benefits by promoting job preparation, work, and marriage."

The welfare bill was built on the then radical idea that work is the pathway to economic freedom and self-reliance. Conservative Republicans wanted to free children from the federal plantation of welfare dependency. Moreover, they could see that liberal social engineering had produced unintended negative consequences. Both Roy and Niger Innis, of the Congress of Racial Equality (CORE), explain:

> It's the welfare culture. The culture of "you owe me something," the culture that "you have to give me something." It pays you to not work. It pays you to have children out of wedlock. It pays you to not save your money. Or worse, it penalized you if you saved money! It penalized you if you got a job. It penalized you if you got married and had children in wedlock. How is that?! How is it that a government program is going to undermine the pillars of a civilization? But that is what the welfare system did.[19]

They are correct. The conservative virtues of hard work, self-reliance, and personal responsibility are the keys to success. It's the model that blacks used after slavery and it is the model that has made America the most powerful and prosperous nation ever. But those virtues are antithetical to maintaining the liberal exploitation agenda. Handing out government cheese and preaching a gospel of victimhood and dependency is what gave liberals an electoral lock on the votes of so many blacks and the poor.

And in the process, this cruel and senseless trading of votes for welfare checks has sentenced poor and inner-city residents to a life overwhelmed by poverty and generational dependency on government. It also robbed generations of black Americans of their ability to achieve independence and success. Is it any surprise that liberals went nuclear when it was clear that, after having vetoed the bill two times before, President Clinton signed the Republican Congress' welfare reform bill? Outraged by the initiative, Democrats took demagoguery to a new level. Although the Republicans named the bill "Ending Welfare as We Know It," Massachusetts senator Ted Kennedy dubbed the bill "legislative child abuse." New Jersey senator Frank Lautenberg declared that reforming welfare would force poor children to take up "begging for money, begging for food, and even . . . engaging in prostitution." Leftist Marian Wright Edelman, chairwoman of the Children's Defense Fund, said the bill was "national child abandonment" and equated it to the burning of Vietnamese villages. Georgia congressman John Lewis thundered, "They are coming for the children . . . coming for the poor, coming for the sick, the elderly, and disabled."

Hugh Price, the head of the National Urban League, condemned the bill, saying that "Washington has decided to end the War on Poverty and begin a war on children." So complete—and hyperbolic—was the liberal condemnation that the *Atlantic Monthly* featured an article titled, "The Worst Thing Bill Clinton Has Done."[20]

Hardly.

How's this? Giving in to overwhelming public opinion polls and the Republican Congress' demands for a new welfare system that rewarded, not punished, work, self-reliance, and ended massive fraud and abuse was possibly the *best* thing Bill Clinton ever did. At its ten-year anniversary, the legislation stands as a shining example of the superiority of conservative principles over liberal federal largess. In one decade, the welfare rolls plunged from 12.2 million to 4.5 million. From 1996 to 2002 the poverty rate for single women with children fell from 42 percent to 34 percent. And in 2001 the black child-poverty rate hit an all-time low, dropping from 40 percent to 33 percent. Latinos experienced an even greater drop in poverty rates, going from 40 percent to 29 percent. Child-support collections, which were an integral part of the bill, have nearly doubled. Nearly a million and a half fewer children now live in poverty than did ten years ago. In the end, the Personal Responsibility and Work Opportunity Reconciliation Act granted nearly eight million adults and children personal freedom from a lifetime of governmental control and dependency.

"Welfare reform was incredible assistance, because I think it sent a very clear message to those who even thought that they could become dependent on the welfare state, that that was no longer going to be the case," says Robert de Posada. "There is no doubt about it. I mean the more dependent you are on a program or to a union or anywhere that people have control over you, it is a way to control your thoughts, to control your independence."[21]

The day the bill passed, the predictably liberal *New York Times* ran an editorial with the melodramatic headline, "A Sad Day for Poor Children." The piece included this quote: "This is not reform, it is punishment . . . The effect on cities will be devastating."[22] Ten years later, they were hardly in a mood to apologize for their laughably absurd gloom and doom prediction. Instead, the *New York Times* editorial headline screamed "Mission Unaccomplished." The huffy editorial strained to find flaws where few existed. Frustrated by the triumph of a market-based incentive policy that had improved the lives of millions of poor families, the *Times* threw a temper tantrum camouflaged as an op-ed. "An anniversary like this should be a time of reflection," the *Times* lectured. "It is flat-out wrong to declare victory as if the hard part of the journey is over." The same paper that had predicted the disintegration of American cities at the hands of evil conservative reforms then took it upon itself to explain to conservatives that what was needed more than ever was for "conservatives to back stronger government supports for the working poor."[23]

Some people—liberals—never learn.

For the past forty years, liberals have bamboozled people of color by labeling as racist anyone who dared to call for greater personal responsibility in reducing out-of-wedlock birthrates and encouraging strong welfare-to-work policies. From Daniel Patrick Moynihan's 1965 report to the hyper-politically correct culture of today, liberals made any call for personal accountability by blacks and the poor a form of racism, a way of blaming the victim. Liberals do this because their attitudes toward the importance of strong traditional two-parent marriages range from begrudging acknowledgement to downright disdain.

Much work remains to be done. Welfare rates have come down, but out-of-wedlock birthrates have not. Yet as the economy booms and more and more Americans enter the workforce, the resulting increasing economic empowerment has forced liberals to look for new ways to exploit the poor and disadvantaged. It is sad that just as record numbers of Americans are now entering the middle class for the first time, liberals continue to devise new ways to stifle their economic growth and opportunity.

2

ROBBING PROSPERITY

How Liberals Crush Enterprise and Entrepreneurship

Anybody who's looking for a handout is not going to
succeed in America. America is a self-reliant nation. . . .
If you think the government's going to pull you through,
you're going to be sadly disappointed.

—Bill O'Reilly, Fox News anchor

Oprah Winfrey is the embodiment of the American Dream. According to *Forbes* magazine, Oprah Winfrey is one of the richest people in America, and is the richest black person in this country.[1] Winfrey earns an estimated $225 million annually and has an estimated overall worth of over $1 billion. Refreshingly, Oprah doesn't apologize for achieving and living the American Dream. She wears Manolo Blahnik heels and sleeps between Pratesi sheets, and she doesn't care who knows it.

"I have lots of things, like all these Manolo Blahniks. I have all that and I think it's great. I'm not one of those people like, 'Well, we must renounce ourselves.' No, I have a closet full of shoes and it's a good thing. . . . I'm going home to sleep on my Pratesi sheets right now and I'll feel good about it."[2]

You go girl!

For the textile-challenged, a queen-sized set of Italian-made Pratesi sheets retails for about $3,360, making them some of the most luxurious sleeping linens around. Manolo Blahniks, popularized by the hit show *Sex in the City*, can cost more than a mortgage payment. A pair of Lizard Nappa d'Orsay heels will set you back $950, but Oprah can afford it. "I was coming back from Africa on one of my trips," said Oprah. "I had taken one of my wealthy friends with me. She said, 'Don't you just feel guilty? Don't you just feel terrible?' I said, 'No, I don't. I do not know how me being destitute is going to help them.'"[3]

But Oprah Winfrey isn't the only minority success story. As far as Latinos go, Jennifer Lopez is what the Hollywood crowd refers to as "the triple threat." Lopez is the highest paid Latino actress in history. She is also one of the most successful singers and dancers in the world. Additionally, she owns a thriving fashion design and perfume company. Her salary per movie has soared past the $12 million mark, and she controls an empire that easily exceeds $300 million in assets. How did she accomplish this from her humble beginnings in the Bronx? Her parents instilled within her a strong work ethic. They also stressed the importance of assimilation and being able to speak English. According to Lopez: "You get what you give. What you put into things is what you get out of them." Lopez credits family for much of her success:

> I think my mom was very integral in that part of my life because she just kind of made us believe that we could do anything. She always was very big on us being independent, not having to depend on any man, not having to depend on anybody, just being able to kind of survive on your own no matter what. And one of the things that went along with that was working hard—always working hard. And they were great examples. My

dad worked nights most of my life. My mom worked at the school and had a Tupperware job; that was how our upbringing was, so work was always a very big part of my life and also, she really made us believe that we could do anything. You know, we could be the president of the United States if we wanted to, if we worked hard enough—a Puerto Rican girl from New York—and it seems so far-fetched, but when people make you believe that, you do. You're less afraid to try things, anyway.[4]

If only liberals shared Oprah's and JLo's entrepreneurial, pro-capitalist spirit. But they don't, and as a result, the poor—the people liberals champion—suffer. Among minorities—particularly blacks—the economic situation is two-pronged. Up-and-coming talk-radio star Hallerin Hill says that "the state of upper middle-class black America is great. The state of lower-class America is tough, but I think it really revolves around the ideas, the thoughts and the ideas that are driving the people in those different populations. . . . There are people who, in the name of compassion, believe that certain human beings are fundamentally defective and they will never do better than a certain level."[5]

The economic divergence that Hills speaks of affects all minorities. It has rattled many liberals and thus results in a somewhat schizophrenic economic message. On the one hand, liberals must appeal to the reality that entrenched poverty exists in black and Latino communities. On the other hand, they recognize that for a significant number of minorities, such appeals are irrelevant to their circumstances.

The 2006 U.S. Census Bureau put the black poverty rate at 24.9 percent, for example. Out of context, such a number justifies the arguments of the liberals that "the government dole is your sole supporter and friend." By putting the national spotlight on the very real and tragic consequences of poverty, such as were witnessed in the wake of Hurricane Katrina, liberal leaders hope to invoke both sympathy and white guilt over the plight of the poor.

In his book *White Guilt*, Shelby Steele explains that white guilt remains one of the liberals' greatest sources of power. "In the age of white guilt," writes Steele, "whites support all manner of silly racial policies without seeing that their true motivation is simply to show themselves innocent of racism."[6] The bamboozlers know of this phenomenon and exploit it regularly.

But on the other hand, the economic achievement of middle- and upper-income minorities is so significant that even liberals—who never miss an opportunity to bash America as an oppressive, evil, racist nation—can't ignore it. As Cabinet Secretary Elaine Chao (who as Secretary of Labor has made minority job opportunity and growth a key goal of her department) stated: "I think we should pay heed to the overall core value of this country, and equal opportunity applies for all and that should be the same standard for everyone." The numbers don't lie. Blacks and Latinos today enjoy explosive economic and entrepreneurial successes and opportunities that eclipse anything people of color the world over could ever dream of.

Take, for example, the African population that lives around Lake Victoria. Lake Victoria is the second largest fresh-water lake in the world and is in the western part of Africa's Great Rift Valley. This area, which is nearly twenty-six thousand square miles, borders Uganda, Kenya and Tanzania. It hosts some thirty million Africans—almost as many as the total number of blacks in the United States—yet their annual income is roughly $250.[7]

In contrast, according to the U.S. Census Bureau data, in 2005, the black American median household income was $30,134 and the median income for Hispanic households was $34,241.[8] The numbers are less than that for white households, but they are significantly better than the incomes for much of Africa.[9] As for the differences between minority and white household incomes, the prevalence of single-parent led families in the black and Latino community contributes greatly to the disparity.

Nevertheless, there is such a thriving middle class in both communities that this category now counts for half of all black families in America, in the Latino community, middle-class households total roughly 40 percent.[10] Importantly, the income growth among Hispanics has been nothing short of explosive.[11] But blacks in America are quite accomplished as well. The achievements of black Americans have combined to create a black American market that now commands a jaw-dropping $762 billion in buying power that is expected to reach $981 billion by 2010.[12] Hispanics are close behind with purchasing power today of $700 billion, and they are projected to reach $1 trillion by 2010.[13]

Not surprisingly, liberal talking points seldom include these positive and impressive economic achievements. To be sure, as the previous chapter made clear, conservatives have much work left to do in dismantling the nanny state erected by liberals that continues to hobble individual advancement. Moreover, all Americans must take responsibility for self-defeating choices and destructive behavior. Because the truth is that when conservatives enact policy reforms that brighten the economic futures of all Americans—such as welfare reform, child tax credits, and small business incentives— liberals lose their ability to exploit minorities for electoral gain.

Cynically, when liberals aren't busy bamboozling citizens into believing that their success in life is Uncle Sam's responsibility, they are hard at work convincing women, blacks, and Latinos that callous conservatives are out to disenfranchise them economically and take what is rightfully theirs. Think of it as the "Kanye West Doctrine": conservatives don't care about poor people and they support policies designed to economically disenfranchise them. By engaging in propaganda campaigns, combined with outright distortions and related falsehoods, liberals have economically crippled and exploited many of the poor and most needy Americans. Instead of sound arguments rooted in economic facts and analysis, liberals offer hyper-emotional sound bites. Sadly, too many minorities have fallen for these tactics.

Aided by an often complicit and sympathetic news media, liberals have successfully painted conservatives as greedy whites—folks who cling tightly to their stock portfolios in fear that some poor American might swipe their hard-earned money. And according to liberals, these conservatives actively conspire to keep minorities from owning their own businesses, homes, or engaging in any self-empowerment in general. Just ask my good friend, liberal columnist and commentator Dr. Julianne Malveaux:

> George Bush doesn't care about black people. George Bush does not care about black people . . . He has been racially insensitive, he has been anti-affirmative action . . . He's talked about minority business, but he does not support the Small Business Administration's efforts to do long term minority business in a way that he could.[14]

I know Julianne Malveaux believes these things and means well, but the reality is far different. In addition to appointing more women and people of color to senior positions in his administration than any other, President Bush's "compassionate conservative" agenda has included the landmark No Child Left Behind education initiative, welfare reform that provides grants to encourage marriage, and one of the largest increases in funding to combat the international AIDS crisis in Africa.

But it isn't just the record of Republicans that is often distorted. Many times minority leaders reject outright the idea that free markets and capitalism are attractive options for blacks and Latinos. "African-Americans have not identified with economic conservatism," says Congressman Jesse Jackson Jr. "*Laissez faire* economics has not changed the condition of blacks, poor whites or working-class Hispanics since the inception of the nation—there is no doubt about that."

The truth is far different. Some of the most successful minority entrepreneurs are open to or have embraced the economic ideas of conservatives and Republicans. One such individual that I've had the pleasure of meeting is Frank Mercado-Valdes. By age thirty-five, Mercado-Valdes had turned a passion for movies with black actors and themes into a $50 million company, the African Heritage Network. At the time, AHN was one of the largest independent, minority-owned syndication companies in the United States.[15] But that isn't the only thing that sets Mercado-Valdes apart. As he says:

I was a Republican before I went into business. I became a Republican in college when I registered to vote. It was 1980. Ronald Reagan was running for president. I was an eighteen-year-old Marine, and when they registered us to vote on our base, I registered a Republican because I liked the message of hope and the anti-Communist message of Reagan at that time. And I thought that Reagan's basic points of self determination were important for African-Americans to hear as it related to their forward progress. Some of it was naive I admit. As you get older, it isn't so black and white. But that's why I initially joined at eighteen and was drawn by his anti-Communist stances, and I was drawn by his beliefs in economic empowerment.

Mercado-Valdes believes that economic empowerment and equality are one and the same. "The key will be to approach African-Americans on the issue of economic empowerment, lasting economic empowerment, which ultimately reduces the effects of discrimination," says Mercado-Valdes.

Another business titan who has kept an open mind and an open door to conservatives and Republicans is media mogul Russell Simmons. Often referred to as the "Godfather of Hip Hop," Simmons is the creator of the Def Jam Record label and Phat Farm, an urban apparel line (which he sold in 2004 for $140 million).[16] I had the pleasure of interviewing Simmons at a fundraiser my husband and I co-hosted for former lt. governor Michael Steele's United States Senate campaign. Simmons has been extremely critical about the Bush administration's handling of Iraq, even going so far in one interview as to call the Bush administration the "gangsta government." So it surprised many when Simmons made the announcement that he intended to support Maryland Republican Michael Steele.

But during our interview, he told me, "I am supporting Michael Steele because of his views. We have to be successful in ending this war on poverty. It's not about Republican versus Democrat, it's not even about liberalism versus conservatism, it's about saving our people in the inner city, especially our black men."

Frank Mercado-Valdes and Russell Simmons are by no means the only minority entrepreneurs open to Republican ideas. But their wealth and willingness to break from the bamboozler's grip make them unique. Unfortunately, many of the poor in America have been hoodwinked into opposing the very ideas and policies that stand to empower them the most. Most cynically of all, liberals lower a rope of "economic compassion" into the same poverty hole that the liberals themselves created.

Ironically, poor people—black and white—have the most control of their own destiny. One simple step—the equivalent of swallowing an "antipoverty pill"—is graduate, take and keep a job, marry, and then have kids. This action alone would allow poor people to reduce their chances of living in poverty by over 300 percent.

It's been ten years since the Republican Congress repealed the old sixties-era welfare program. Today we can see that kicking the welfare habit has helped, not hurt, blacks and whites alike by raising incomes and decreasing poverty. How many of these success stories no longer feel obligated to support big government and liberal policies?

"My belief comes from what [Frederick] Douglass used to say almost continuously," says former Ohio secretary of State Ken Blackwell, "that African-Americans need to be part of their own empowerment, that we are agents of moral authority, we can make decisions that are in our interest. And we have not just the moral agency, but we have the capacity to be participants in our own upliftment."[17]

The self-reliance that produces the kind of economic uplift that Blackwell describes flies in the face of the collectivist, socialistic policies that drive the liberal agenda. By tying minority prosperity to the advancement of liberal programs and policies, Democrats serve up enough governmental crumbs to keep them loyal, but never allow them to taste the cake of economic success.

Liberal leaders must keep women and people of color from adopting the capitalist, entrepreneurial enthusiasm of someone like Oprah Winfrey. I interviewed Congressman Jesse Jackson, Jr., whom I respect, even though his point of view puzzled me. Here's what he told me:

Historically, however, en masse, African-Americans have not identified with economic conservatism. That is, the failure of states and federal governments to invest in housing, health care, and education so that the vast majority of Americans can work their way out of their economic condition. *Laissez faire* economics has not changed the condition of blacks, poor whites, or working-class Hispanics since the inception of the nation—there is no doubt about that. The Roosevelt era not only benefited working class whites, but it also benefited and eliminated poverty en masse for working class African-Americans, Hispanics, and other immigrant groups who found themselves at the end of a hard day's work, still trapped in a condition of poverty.[18]

Our society is a democracy that gives us the freedom to hold whatever opinions we may choose, and the good people of Chicago elected him. However, his comments are indicative of so much that is wrong with the belief by some Democrats for income redistribution and a state-controlled economy. Put simply, they are stuck in a bygone industrial economic age, an age of the past. Today, anyone using a free public library computer could launch his own small business. This new economic world demonstrates, once and for all, that liberals have lost the economic argument; capitalism abounds and continues to flourish. And under the leadership of the Bush administration, Labor Secretary Elaine Chao and former head of the Small Business Administration Hector Berrato have worked aggressively to bring that reality to many women and communities of color all across America.

Capitalism abounds and continues to flourish. Under the guise of fighting—liberals are always fighting for something—in this case for those "trapped in a condition of poverty," as Jackson puts it, liberals resort to what constitute economic cons. Their goal: convince voters that conservative fiscal policies are anti-American. These cons include attacking conservatives who oppose raising the minimum wage as being indifferent to the poor; labeling affirmative action opponents bigots; and misleading voters about the GOP track record on minority home ownership, income, and entrepreneurship. As we will see in later chapters, these misguided and dishonest efforts and policies haven't actually helped the poor. In fact, in many instances these liberal policies have robbed prosperity.

Conservatives are actually for the "little man"—the small business owner. Let's take the minimum wage for example. Most conservatives oppose raising the minimum wage. Liberals would have you believe that opposition to a minimum wage hike is intended to hurt people of color and the poverty stricken. But what they don't tell you is an increase in the minimum wage would actually hurt minorities.

It seems simple enough: If blacks, Latinos, and women experience higher rates of poverty and the goal is to increase their standard of living (and it is), then just raise low-income workers' pay by raising the minimum wage. Easy, right? It seems like the humane position to take. Who's against helping the little guy get a leg up? It's only a buck or two. How could that be wrong? Plus, opposing an increase in the minimum wage isn't easy. Most people support the idea. In April 2006, the Pew Research Center found that 83 percent of those polled said they favored a federal minimum wage hike, including 72 percent of Republicans.[19] Many Americans agree with the sentiment expressed by liberal congresswoman Maxine Waters (D-CA):

I am really ashamed to be a Member of Congress at this point. The Republicans are playing tricks again. They have coupled another tax break for the richest in America with this minimum-wage increase. Since 2001, this Republican Congress has cut taxes by $1.8 trillion, and most of these tax cuts have gone to the wealthiest one percent of Americans. Yet when it comes to helping low- and middle-income Americans, the Republican Party is nowhere to be seen. The increase in the minimum wage is about one thing, Mr. Speaker, justice for American workers. Without an increase in the minimum wage, the

American worker cannot enjoy life, liberty, and the pursuit of happiness. Quality of life is indeed important. Freedom to pursue one's dreams, whether it is in education or a new home, is freedom. Happiness is about fulfilling dreams. Workers earning the current stagnant minimum wage are simply not as happy as they should be in America. I oppose this legislation as drafted. I am ashamed to be here with these people who are denying the poorest of our society a decent living.[20]

Well, there you have it. Greedy Republicans hate poor people and therefore are committed to "denying the poorest of our society a decent living," just as Rep. Maxine Waters would have the poor—indeed, all Americans—believe. One person who refuses to take the liberal bait is Frances Rice, president of the National Black Republican Association. "I am appalled. This happens every election cycle. The Democrats will go into black communities and preach hatred against the Republican Party. Democrats have been running our inner cities for the last thirty or forty years. Those cities are in deplorable condition due to their socialist policies of living on handouts. Yet, they have the gall to blame Republicans for what is going on in these communities."[21]

According to the U.S. Department of Labor's Bureau of Labor Statistics, in 2004, only 520,000 workers made the minimum wage.[22] We're a nation of nearly 300 million people and yet barely more than a half-million people are paid at the minimum wage. Who are these people? Most minimum wage workers are young; over half are less than twenty-five years old. Nearly three percent of white hourly-paid workers earn the minimum wage or less, compared with about two percent for both blacks and Latinos.[23]

Rice and others are wise to denounce liberals' economic scapegoating, especially as it relates to the minimum wage. Indeed, individuals who know anything about economics view the consequences of wage controls differently, *very* differently. "The high rate of unemployment among teenagers, and especially blacks and Latinos, is both a scandal and a serious source of social unrest. Yet it is largely a result of minimum wage laws," says the late Nobel Prize-winning economist, Milton Friedman. "We regard the minimum wage law as one of the most, if not the most, antiblack laws on the statute books."[24] Friedman was not alone in opposing wage controls like the minimum wage. Surveys of professional economists routinely show that an overwhelming number of economists (90 percent in one poll) recognize that minimum wage hikes cause job losses.[25] So what's the deal? Are all economists surrogates for the GOP and conspiring to hold a good people down?

Hardly. While most Americans, including me, will never be award-winning economists, it fortunately doesn't take one to see the folly of wage controls. All it takes is a little simple math. Consider the following: imagine you own a small business. Let's make it a mom and pop restaurant that stays open for ten hours a day and has ten employees. To keep it simple, let's imagine that the minimum wage at the time is $5 and that lawmakers decide to raise it to $8 an hour, close to what's been proposed. That means your labor costs for one hour of operation just jumped from $50 an hour to $80 an hour, a difference of $30 an hour. Since the restaurant stays open 10 hours a day, that means you, the restaurant owner, must now find an additional $300 a day, or $2,100 a week, to pay your employees. Now, $2,100 a week multiplied times the number of weeks in a year works out to be an added annual cost of $109,200. Again, this added cost, a tax really, isn't producing more output or efficiency. No, all it does is prevent your restaurant from churning out salads and burgers at the same price it once did.

Hmmm . . . I wonder what will happen next?

Obviously, the small business owner will be forced to lower his costs or reduce services. Cutting jobs is one obvious place to lower costs. But the owner has no choice. While the owner could raise prices, he can't set prices at an uncompetitive level. How many customers, for example, would buy a $30 hamburger? Not many. So to recoup the $30 of added hourly costs, the employer will likely fire— at a minimum—three workers. This will reduce the workforce from ten to seven. Still, firing three workers only recouped $24 hourly of added cost (three workers at $8 an hour). That means you still have $6 additional of hourly costs—$21,840 annually—to make up for somehow. That is if your small business is to remain at the same level of profit you were at before Representative Maxine Waters "stood up for the little man." Ultimately the prices charged at the restaurant will likely rise as well. End result: fewer jobs and higher prices for goods and services.

The restaurant illustration above is apt. According to the National Restaurant Association, following the 1996 minimum wage increase, at least 146,000 restaurant workers lost their jobs.[26] Furthermore, according to the president and CEO of the U.S. Chamber of Commerce, Thomas J. Donohue, raising the minimum wage just $.50 an hour in 1996 destroyed 645,000 entry-level jobs despite the robust economy at that time.[27]

Even if many low-wage workers are lucky enough to survive the nationwide firing spree triggered by a minimum wage increase, the prices they pay for goods and services can be expected to increase as well. This dilutes their actual purchasing power. Additionally many businesses resort to cost-cutting technologies to offset higher labor costs. Think about it. How many local gas stations still have gas attendants waiting to wipe your windshields, check your oil, and provide you and your car with full service? Not many. Today pay-at-the-pump credit card machines have turned customers into both gas attendant and cashier. The same goes for self-scan checkouts at your local grocery store or Wal-Mart. The higher the minimum wage goes, the greater the incentive for businesses to implement these cost-cutting technologies.

Ironically, Democrats, many of whom profess to loathe "sinister" big businesses like Wal-Mart, are unwittingly doing the bidding of large corporations. Like many mega-corporations, retailer Wal-Mart supports increasing the minimum wage. Could it be because they know what a minimum wage increase does? Could it be that it will crush small business competitors or mom-and-pop operations that can't absorb the higher annual costs? In our fictitious small business diner example above, a minimum wage hike would have forced the owners to pay over $109,000 in added costs, despite the fact that the increase in rate wouldn't guarantee any gain in productivity.

But more devastating than the costs to business owners, including women and minority business owners, are the costs to black and Latino male teenagers. Black conservative author and award-winning economist Thomas Sowell points out that higher labor costs result in fewer jobs. Because the workforce is made up of individuals with varying skill levels, minimum wage laws disproportionately impact young, unskilled workers with limited experience. "In the United States," says Sowell, "the group hardest hit by minimum wage laws is black male teenagers. Those who refuse to acknowledge that the minimum wage is the reason for high unemployment rates among young blacks blame racism, lack of education, and whatever else occurs to them."[28] And Latinos are in a similar situation. They are overrepresented among minimum wage workers; while they are nearly 12 percent of the U.S. workforce, they are nearly 20 percent of those on or near the minimum wage.[29] A sharp increase in the rate will hurt them the most.

The minimum wage was never meant to be a living wage that could support a family. "Raising the minimum wage doesn't do anything in and of itself," says former lt. gov. Michael Steele. "I don't see the minimum wage as a minimum wage. Because that is not the most money anyone should ever make in their lives. It should be, or what I think it should be, is a training wage—a wage to train someone so that they will eventually be able to get on a pathway to creating ownership and more importantly, a greater earning power."[30]

Steele is correct. This data means little to liberals. Because advocacy for minimum-wage increases is popular with the public and minorities in particular (even though they are most susceptible to the harm created by wage controls), liberals can ignore the facts and instead trumpet unfair claims that conservatives are indifferent to the poor. Democrats even use the tactic when running against minority and female Republican candidates.

During the 2006 race for Pennsylvania governor, NFL superstar-turned-GOP gubernatorial candidate Lynn Swann was smeared by his Democratic opponent, Gov. Ed Rendell. Using a series of radio ads, he alleged that Swann was a carbon copy of President Bush and that he, too, opposed raising the federal minimum wage. I asked Swann about the issue. He explained that his position was that it would be irresponsible to raise Pennsylvania's minimum wage without first studying how it would affect state workers and small business owners. "It was misleading to the African-American community and it's divisive," said Swann. Unfortunately, Swann wasn't able to get that explanation out to the voters.

Conditioned by decades of bamboozling by the Left, black voters responded exactly as Democratic Party leaders knew they would: 90 percent voted for Rendell over Swann.[31] Swann's independent thinking made him a ripe target for liberals. Standing athwart ineffective feel-good legislation shouting "Stop!" is seen as a betrayal of those struggling to get their footing on the lowest rung of the economic ladder. Yet raising the minimum wage hacks the lowest rungs off the ladder altogether. But economic logic doesn't wash with liberals who are intent on inflaming class warfare.

I had the pleasure of speaking at length with Sean Hannity about the exploitative liberal agenda. He mentioned to me that he had an interesting interview with the Reverend Jesse Jackson on this very subject. He asked Reverend Jackson how much a person needs to make in order to be considered "rich." Jackson was hesitant to put a number on it, but declared that "it doesn't stand to reason to be fighting for real estate taxes for the wealthy and not raise the minimum wage for working people."[32]

Never mind that opposing minimum wage hikes is the right thing to do for lower income Americans, most especially black and Latino teens. No, what matters is towing the liberal line. Better to seduce voters with monetary mirages than to support policies that clear a path toward long-term, lasting prosperity and independence.

In the wacky political universe of liberals, when minorities fight to protect jobs, it is seen as selling out, as being counterfeit and antipoor. And standing up against ineffective feel-good legislation is seen as a betrayal of minority solidarity.

Liberals' economic shortsightedness and their desire to demonize conservatives in an effort to exploit women and minority voters go beyond the minimum wage. In addition to pushing wage controls that hurt the poor, liberals also want you to believe that conservatives are indifferent or outright hostile to the interests of the poor. They consistently mislead the public and minorities about the GOP track record on home ownership and entrepreneurship. These misguided and dishonest efforts haven't produced an economic uplift for the poor, but they have enabled an entrenched liberal bureaucracy to stay in place far past its usefulness. Rather than seek solutions that will make a difference in the lives of the poor, they push failed policies that divide America.

One such policy is affirmative action quotas. Women, Latinos, and blacks are now educated and hired at record levels. Indeed, female college enrollments and graduation rates now surpass men. But barriers to academic entry and professional advancement still exist. What's more, even independent black leaders like former secretary of state Colin Powell and former lt. gov. Michael Steele have recognized that affirmative action policies undoubtedly aided their path to the successes they've obtained.

Most people agree that unfair or discriminatory practices in hiring or college admissions should be dealt with strongly and swiftly. Racism and bigotry are still with us, albeit far less than they were a generation ago. Title VII of the Civil Rights Act of 1964 makes it illegal to discriminate in employment, and its guidelines cover all employers public and private. The Equal Employment Opportunity Commission (EEOC) is tasked with ensuring that alleged violations of the law are investigated and resolved, through legal sanctions if necessary.[33] But this is not what much of today's debate over affirmative action is about. It's about racial preferences cloaked in the language of victimology. The quota model of affirmative action is harmful in every field in which it is tried. Whether in the worlds of business or universities, lowering standards to achieve diversity robs minorities of personal achievement and imposes a stamp of implied inferiority.

"I grew up in segregation," says *New York Times* best-selling black conservative author Shelby Steele, "so I really know what racism is. I went to a segregated school. I bow to no one in my knowledge of racism, which is one of the reasons why I say white privilege is not a problem . . . Racism is about eighteenth on a list of problems black America faces." Steele, who is a research fellow at the Hoover Institution at Stanford University, and a recipient of the National Humanities Medal, says that the barriers to educational access have been largely leveled:

> If I'm a black high school student today, there are white American institutions, universities, hovering over me to offer me opportunities. Almost every institution has a diversity committee. Every country club now has a diversity committee. I've been asked to join so many clubs, I can't tell you. There is a hunger in this society to do right racially, to not be racist . . . You owe us a fair society. There's not much you can do beyond that. There isn't anything you can do to lift my life up. I have to do that.[34]

It's easy to understand why Democrats, whose party has a century-old record of oppressing and brutalizing minorities (covered in Part 2), would exploit policies like affirmative action. Ironically, they like to use it as a way to showcase their newfound commitment to racial equality. But in the characteristic fashion of the bamboozler, their idea of affirmative action promotes symbolism over substance. It cruelly sacrifices economic access on the altar of groupthink retribution.

Quotas don't work and they're unpopular. A 2003 Supreme Court decision upheld a general affirmative action admissions policy at the University of Michigan's law school. In response, opponents put an initiative banning the race-based admissions policy on the ballot in time for the 2006 midterm elections. On November 7, 2006, Michigan voters became the third state to ban preferential treatment based on race, gender, color, ethnicity, or national origin for public employment, education, or contracting purposes. This loss is a bitter reality pill that liberals are only now beginning to swallow.

The self-appointed voice of the people on affirmative action, Reverend Al Sharpton, told me, "With the entire sweep of the Democrats, we still lost affirmative action on the ballot in Michigan where whites and blacks went to the polls, elected a woman, a white woman governor, reelected her and reelected a white woman senator, but they voted overwhelmingly . . . against affirmative action," Sharpton said. "So we are in a situation where race is being denied and racial progress, in our opinion, is regressing."[35]

Quotas aren't only intellectually demeaning, they're also ineffective. Like the minimum wage, quotas often produce a result opposite of their intent. "One of the most troubling effects of racial preferences for blacks," writes Shelby Steele, "is a kind of demoralization . . . an enlargement of self-doubt." Other conservative blacks like John McWhorter, author of *Losing the Race*, believe that affirmative action in business can still serve a positive role to supplant the consequences of slavery (which severed social networks and relationships). But McWhorter joins Steele in opposing college quota policies. In my interview with McWhorter, he argued that the educational gap in higher education is "due to a sense of separation from scholarly endeavor internal to African-American culture." According to McWhorter, blacks' lower educational attainment is a logical outgrowth of a black American culture that has rejected academic achievement as "acting white"—not a function of "institutional racism," as liberals would have people believe.

And as the minority graduation rates have dropped, liberals have consistently sought to mask the rationale. Liberals aren't so interested in the real results, they prefer style over substance. As long as there are enough black and Latino faces to photograph and sprinkle through the public relations propaganda booklets and admissions brochures, liberal administrators are content; they have proved their commitment to racial equity and have fought for those who can't fight for themselves. This brand of racial conde-scension is so utterly insulting. The emotional self-satisfaction and sheer exploitation of using black and Latino students as proof of one's commitment to diversity is a cruel twist of the cause of civil rights; but for liberals, that's enough.

Liberals' devotion to keeping up a façade of diversity means they support admissions policies that undermine the best interests of minority students. As former Black Panther-turned-conservative activist David Horowitz has observed, "it is a poignant irony that the college that comes closest to racial equality in actually *graduat-ing* its students in the era of affirmative action is Ole Miss, once the last bastion of segregation in the South." I know a little something about blacks who graduate from Ole Miss because I'm one of them; Ole Miss is my alma mater. The admissions office does not use race-based admissions policies. As a result, 49 percent of all white students who enter Ole Miss earn their degree and graduate. For black students, the number is almost identical: 48 percent.[36]

But that approach doesn't appeal to liberals. They push this divi-sive social scheme no matter what the results. Using black and Latino students as public relations pawns on the chessboard of political correctness is wrong. Admissions that lower standards for any reason—parental legacy, donations, or even athletic prowess—are unfair and ultimately self-defeating.

It is sad to see that in the end, liberals are far more concerned about showcasing their commitment to diversity than doing what is in the educational—and thus, economic—long-term interests of minority students. Yet once again, minorities have been bamboozled into believing that conservatives who oppose race-based admissions policies do so because they are racist. Question: is it the quota admissions' policies that are racist, or is it the conservatives who oppose them? You decide.

Another way liberals hinder the economic prospects of minorities and the poor is by demonizing Republican presidents as hostile to their interests—particularly with regard to home ownership and income earning. Through tireless repetition of this lie, liberals have successfully kept minority voters from fleeing the federal plantation and returning home to the political party that helped win emancipation. In June 2006 Americans rated Ronald Reagan as the greatest president in American history, according to CBS News.[37] Yet at the end of the Gipper's two terms in the White House, the Harris Poll found that an astounding 80 percent of blacks believed the Reagan administration had been "oppressive."[38] What explains this? Put simply, the better a Republican administration is for blacks and the poor, the more liberals work to excoriate and degrade his standing among them in order to prevent defections to the party of Lincoln. "Reagan believed in states' rights and Jefferson Davis," the Reverend Jesse Jackson said brazenly on CNN. "I believe in the Union and Abraham Lincoln."[39]

Jackson's statement is breathtaking in both its ignorance and deception. Apparently confident in the knowledge that blacks would forget that Jefferson Davis was a *Democrat* and that Abraham Lincoln was a *Republican*, Jackson's smear of Ronald Reagan is standard operating procedure for bamboozlers, who act confidently in the belief that women and minorities will never dare study the data or learn the history of the two political parties.

Maybe the Rev. Jackson doesn't know that the first black U.S. senator, Republican Hiram Revels, assumed the seat vacated by Democrat Jefferson Davis when he became president of the Confederate States of America? Or maybe he just doesn't care? Perhaps he figures: why bother with facts when fiction has been so good to me and the Democrats?

Either way, his comments bamboozle women and people of color.

But luckily, the always brilliant Michael Novak has looked into the real record of Reaganomics, particularly its impact on blacks:

> During the Reagan Administration there were 19 million new jobs created. Between the end of 1980 and the end of 1988, black Americans alone got 2.4 million of these new jobs. The numbers of blacks employed jumped from 9 million to 11.4 million in that short period—a jump of more than 25 percent. Black income jumped, too. In constant 1988 dollars, the total annual income earned by all 30 million U.S. blacks together rose from $191 billion at the end of 1980, to $259 billion by the end of 1988. That sum was larger than the GDP of all but ten nations in the world. The number of black families earning more than $50,000 per year much more than doubled, from 392,000 in 1982 to 936,000 in 1988. The median salary/wage of black males increased from $9,678 in 1980 to $14,537 in 1988 (in current dollars). Median means half earned more than that, half less, so more than half of all black males improved their income by more than 50 percent.[40]

Funny, Rev. Jackson failed to mention any of that. I wonder why? Guess all those numbers made it hard to make a Jesse-esque rhyming jingle: "Black families earning more than $50,000 per year doubled—Ronald Reagan never caused us no trouble! Black Americans alone got 2.4 million new jobs—the Democratic Party is the one who robs!"

Yes . . . maybe it's best that the Rev. Jackson steered clear of the facts and numbers.

Let's take a look at President Bush's ambitious goal to increase minority home ownership. One of the many nasty lingering legacies of slavery and Jim Crow has been that black Americans as a group hold fewer assets, such as land, homes, or other real estate.

The goal of acquiring financial assets and related property ownership, therefore, is one many black Americans strive toward.

"My dad was a devotee of Booker T. Washington and his whole thing was getting an economic niche and striving for ownership," says former Ohio Republican secretary of state Ken Blackwell. "He never discouraged academic pursuits or the pursuit of a high school or college or post-graduate degree, but it was a real nice balance between academic pursuits and pursuing ownership, whether that is something that is as basic as home ownership or owning your own business."[41]

As Lloyd Williams, president and CEO of the Greater Harlem Chamber of Commerce, put it to me, "The more you need access to capital, the less likely it is that you're going to get it."[42] Former lt. gov. Michael Steele calls this conundrum the challenge of building "legacy wealth," which he says represents the next phase in the cause of civil rights.

I interviewed Congressman Jesse Jackson, and afterwards I realized there was much he said that was factually accurate and that conservatives would not dispute: "There are still significant gaps that exist between African-Americans and the income that they receive compared to the broader population," he said. "There are significant gaps between African-Americans and Hispanics in terms of income. Our housing situation in the urban core of our nation, where many African-Americans live, is still lagging far behind many other ethnic groups, our education levels and standard still lag behind."[43]

There is little in the congressman's statement to disagree with. Surely black income and home ownership, which are inextricably linked, lag behind the rest of the American family. But how could they not? With marriage rates among blacks at historic lows and 70 percent of black children being born out of wedlock, it's hard to see how a single, often young, black female (who may lack a college or even a high school diploma) will be able to compete with the incomes of stable two-parent families. It's hardly rocket science. Two incomes are twice as much as one income.

Yet even when Republicans attempt to raise these factors in the public eye, as President George W. Bush has done while encouraging the creation of the Ownership Society, liberals castigate conservatives for not doing enough to help minorities or because the gains haven't occurred fast enough. This is particularly galling when often the policies of liberals either caused or exacerbated the problems in the first place.

It is in this context that President Bush announced that his administration would try to improve minority home ownership. In an interview with President Bush's Secretary of Housing and Urban Development (HUD), Alphonso Jackson, he explained to me the challenges and successes inherent to the president's ambitious vision:

In August of 2002, the president said that he wanted to close the home ownership gap that existed between black, Hispanics, and whites. And he challenged us to create 5.5 million new minority homeowners, black and Hispanic specifically, by 2010. So what I said to the president was that we were going to do that and there were two things that we must do. The most difficult problems that blacks and Hispanics are facing is the down payment and the closing costs. Secondly, it's the Housing Council. I said that we can't help blacks with $8 million a year for the Housing Council. That's what it was when we started here. Today it's $47 million . . . We have created 2.7 million new black and Hispanic homeowners in this country. We'll get 5.5 before 2010. The key to it is that this president is committed . . . since President Bush has been president—Defense, Homeland Security, and Housing and Urban Development. When we walked in here, our budget was $29 bil-

45

lion. To date, it is $35 billion. So when they say he is not committed to making life better for black, Hispanic, and other races, they are truly off base—he is very committed.[44]

Robert de Posada, former president of the Latino Coalition, agrees: "Home ownership is increasing dramatically, and that is because the president specifically addressed his policies to help those communities, specifically targeted ways to help the first-time homeowners to be able to purchase that first home—to give them assistance in that process, that initial confusing process," says de Posada. "What you have seen is an incredible outtake in the number of new home owners. And at the same time, by reducing the tax burden on small businesses, you have seen that that has been a great generator of new economic activity. . . . There is a significant increase in the number of Hispanic small businesses in the country. It is the fastest growing segment of our small business community."[45]

And despite a very high poverty rate among minorities, black and Latino wealth and income has grown under, dare I say it, yet *another* Republican administration.[46] The data tells the story:

- Black unemployment is lower than the 9.5 percent average realized between 1995 and 2000 (the height of Clinton's so-called economic miracle).[47]
- Unemployment for women reached the same level as men (5.1 percent) in 2005.[48]
- In 2005, Queens, New York, became the first county in the United States where black household incomes surpassed those of white households.[49]
- Unemployment for Hispanics reached 5.8 percent in January 2006.[50]

- In 2005, the White House reported that SBA business loans for minorities increased by 40 percent and for black Americans by an astounding 75 percent.
- As part of President Bush's Minority Entrepreneurship effort, millions of dollars have aided minority business development, including the awarding of $127 million in tax credits for equity and debt financing of businesses in low-income areas.
- According to the University of Georgia's Selig Centre for Economic Growth, black buying power has gone from $318 billion in 1990 to $723 billion in 2004 and is projected to soar to $965 billion by the end of Bush's second term.[51]

Despite the best efforts of bamboozlers to convince them otherwise, minorities have and continue to experience historic economic expansion under Republican administrations. Indeed, a rising tide lifts all boats. By lowering taxes, decreasing bureaucratic barriers to small businesses, and decreasing the regulatory restrictions that crush entrepreneurial opportunities, Republican policies have created a climate where small businesses can sprout and economic opportunities can flourish. But the bulk of the economic credit will always go to the American worker—the real engines of economic expansion and entrepreneurship. Governments can't create prosperity—they can only slow its accumulation and growth.

Unfortunately, liberals don't trust free market capitalism to create wealth for the same reason they don't trust Americans to keep the money they earn. Liberals believe they, not individuals, know what's best for citizens. As the old saying goes, "money *is* power," and the more money the government takes, the more power it has over individuals. Furthermore, Democrats realize that growing incomes increase the willingness of minorities to support economic policies that allow people to keep more of what they earn. Bonnie Erbe, host of the PBS news show *To the Contrary*, the first of its kind to feature an all-woman panel, says that "overall, lower income women who tend to be single, whether widows or never married or young, to-be married women, lower income women tend to be more progressive. The more money women get, the more they worry about tax cuts, and the more they tend to turn Republican and conservative."[52] The data on voting behavior support Erbe's analysis.

Liberals are quick to say this is proof that conservatives and Republicans only care about rich folks. This, they say, is further evidence that the GOP is funded and controlled by the super rich. But as best-selling author and Hoover fellow Peter Schweizer has demonstrated, millionaire donations to the Democrats far outpace those given to the GOP by a ratio of 12 to 1. Indeed, the average donation to the Republican National Committee is roughly $50, hardly George Soros territory. What's more, he notes the left-wing newsmagazine *Mother Jones* reported that eighteen of the top twenty-five individual donors to all political campaigns were Democrats, not Republicans. According to Schweizer, "Ironically, Democrats, who talk about income inequality and plutocracy, are now the party of the super rich."[53] Instead of being concerned about the wealthy, Republicans are concerned about creating an economic environment where wealth generation is possible. The truth is that as more women and people of color obtain wealth, they become more willing to recognize that their own efforts and choices are superior to those of the liberals in Washington.

The bamboozlers have cast themselves as the saviors of the poor for decades. Democrats substitute race-baiting rhetoric and emotional appeals to fighting for the little person (it's politically incorrect to say man, you see) instead of relying on rational thinking and policies rooted in reality. The way liberals see it, they courageously stand up to those evil conservatives who won't raise the minimum wage and reject quota policies, and they also fight the oppressive economic policies of Republican administrations. Yet in each case the reality is different. The minimum wage destroys the jobs and opportunities of those who need them the most. Race-based hiring and admissions policies stigmatize minorities. And finally, it is the very policies of Republican presidents like Reagan and Bush that have lowered unemployment rates, yielded soaring home ownership levels, and led to a boom in minority enterprise, all of which have contributed to the existence of the most prosperous and powerful minority middle class in the history of the world.

Boy, those conservatives and that evil George W. Bush sure know how to stick it to minorities!

3

AN EDUCATION IS A TERRIBLE THING TO WASTE

The Achievement Gap, Denying School Choice, Union Bullies, and the "Soft Bigotry of Low Expectations"

After spending $125 billion of Title I money over twenty-five years, we have virtually nothing to show for it.

—Secretary of Education Roderick R. Paige

It is official: America has now reached the point when it is no longer possible to have a serious public discussion about the chasm separating black and Latino academic performance from Asian and white achievement. It's something that scholars call the "achievement" or "racial gap" in learning.

It is easy to get discouraged when confronted with the dizzying data on educational attainment in America, specifically when looking at the abysmal failure of our educational system for minorities. For some, the troubling results may make the challenges seem intractable—hopeless, even. But if we are going to craft solutions, we must be willing to see the problems as they are. Moreover, our children, particularly those in the inner city, deserve better than they have received.

One particularly useful tool to measure educational achievement is a federal law, the National Assessment of Educational Progress. Enacted by Congress in the first year of the Nixon administration, the NAEP assesses students and schools regularly, and its reports are often referred to as the nation's education report card.

Recent NAEP data, particularly the assessments of blacks and Latinos, should anger and alarm all Americans.

- By twelfth grade, the average black and Hispanic student has attained academic skills equivalent to only an eighth-grade level.
- In five of the seven categories covered by NAEP, a majority of black students perform below the minimum. Hispanic students perform only modestly better.
- 77 percent of white students read at a higher level than the average black student.
- Only 184 black students in the United States scored over 700 out of a possible 800 points on the verbal portion of the SAT, and only 616 black students scored above 700 out of a possible 800 points on the math portion of the SAT.
- In 1999, 90 percent of white students scored higher on science comprehension tests than the average black student.

It is easy to understand why some Americans recoil from facts like these. The data make us uncomfortable. They remind us that there is much work remaining to be done. It would be nice to conclude that no one—liberal or conservative—would want to see children flounder. But policies have consequences. And averting our eyes won't solve the problem. Nor will blithely blaming these results on racially biased tests, as some have chosen to do. As an aside, I've yet to hear a liberal explain exactly how a mathematical equation can be racially biased.

In fact I'd love to see Reg Weaver, the president of the National Education Association, explain how learning the periodic table, the process of photosynthesis, or the way a heart valve operates constitutes a racist educational curricula.

The stakes are simply too high for our nation's youth, and the consequences too significant for us to indulge in these silly distractions. And as a result of globalization, America needs its entire workforce operating at full capacity, now more than ever. "What we're talking about is the success of the next generation," says Assistant Secretary of Education Tom Luce. "We have to run faster to stay ahead."[1]

We can't solve this problem if we can't even discuss it. But the left would prefer that we simply not talk about this problem.

Just ask Robin Zhou, an eighteen-year-old student newspaper columnist at Alhambra High School in Los Angeles, California. In 2005, Zhou's assistant principal, Grace Love, told a group of student leaders that their school had made small gains in narrowing the achievement gap on state tests in 2005. But Zhou saw little reason to celebrate. He asked, "Why was the gap there in the first place?" So, according to the *Los Angeles Times*, Zhou studied the issue and then wrote a column.

Using test scores as a measure, he wrote that Latino students were "not pulling their weight." Zhou went on to explain that the reason for the achievement gap was largely cultural. Asian parents, he wrote, were more likely to "push their children to move toward academic success, while many Hispanic parents are well-meaning but less active."

One of Zhou's newspaper colleagues, Sara Martinez, sixteen, read Zhou's article before it went to press. "My first reaction? Robin's gonna get beat up," she said. She had no idea how bad it would be.

When Zhou's article finally ran, one math teacher scrawled "racist" across the article and posted it on the blackboard. Soon,

Zhou's friends began receiving word that Latino students were preparing to beat him up and pelt him with paintballs at graduation. On March 30, 2005, virtually the entire Latino student body and a few white and black students showed up to school wearing brown T-shirts with statements of Latino pride, including "Hecho en Mexico" and "Stay Brown Chicanas!"

The groundswell continued. Latino parents were incensed. They wanted action. They demanded an explanation. Not an explanation as to why there was an achievement gap, or whether Zhou's cultural argument was in keeping with the scholarly literature on the root causes of the achievement gap. No, they wanted an explanation as to why Robin Zhou had the audacity to say out loud what the Left has decreed that no one should be allowed to discuss.

Over thirty parents contacted the school's principal, Russell Lee-Sung. Their sharp criticisms were directed at Zhou, the school newspaper, and Principal Lee-Sung himself for not preventing the publication of the student's article.

To accommodate the concerns of the parents, Principal Lee-Sung formed an Action Planning Committee, hosted several staff discussions, and then held several student committee meetings to allow open discussions of Robin Zhou's egregious offense. It made little difference, however. Latino parents and students were unsatisfied.

Fortunately, Robin Zhou wasn't physically harmed. And by the May 10 issue of the school newspaper, Zhou tried to provide a final resolution to the issue: "I realize that pointing out a disparity between two of the major student groups on campus has the potential to divide us, to turn students against classmates and neighbors against each other. My deepest regrets to those who have been hurt. It was not my intent to make anyone feel they are inferior or unable to succeed, but rather to address an issue in desperate need of attention."

One ray of hope pierced through the controversy. By year's end, the percentages of Latino students passing the English Language Arts exam and all but one of the math tests had improved over the previous year. More Latino students also applied for Advanced Placement (AP) classes. Lee-Sung, the school's former principal, says he thinks it was Zhou's article that sparked action.[2]

As the story of Robin Zhou demonstrates, our politically correct culture has made it all but impossible to have a candid dialogue about the state of academic achievement by blacks and Latinos in America. To be sure, these discussions must be conducted with sensitivity and respect, but they are discussions that must be had.

And the challenges we face aren't solely attributable to cultural differences. In many instances the failings are the result of a bureaucratic public education system largely indifferent to how it affects inner-city children.

Listen to New York Council member Gifford Miller, "Good Day Street Talk":

> I was in a 4th grade class the other day and there were 31 kids in this teacher's class. And you know what the teacher said to me? . . . She said, "I pray for the flu." Because when the flu comes, eight or nine kids are sick and he feels like he's teaching instead of just maintaining order.

A key step toward closing the achievement gap will depend on our ability to accurately diagnose the problem. And that, unfortunately, is where liberal Democrat interests and the interests of the children begin to diverge. Bamboozlers on the Left cite at least three major reasons to explain the causes of the perpetual achievement gap. Not surprisingly, these explanations typically are designed to pit poor people against Republicans. But the convoluted theories liberals espouse are, in fact, wrong. Instead of data, they often rely on outdated arguments cloaked in liberal "compassion."

Liberals often say that poor students lag behind other pupils because they lack funding. Selfish, rich Republicans, we are told, don't want to help poor black children. Think I'm exaggerating? Here is the script from one radio ad sponsored by Democrats in Missouri that ran on urban stations: "When you don't vote, you let another church explode," the ad warned. "When you don't vote, you allow another cross to burn. When you don't vote, you let Republicans continue to cut school lunches and Head Start."[3]

Liberal columnist and commentator Julianne Malveaux echoes this claim:

> Education K to 12 is in really bad shape in inner cities and that's where many African-American kids are being educated. . . . We have to create a safe, clean, attractive learning environment . . . we should be spending billions of dollars on school reconstruction in inner cities. Suburban schools are fine, by and large, not completely, but by and large. Suburban schools are fine. Inner-city schools, as long as you fund education through the property tax, you're going to end up with educational inequality. . . . I mean, I was superintendent of schools; I'll burn my school to start over. I mean, I really would and just start over.[4]

But for those who care to check, the facts are far different. In 2000, the United States ranked the highest among the G8 countries (among the wealthiest countries worldwide) for per student expenditures for both primary and secondary education as well as higher education.[5] As Jay Greene, author of *Education Myths*, explains, "If money were the solution, the problem would already be solved . . . We've doubled per pupil spending, adjusting for inflation, over the last thirty years, and yet schools aren't better."[6] According to the U.S. Department of Education, in constant 2002 dollars, total U.S. K-12 spending increased from $4,505 per student in 1970 to $9,553 in 2002. Despite the surge in spending, student performance on SAT scores actually fell, from 1049 in 1970 to 1026 in 2003.[7]

But liberals continue to argue that the problem is funding, and in some instances they've convinced the public that it must be true. In 2006, the Rose and Milton Friedman Foundation sponsored a poll of Floridians. They were asked how much money they thought their state spent per child on public education. Half of Floridians (50 percent) thought the figure was no more than $4,000 per pupil per year on operating expenses for K-12, not including school construction. Almost two-thirds (62 percent) thought Florida spent no more than $6,000. Only 5 percent gave the correct response: between $7,000 and $8,000. Surprisingly, when Floridians were asked what they thought the appropriate amount of state spending per pupil should be, two-thirds responded with an amount *less* than or at the current level of what is being spent.[8]

And some parents in the District of Columbia know perhaps better than anyone that money does not equal pedagogical excellence, because if it did, they would have the best school systems in the United States. The District of Columbia—whose school district enrollment is predominantly black—spends more per pupil than any school district in the nation. In 2005, the District of Columbia spent a whopping $13,328 per student, when the national average that year was just under $10,000.[9] And how does it fare? Its scores are among the worst in the nation.

"The only thing the Washington, D.C., public schools train our children to do is to go to jail, to graduate to jail, to graduate to a life that is not going to be successful," says Niger Innis. "Throwing more money at the beast, if you will, that is depriving our children is not the solution."[10]

It's not just D.C., however. In 2000, a *New York Times* analysis of New York public schools found that "across the city, the school districts that rank highest academically have, in most cases, the smallest per-student budgets." Less Money = Better Schools might not exactly make the best political bumper sticker, but at the very least the data prove that more money does not equal better schools.[11]

And the dirty little secret is that rather than spend the resources they have to see to it that black and Latino students attain a mastery of the basics, much of these funds are wasted on a multicultural curriculum and other untested education schemes. In 2003, the Joint Center for Political and Economic Studies reported that while 54.9 percent of whites believe their public schools are excellent or good, only 35.2 percent of black Americans felt the same.[12] Is there any wonder they feel this way?

In making the funding argument, the bamboozlers bemoan the fact that public school funding equations are often derived from local property taxes. This, they claim, results in wild variances in funding between poorer neighborhoods, which are disproportionately black and Latino, and more affluent ones, which are more likely to be white.

"It's not about the money," says Ben Chavis, a former public school principal who now runs an alternative charter school in Oakland, California. "That is the biggest lie in America. They waste money," he said.

ABC News reporter John Stossel cites Chavis as a model of fiscal efficiency. To be sure, Chavis is a tight manager of resources. He requires his students to do things like remove trash from the school grounds and set up lunch tables. For physical education, instead of needing expensive equipment, students simply run laps around the city block and perform basic exercises—things that require minimal equipment. But these cost-cutting measures free up funds for teaching. And remarkably, without spending more per pupil than public schools, Chavis pays his teachers more than public school teachers are paid. He also regularly appears in each and every classroom and often uses gimmicks like small cash payments to encourage student classroom attendance. Since Chavis took over four years ago, his school has gone from being among the worst in Oakland to being among the best. His middle school has the highest test scores in all of Oakland.

"Give me the poor kids, and I will outperform the wealthy kids who live in the hills," says Chavis. "And we do it."[13]

The proliferation of charter schools over the last five years has yielded dozens of Ben Chavis–like examples. Even when controlling for poverty levels among various school districts, the lack-of-funding argument is unjustified. NAEP data from 1999 to 2000 show that among the most affluent public school districts, the average per pupil expenditure was $8,957. Yet in those districts with the highest levels of poverty, the average per pupil expenditure was $8,503, a difference of $453 a year per student. What's more, these numbers do not reflect the estimated 15 percent more in federal funds that lower income schools receive to administer programs such as Head Start. No, the gaping disparity in test scores between minorities and white students can hardly be explained by a difference this small.

Here's the truth: if closing the achievement gap could be done with a swipe of the federal credit card, the problem would have been solved long ago. But we have a record of thirty years of spending, and lack of money just isn't the problem.

The second critique that the education bamboozlers make is that minority students are hamstrung by a dearth of minority teachers in public schools. This view assumes, of course, that black and Latino students learn more from black and Latinos teachers and, presumably, that white students learn more from white teachers. The fact that there is little to no research that proves this argument doesn't seem to matter. In the world of the committed liberal there is no virtue more valued than that of diversity. Of course, they define diversity solely in terms of skin pigmentation.

Without any scientific justification, liberals hoodwink black and Latino parents into believing that having more minorities teach their children will improve their performance. When George Wallace, Lester Maddux, and Bull Connor supported doing this we called them racists. Isn't it ironic that many of the advocates of this policy today belong to the same party as George Wallace and Lester Maddox?

But unlike the bigots from the Jim Crow era, today's opponents of a sound education for blacks and Latinos have academic credentials and even have lobbyists in Washington, D.C. With its 2.4 million members and $1.25 billion—that's billion with a "b"—annual budget, the liberal National Education Association (NEA) is one of the most influential teacher advocacy organizations in the United States. It also has the distinction of being one of the largest contributors to the Democrats. They, too, are on the diversity bandwagon.

When I spoke with former secretary of education Rod Paige, he explained that "the NEA is a national organization that masquerades as a teacher's organization, when it is really a lobbying organization. All you have to do is look at the issues that they address. A lot of them have nothing at all to do with education. . . . I don't want to be misunderstood here and have people think that I am opposed to unions. I do not oppose unions. In fact, there are many places in history where as a race, we were greatly benefited by unions." Nevertheless, says Paige, today's "teachers' unions, and especially the NEA, represent the greatest barrier to effective education for minority children than any other force. I think the nation is not paying attention to this issue."[14]

But their actions are quite revealing. Demonstrating that they're more interested in the rights of teachers rather than students, in 2005, the NEA spearheaded a national campaign to change the No Child Left Behind Act's provisions relating to minimum standards for teacher entrance exams. While attacking the minimum standards, they didn't admit that unqualified teachers hinder the educational attainment of students; they claimed that the standards imposed on minority teachers would harm diversity in the classroom. Below is the actual language from the NEA's 2004–05 "Focus on Blacks" report:

> Few can doubt the connection between student achievement and a highly qualified teacher workforce. Yet, the necessity for teacher diversity is often overlooked rather than accepted as central to school reform. High-stakes tests impede efforts to expand the pool of prospective teachers of color, and the logistics of the No Child Left Behind Act (NCLB) continue to create significant barriers to recruiting teachers of color . . . In most instances, fewer than 50 percent of African-Americans pass teacher entrance exams. This pattern prevails across time, location, and types of tests. The Collaborative [NEA task force] is proposing solutions that include revising NCLB measures to clearly spell out diversity as a critical element of a "highly qualified" teacher workforce, identifying and eliminating the obstacles faced by minority teachers in passing entry tests, and developing programs that support teachers of color both in the pipeline and in the classroom.[15]

Yes, the liberal solution to help black and Latino students overcome the Mt. Everest-sized academic deficiencies that separate them from their Asian and white classmates: force poor children to be taught by teachers who can't even pass a basic teacher competency exam.

Brilliant! Lester Maddox would be proud.

Is there any wonder why our black and Latino students remain academically uncompetitive and, on average, graduate high school with an eighth-grade education?[16]

Tragically, these policies are pushed in communities that can afford it least. For example, in 1997 Jerome Clark, the school superintendent in Prince George's County, Maryland, hired 600 new black teachers, many of whom were uncertified. Clark was belligerent about this decision—a measure which could be considered a horrific sacrifice of needy minority children on the altar of diversity. "We make no apologies for bringing into our school system people who may not be fully certified but are fully dedicated to our children," said Clark.[17] No one is arguing that we shouldn't have more black teachers in the schools, or white ones for that matter. The issue is that every teacher must be qualified. An affirmative action quota plan like Mr. Clark's is self defeating and will ultimately hurt children—it is a return to the pre-*Brown v. Board Education* second-class schoolhouse. This is reminiscent of taking blacks back to the Southern plantation, forcing them to only learn the limited skills that the slave master would allow. While certification is not an automatic indicator of teacher quality, neither is the color of one's skin.

There was yet another instance of pigmentation being viewed as more important than competence in California. In this instance, a group of minority applicants who failed the California Basic Educational Skills Test (CBEST) decided to sue the state of California on the grounds that the tests were racially discriminatory. One plaintiff, Sara Boyd, was a former teacher and guidance counselor. She stated that she had received many awards and accolades throughout her tenure in the government school system. The only thing holding her back from teaching was the mathematics portion of the CBEST.

During a videotaped deposition, Boyd stated that six of eighty teachers at her school were black, which she then estimated to be 1 or 2 percent. Later she realized that eight teachers at the school were black. "So, in fact, 10 percent of the faculty is African-American," the defense attorney reminded her.

"No," said Boyd.

"What percent of eighty is eight?" the defense attorney asked.

Boyd stood in silence for a full 40 seconds. "Can you rephrase that? I'm drawing a blank here," she said.

The attorney obliged.

Boyd then answered: "That's about 1 percent."[18]

These examples would be funny if their consequences weren't so disastrous. Moreover, as Niger Innis demonstrates, they illustrate a huge values chasm between liberals and conservatives.

So what is the liberal strategy? You handicap children from K through 12 education and then push them along through affirmative action once they are already in college and moving in their professional lives? That's not going to work. The way to truly help the community, they way to truly provide opportunity for individuals that would seek it, is to liberate the public schools and actually liberate the parents of children who are in the public schools so that they should have as many options as possible to educate their children properly.[19]

Placing diversity—defined narrowly as skin color alone—above teacher quality is not compassion. It is cruelty. And saddling black and Latino students who are already miles behind educationally with teachers who can't even pass a minimum skills test is inexcusable.

After learning about the high rate of failure on teacher licensing exams, one angry Latino mother from Cicero, Illinois, put it best when she said, "If they can't learn, how can they teach?"[20] Long after the bamboozlers have renegotiated their latest union contracts, black and Latino children will be the ones left to deal with the aftermath of having been taught by teachers, of whatever race, who don't know that eight is 10 percent of eighty.

It bears repeating that there is very little existing research that supports the idea proffered by the education establishment that a teacher's race directly influences a student's academic achievement. In contrast, if a teacher can't even perform simple division, there's no research needed to know that the consequences for the students will be significant. What's more, instituting a policy requiring teachers to teach students of their own race would not only be a breathtaking reversal of the landmark Supreme Court decision *Brown vs. Board of Education*, but, according to Harvard University professors Abigail and Stephan Thernstrom, it would be almost impossible:

> If minority students truly need minority teachers in order to learn, the racial gap may be impossible to close. There are proportionally many more white teachers than white students, and many fewer black, Hispanic, and Asian teachers than students from those racial and ethnic groups. To obtain a teaching force that perfectly mirrored the racial mix in the student population, the number of black teachers would need to be more than doubled, while the number of Hispanic and Asian-American teachers would have to almost quadruple.[21]

The bottom line: inner-city parents want what all parents want—the highest quality teachers available, regardless of skin color. Politically correct diversity policies serve no one and come at too great a price. If we want to narrow the achievement gap, we must get serious about improving teacher quality. In the final analysis, black and Latino students deserve better than what the education bamboozlers and their NEA cronies have given them.

America can and must do better for its students, says former Ohio secretary of state Ken Blackwell: "My position is that the standards are standards against which every child should be measured because the standards ought to reflect what they are going to need in an increasingly competitive global economy . . . all too often these young people are met with the bigotry of low expectations."[22]

Parents are growing impatient with the sluggish progress they've seen from public schools; some are beginning to see through the smoke screen created by liberals. What some of these parents don't realize is that the automatic support that many inner-city parents give to the Democrats is at cross-purposes with what these parents value most—their children. Why? Because most of these Democrats are in the pocket of the teachers' unions—one of the biggest financial backers of the party.

All too often, liberal lawmakers and the left-leaning teachers' unions—working in tandem—block the road for real education reform. "In the 1960s, Democrats blocked school doorways while Republicans pushed desegregation legislation," says black conservative columnist La Shawn Barber. "In 2004, Democrats continue to block school doorways while Republicans push school choice, the only hope many inner-city parents have to ensure their kids get a decent education."[23]

The final excuse the left-wing education bamboozlers use to explain the achievement gap is differences in class and income. According to this explanation, minorities are the victims of stifling poverty, a shameful residue of the horrors of slavery, and this, we are told, accounts for much of the achievement gap. There is no doubt that slavery and the terror unleashed by the KKK Democrats against blacks (the shocking history of which will be revealed in Part 2) after the Civil War has had a significant effect on the wealth and income of blacks. But it can't be shown that this affects the scores today. In fact, most studies show little to no correlation between a family's income and academic achievement in the minority community. Today, over a third of all black Americans live in a suburb, and 31 percent of blacks live in households that make more than $50,000 a year. While these numbers are still significantly below white households, they are hopeful signs of progress. Moreover, it indicates that there is a sufficient population available for testing the hypothesis that income explains academic achievement.

It is generally true that family income correlates positively with SAT scores. On the other hand, the black-white test score gap remains for even affluent blacks who live in suburban neighborhoods. Based on 2005 data from the College Board, the *Journal of Blacks in Higher Education* reported the following:

- Whites from families with incomes of less than $10,000 had a mean SAT score of 993. This is 129 points higher than the national mean for *all* blacks.
- Whites from families with incomes below $10,000 had a mean SAT test score that was 61 points higher than blacks whose families had incomes of between $80,000 and $100,000.
- Blacks from families with incomes of more than $100,000 had a mean SAT score that was 85 points below the mean score for whites from all income levels, 139 points below the mean score of whites from families at the same income level, and 10 points below the average score of white students from families whose income was less than $10,000.[24]

No matter how you look at it, you have to admit that there just isn't any way to claim that the problem is related to income. These findings are heartbreaking, as Stephen and Abigail Thernstrom confess. Moreover, they can leave one feeling defeated, as if there is no hope for positive change. *If economic status holds little promise in closing the achievement gap*, one wonders, *what ever will?* If the explanation proffered by bamboozlers for the achievement gap—inadequate funding, a shortage of minority teachers for minority students, and parental income/class—does not account for minority underperformance, then what does? Better still, how will inner-city parents ever be able to ensure that their children achieve their full potential? While there are no easy answers to solving the complex problem the achievement gap presents, many conservatives believe there are three core tools that will improve black and Latino student academic achievement: 1) school choice that empowers parents and students, not the education bureaucrats; 2) curricula that reject fads and politically correct distractions and instead embraces a back-to-basics approach; and 3) instilling and reinforcing the "soft skills"—the skills that influence how humans successfully interact, including such abilities as effective communication, creativity, analytical thinking, and the like. This is both in the classroom and, importantly, at home.

The parents of blacks and Latinos are beginning to see that it is conservatives and Republicans who support school choice programs and that it is the NEA, liberals, and most Democrats who fiercely oppose them. Why do conservatives support school choice and voucher initiatives? For a simple reason: vouchers work. School choice programs allow parents to direct funds earmarked by the government for education to a school of their choosing, whether public, private, or religious.

On the NEA website there are long, detailed arguments against allowing parents the option of choosing which school their child should attend. The website even includes a list of "talking points." But funnily enough, these talking points such as "Voters, for the last thirty years, have rejected vouchers every time," are belied by the significant effort put into debunking the concept. When a link reads, "Next time someone puts you on the spot, use these talking points to debunk the most popular voucher claims," the NEA has implicitly acknowledged that school choice is both popular and legitimate.

In a February 2006 *New York Times* article, columnist John Tierney explains that Democrat leaders are scrambling to figure out how to walk the tightrope between satisfying the teachers' union's opposition to vouchers for low-income families on the one hand, and avoiding a massive black voter revolt on the other. "Governor Jim Doyle, a Democrat, looks like public enemy number one for black schoolchildren," the *Times* columnist writes. "'He's throwing away my dream,' one Milwaukee student says in a TV commercial supporting the city's school voucher program for low-income families. Another commercial shows a black father on the verge of tears saying, 'School choice is good enough for the governor's family. I ought to be able to have it, too.'" The radio ads against the governor were equally powerful. One of the ads featured Ken Johnson, the black leader of the Milwaukee school board. That's right, the head of the public school board supports giving kids the chance to escape public schools.[25]

Why? Because Milwaukee's voucher program, which has served as the nation's school choice laboratory for fifteen years, has been a smashing success and has won numerous converts, except, as Tierney notes, the "Democrats [who are] terrified of teachers' unions." Indeed, black voters are beginning to see where the Democrats' true allegiance lies. Even after years of scare-tactic headlines, Milwaukee's black support for school choice continues to soar. Many of these scare tactics are so intellectually insulting that they border on the absurd.

Take a look at the September 2000 issue of *Essence* magazine, which ominously intoned: "Reading, Writing, Roulette: School Voucher Programs in Milwaukee, WI: Offering parents questionable choices, Milwaukee's ten-year-old experiment with voucher schools may be gambling with poor children's education." Although the public at large doesn't appear persuaded by these tactics, the so-called political leadership—particularly on the Left—appears to be immobilized by them. In a game of brinksmanship, Democrat Governor Doyle has consistently vetoed bills passed by Republican legislators to expand school choice throughout the state. Republicans, however, were able to win a showdown over the governor's proposed capping and rationing of the program.

As John Tierney's *New York Times* article questions, one wonders, "How long will blacks vote for a party that opposes the voucher programs they strongly favor? And how can Democrat leaders continue preaching their devotion to public schools while sending their own children to private schools?"[26]

Democrats' purported "strong support for public schools" is a joke, and has been for some time, as lawmakers on the state and federal level frequently send their children to private schools. Senator Hillary Rodham Clinton represents a striking case of hypocrisy and demagoguery on the issue. Clinton, who sent her daughter, Chelsea, to a private school, has resorted to outrageous scare tactics over the issue of school choice:

First family that comes and says, "I want to send my daughter to St. Peter's Roman Catholic School," and you say "Great, wonderful school, here's your voucher," Clinton said. Next parent that comes and says, "I want to send my child to the school of the Church of the white Supremacist. . . ." The parent says, "The way that I read Genesis, Cain was marked, therefore I believe in white supremacy. . . . You gave it to a Catholic parent, you gave it to a Jewish parent, under the Constitution, you can't discriminate against me." So what if the next parent comes and says, "I want to send my child to the School of the Jihad"? . . . I won't stand for it.[27]

Yes, Senator Clinton, and neither will the law. Under federal law, no one is permitted to create a school that advocates violence against the country.[28]

But even more striking than the over-the-top rhetoric and hypocrisy of Senator Clinton, has been the sizable exodus from the public schools by children whose parents teach at, well, public schools! According to a recent report by *USA Today*, children of urban school teachers are twice as likely to attend private schools. And nationwide, nearly a quarter of all public school teachers send their children to private schools. This raises a profound if obvious question: if America's public school teachers have lost faith in our public school system, why shouldn't the rest of us?[29]

Competition forces lackluster public schools to get their act together. As school choice advocate and former D.C. councilman Kevin Chavous says, "Bad schools closing is a good thing. That's a *very* good thing!"[30] The NEA fears school choice because it threatens their powerbase and membership dues. And elected officials who rely on those campaign donations are beholden to the NEA's view, whether it is legitimately supported by their constituents or not.

But once the public school monopoly is broken up, dwindling union funds will mean an atrophy of influence. Worse still for liberals, their grip on black parents appears to be weakening on the issue of education, as vouchers are extremely popular with black voters. Most polls find that the black level of support for vouchers hovers between 65 percent and 75 percent, depending on a person's age. The younger you are, the more likely you are to support them.

There is yet another troubling trend facing the Left's exploitation agenda. By allowing parents to choose their child's school, parents will be better able to navigate around public schools that value spreading the tenets of liberalism more than learning. This is especially important for black and Hispanic parents whose children are often targeted by liberal education administrators and planners. These "educrats" foist an untested multicultural curricula that teaches self-esteem and tolerance instead of mastery of the education essentials including writing, mathematics, and science. School choice gives parents an escape hatch, and that's something the NEA and the liberals simply can't allow.

Even after liberals trotted out the Rev. Jesse Jackson to try to gin up opposition to school choice, they were unable to bamboozle blacks into opposing this reform. "Vouchers are no substitute for a quality program for all," warned Jackson. "It is a rope for a few rather than a net for all."[31] The message continues to fall on deaf ears as blacks and Latinos continue to overwhelmingly support the free market approach to education that Republicans and conservatives have pioneered. And besides, who wants to be trapped in a net?

The secular constituency of the Democrats also makes it hard for the DNC as a party to formally support voucher programs. Why? Because vouchers might allow parents to choose parochial and Christian schools. But here again, blacks and Latinos find themselves standing on another electoral fault line that separates liberals from conservatives.

As we'll see in chapter five, the rift between people of faith and the Democratic Party is widening, not contracting. Black Americans make up one of the strongest faith communities in our nation. Many blacks are impervious to Democratic arguments about the "dangers" of Christian influence in politics. Why? Well, because the last time they checked, Dr. Martin Luther King Jr. was himself a Baptist preacher. Moreover, much of the Abolitionist movement was fueled by churches and Christian organizations. And perhaps most importantly of all, evangelical faith is hardwired into the black community. Politicians who fail to understand and respect this dimension of black and Latino America do so at their own electoral peril.

"There's a very strong foundation of Christian faith in the black community," news commentator Bill O'Reilly said during our interview. "Churches are the cornerstones of most neighborhoods, so that black Americans understand that the country was founded on Judeo-Christian philosophy, and this philosophy is good. . . . By their very nature, they're traditionalists. They don't want to wipe out, as the secular-progressives do, all spirituality from the marketplace. They think that's wrong."[32]

The NEA and other teachers' unions argue that vouchers undermine and erode the quality of American education. That's spin, and parents know it. Competition breeds innovation and efficiency. And besides, if American parents can't be trusted to decide what's best for their children, who can? As usual, the liberal answer is, "We can! We know what's best for your child!" "No thanks," parents seem to be saying. "We saw what you've done to our children for the last thirty years. We'll pass."

Public schools can be made to serve poor students well. But these successful schools often come about as the result of creative partnerships between private organizations and professionals. Here again, success stories exist that demonstrate the legions of "angels in the vineyard" doing the hard and often thankless work required for educational reform. One such individual is David Banks, principal of the Eagle Academy in Bronx, New York. During my tenure at

News Corporation as Director of Government Affairs and Diversity Development, I was approached by David Banks about starting up an all-male charter school in the Bronx. At the time, Banks, a member of the influential black professional organization, "One Hundred Black Men of New York," was principal of the School of Law, Government and Justice. As a result of News Corporation's nearly $500K grant and other corporate and community support, he was able to found the Eagle Academy, the first all-male public high school in the nation. When I recently spoke with him, he said:

> The school was started as the response to a growing national crisis that is impacting our young boys, and particularly young African-American and Latino men, who are not making it to the finish line. They are dropping out of school. They are continuing to fill our prison systems. We have more young people, young men of color, incarcerated than we have in college . . . We decided to use this as a real call to action. . . . So we are a college-bound preparatory academy where our intention is for all of our students to graduate and to go on to college.[33]

The Eagle Academy, which has a five-year strategic plan to put fifteen to twenty Eagle Academies throughout the metropolitan area, uses a rigorous academic curriculum tied to the learning styles of boys and emphasizes leadership and character development. Monday through Thursday, boys wear uniforms, including a tie decorated with eagles. On Fridays and Saturdays boys are free to wear polos and slacks. The Saturday Institute was started, Banks says, because "we believe that idle time is the devil's playground." So the Eagle Academy offers a series of extracurricular activities geared toward boys, including a trumpet academy; a chess program; a debate team that engages in Lincoln-Douglas-style policy debates; a robotics club that merges math, science, and technology; and a martial arts program that emphasizes self-discipline.

Beyond the intellectually rigorous core curriculum, the young men are expected to participate in community service projects and are each assigned a male adult mentor who agrees to serve as a mentor for the full four years of his student's high school experience. Banks says that the mentorship is one of the creative components that set the school apart:

> For each and every student in the school, a one on one mentor, men who are professional men, most of whom are men of color, but not all, but professional men who recognize that this is a serious crisis. These are men who do not have the time to do it. They're in their own professional careers. They have their own families. And yet they have decided to give further of themselves . . . these young men need to see positive male role models. You see, in the 'hood, young men don't see the investment bankers, and there are a lot of good brothers that are out there that are doing the right thing. And they don't all have to be investment bankers. They're police officers. They're firemen. They're sanitation workers. They're men who love and take care of their families. And a lot of the young men don't have enough interaction with these positive men. Far too many of them have very negative experiences with men—that father who constantly disappoints them or keeps telling them, "I'm coming to see you, son. I'm coming to see you. I'm coming next week. I'm coming next week." And they never show up. And this serves to really harden these young men emotionally, and so they put on a very tough exterior. And so unless you are exposing them to these other positive men, they only have negative images to deal with.[33]

Banks says that the core values of self-reliance, character, and leadership are at the heart of what the Eagle Academy strives to instill in its young men. He says that turning back the tide of fatherless homes, criminal delinquency, and disappointing academic achievement will only come when parents and teachers get serious about holding themselves to higher academic standards. Only they can create a "culture of cool" that includes a level of academic excellence and moral integrity that elevates and empowers the individual:

> Too many of our people have developed this sense of victimiza-
> tion—somebody is always supposed to do something for us . . . I
> don't think that that's what government should be designed to do,
> and we should never be so overly reliant on any government or any
> entity for our success. The Eagle Academy is really kind of represen-
> tative of that. It's a school where we're essentially saying that the
> most at-risk population—the young black male—can in fact change
> that circumstance once our minds are made up to do that.[34]

America needs more David Banks, more angels in the vineyards.

Another success story in the growing alliance between conservative policymakers and parents has been the explosion of charter schools. Since 1991, roughly 3,000 charter schools have been created, serving an estimated 750,000 school children nationwide. Charter schools are public schools that are open to all, free of charge, but that are not bound by the same regulations that limit traditional public schools. Charter school principals, for example, can fire incompetent teachers much more easily than in a traditional school.[35] As was the case with award-winning Oakland charter school principal Ben Chavis, charter school principals are given the freedom to structure classes, salaries, and just about anything else as they see fit.

There is no easy way to compare the performance standards of charter schools with traditional public schools, because many charter schools serve high populations of children who enter with far lower scores and aptitudes than their traditional public school counterparts. Still, the "parents will do what's in the best interests of their child" rule applies. Individual freedom and self-determination may be anathema to the collectivist, government-control impulses of liberals and many Democrats. But many parents are beginning to see clearly that big government approaches to education harm their children.

There is a great liberal myth that poor people somehow inherently love big government. That's false. It is true that a people in crisis will always seek a helping hand, but no one wants a lifetime of control. What many have come to realize is that the liberal/NEA public school system is holding their children back, not propelling them ahead.

This dawning reality is spreading in ways that are often hard to predict. It explains why in 2005, hip-hop rap mogul Russell Simmons met with Republican National Committee chairman Ken Mehlman to discuss poverty and related social ills. Asked how the meeting went, Simmons told the *Washington Post*, "There are practical solutions to the poverty problem and education problem that sometimes come out of Republican thinking. I don't have to agree with them on everything, but we have to be able to listen."[36]

I spoke with Russell Simmons, and his response might surprise many leftists. He stated that:

We can only win this war on poverty by having a real anti-poverty campaign. We want a guarantee of equal opportunity, not equal outcome. The GOP's fight for civil rights has always been a fight for opportunity; it's been about leveling the playing field to allow black Americans to compete. The strong Christian current that runs through the black community also means blacks believe that not everyone finishes the race in the same place; it is up to the individual to choose his or her own path that leads to hope and promise.

Issues like school choice expose the true intentions of liberals and should make women and minorities question whether they truly care about their interests. Increasingly, a new generation of blacks and Latinos are less willing to blindly advocate the failed liberal programs of the past. This is especially true for younger blacks whom polls show are much more open to Republican ideas and solutions achieved through private enterprise. Younger men like Jason Fields, a first-term state legislator who has defied his fellow Democrats by supporting vouchers, are a good example. "If the Democratic Party is supposed to be the party of the little guy, where do we get off opposing a chance to help those with the least of all?" he asked. The answer he's received from members in his own party has been that supporting vouchers and bucking the teachers' union will result in the union backing another Democrat to defeat him in the primary. "If they run someone against me, so be it," Fields says courageously. "I'm willing to leave it up to the voters to decide who really cares about African-Americans, and who's just spitting out rhetoric."[37] It's precisely this kind of independent thinking that has Democrats afraid that their overwhelming grip on minority voters is beginning to loosen.

In addition to increasing school choice, the second component of closing the achievement gap will demand that we get serious about the curricula teachers use. For centuries, teachers have relied on core teaching principles based on testing. This rigorous approach has produced impressive results. Instead of fashionable "flavor of the month" theories, students need a firm foundation based on essential skills in math, science, English, and humanities. One question we might do well to ask ourselves is: what characteristics would a great school embody that could promote black academic excellence?

Luckily, we have some guides. Indeed, black academic achievement hasn't always been as out of step with whites as current trends suggest, as Thomas Sowell's historical resarch demonstrates:

> In 1899, there were four academic public high schools in Washington, D.C.—one black and three white. In standardized tests given that year, students in the black high school averaged higher test scores than students in two of the three white schools. . . . That same school repeatedly equaled or exceeded national norms on standardized tests in the 1930s, 1940s, and early 1950s. . . . As of academic year 1892–93, of the known occupations of these parents, there were 51 laborers, 25 messengers, 12 janitors, and *one* doctor. . . . Over the entire 85-year history of academic success in this school, from 1870 to 1955, most of its graduates went on to higher education. . . . When black educator Horace Mann Bond studied the backgrounds of blacks with PhDs in 1970, he discovered that more of them had graduated from M Street-Dunbar than from any other black high school in the country.[38]

Sowell found that the average IQs of Dunbar students were near the national average, so he wanted to know what other factors might have produced such impressive results. The traits he identified were: less absenteeism and tardiness than white schools; well-trained principals, including the first black man to graduate from Harvard in 1870, and two later principals from Harvard as well; above average pay for Dunbar's teachers, despite having an extremely low operating budget; a non-Afrocentric curriculum that included, among other things, such Eurocentric courses as Latin and Greek; and an unyielding commitment to hard work and standards.[39]

Embedded in the miracle of Dunbar High School are the seeds for transformational education reform. While the GOP's first step of breaking up the education monopoly that Democrats and the NEA so fiercely guard is essential, it will be the job of parents to ensure that school curricula are grounded in sound educational practices.

Schools like this can only exist if voters reject what President George W. Bush has eloquently labeled the "soft bigotry of low expectations." The condescendingly low expectations for minority schoolchildren, and the aversion to high standards (teacher accountability and time-tested principles of pedagogy, i.e., phonics) that bamboozlers and teachers' unions have foisted on us for over 30 years, have wreaked havoc on minority children. And minority students and parents seem to resent the low expectations most of all. "When we answer a question wrong, they say, 'It's OK. You're really trying hard.' It's like, OK, but what's the answer?" said one student.[40]

Likewise, Joyce Croffitt, a black parent, said that the Atlanta public school her children attend did not expect enough from her two children. "I got the impression that with so many of our boys having a problem, they almost assumed [my son] would. And with my girl, I've found they tend to baby her."[41] What was intended as a way of boosting self-esteem actually had the unintended consequence of lowering it.

Efforts like the No Child Left Behind Act, which sets high standards, requires accountability for all, and measures improvements through testing, have come under intense fire from liberal Democrats and the NEA. But the No Child Left Behind Act is clearly working.

"The Republicans need to be more explicit about some of the things they are doing which are aimed at black people," says John McWhorter. "The Bush administration has done some really special things in terms of helping black children in particular, such as No Child Left Behind or the faith-based initiatives."[42]

McWhorter is right; the GOP needs to do a better job communicating what No Child Left Behind is and what it's not. For example, a March 3, 2006, *Los Angeles Times* article reported that "in the four years since the federal No Child Left Behind Act took effect, test scores in California have improved significantly, but the gaps between rich and poor, white and non-white, have widened." Well, of course they have! A rising tide lifts all ships. One would therefore logically expect that better teaching would produce an increase across all levels of educational attainment, regardless of race. That's hardly news.

What is news is that these pedagogically sound practices, which the NEA and many liberal Democrats excoriate as "teaching to the test," are producing steady gains for black students. The goal shouldn't be to artificially hold one group back so that the difference between the two will appear smaller on paper. That's ridiculous. Rather, the goal must be to give black students access to teachers and schools where they can receive high quality instruction using the back-to-basics principles that have stood the test of time. The best way to build a child's self-esteem and self-confidence is by giving him something to feel confident about.

The final and most important component of shoring up the achievement gap involves integrating families into the educational equation. Ultimately, parents are the stewards of their child's education. Building a culture of learning inside the home is essential if learning is to take root. Harvard sociologist Orlando Patterson argues that the primary explanation for the glaring racial gap in educational performance is not genetic but cultural. Patterson says that the culture of learning in black homes is often counterproductive to student achievement. This, he says, explains how a child growing up in an affluent black home could still be lagging academically. An individual might be worth an estimated $300 million, but that alone won't guarantee that his children will experience high educational achievement. It doesn't take a village to raise a child, but it does take a family committed to their child's education.

Another component of reinforcing excellence in the home involves honing what Harvard University Professors Stephan and Abigail Thernstrom call the "soft skills," such as decorum, the use of grammatically correct English, eye contact, and public etiquette. In my interview with Bill O'Reilly, he likewise underscored the importance of these subtle yet essential building blocks of success:

> Anybody who's looking for a handout is not going to succeed in America. America is a self-reliant nation. You've got to really get educated and depend on yourself if you want to succeed. If you think the government's going to pull you through, you're going to be sadly disappointed. Hurricane Katrina proved that. But you basically had in the black community a crossroads where many blacks came to the realization that education wasn't important. I don't know why that happened. And they didn't encourage it among their children or with books in the house. There wasn't supervision when the kids went to school. There wasn't proper grammar—people speaking the right way. All these things have to happen before the child wises up and says, "I'm going to have to pay attention in school. I'm going to have to learn how to speak English. I'm going to have to know how to write a sentence, or I'm not going anywhere. I'm going to jail or I'm going to be poor." That's America. This is a hyper-competitive, capitalist society. So the education that has spurred white success has not gripped the poor black precincts, and that's what has to happen. I mean, it has to be encouraged by not only parents, but ministers and leaders, and it isn't being encouraged. School vouchers would be a big plus because then parents who don't have a lot of money wouldn't be confronted with terrible schools.[43]

Because of the enormous flexibility to tailor and customize curricula, many charter schools serving minority populations are chosen to teach and reinforce the soft skills that educators like the Thernstroms stress. Moreover, minority parents whose children attend charter schools are also mentored in the art of extending learning beyond the classroom walls and into the home. "Today most public school principals and other administrators and teachers are very nervous about an education in the soft skills, but I think these are equally important to reading, writing, and arithmetic," says Abigail Thernstrom. "They feel 'oh wait a minute, we're interfering with the culture of the students; we're showing disrespect,' but these habits are going to be disastrous as these students get older. If you do not learn these soft skills, you will not climb the ladder of economic and social opportunity in America."[44]

One of the exciting trends that school choice has produced is the integration of exactly these soft skills into the design of charter schools. Charter schools, like the award-winning KIPP Academy in Houston, Texas, are teaching parents how to transform their homes into places of intellectual growth and learning. In other words, they stress that the culture of the classroom must flow seamlessly into the culture of the home. Parents must be parents. If learning isn't being reinforced at home, the lessons of the classroom will wither.

Closing the achievement gap will not be easy. But as former secretary of education Rod Paige likes to say, the best thing for minority students is to make that gap visible, because then we can begin to attack it. The marriage between liberals and the NEA has forced them to choose between what is best for black students and what is politically expedient. Unfortunately, some Democrats have put their allegiance to the liberal agenda above what's best for minority children.

Regardless, black support for school choice remains strong and is growing stronger. Partnerships and collaborations between black parents and conservative Republicans have highlighted the common values shared by both. Together, they have begun to forge alliances designed to narrow the achievement gap. By fighting for greater school choice, demanding high standards from all, and promoting and reinforcing a culture of learning in the home, they are not only fighting for our nation's future, they are beginning to see that they are more alike than different.

For the bamboozlers, that's cause for alarm. For minority children and their parents, it's cause for celebration.

4

"RACIST COPS . . . UM . . . YEAH, THAT'S IT!"

The Liberal Love Affair with Criminal Leniency

Congress should be considering how to make sure young people stay out of jail, not keeping legislation on the books that puts more of them inside . . . but that won't sell well to Red State champions Bill O'Reilly, Rush Limbaugh, and Sean Hannity.

—Representative Charlie Rangel (D-NY)

Why is it that America has the largest penitentiary population in the whole world? It's because they have gotten away from this thing called accountability.

—Judge Joe Brown

When it comes to convicted murderers, rapists, thugs, and pedophiles, Senator Hillary Clinton wants Americans to know that she's not going to take it anymore. She's fed up. Oh, not the part about them murdering, raping, and molesting, mind you. No, she's hopping mad that the felons who did the murdering, raping, and molesting have been "disenfranchised" from voting— for liberals.

"The Voting Rights Act helped take our country forward, helped us to build an America that reaches ever closer to her ideals," said Clinton. "We should not have to plead or to debate the importance of protecting the right to vote in America . . . We also need to make sure that voters have faith in the fairness and accuracy of our voting system and the Count Every Vote Act is an important step toward restoring this covenant. We must be able to easily and accurately count every vote so that every vote counts."[1]

Senators Hillary Clinton and John Kerry have sponsored what could easily be named the "Make Every Murderer and Rapists' Vote Count Act" to lock up the votes of those who are, well, locked up.[2] The four million felons who, according to the bill, are disenfranchised due to varying state laws that restrict or ban convicted criminals from casting ballots are among the most sought after voting bloc by liberals. Today, only Maine and Vermont allow inmates to vote during their prison sentence.[3] The remaining forty-eight states ban felons from voting altogether or require that felons undergo a formal process before regaining voting rights.

It's common sense to most people. But to Clinton and Kerry, it's evidence that a racist system has been created wherein "thirteen percent of the African-American adult male population, or 1,400,000 African-American men, are disenfranchised. Given current rates of incarceration, three in ten African-American men in the next generation will be disenfranchised at some point during their lifetimes."[4] Apparently, the 31 percent of Hispanics that make up the federal prison population aren't nearly as important to Clinton and Kerry as are black felons.[5]

Moreover, imagine how removed from reality you must be to believe that the killers and thugs behind bars are the victims. Here again is another example of liberals acting on their view that people are not accountable or responsible for their actions. What next, allow prisoners to start a petition drive to end mandatory sentencing and repeal the death penalty? When balanced against the victims of these hardened felons one can't imagine why there would be any willingness to consider their views on proposals like these at all. But if you look carefully, this policy just demonstrates how desperate liberals are to keep power at all costs.

Like bank robber Willie Sutton's unapologetic view that the reason he robbed banks was because "that's where the money was," liberals like Hillary Clinton push felon voting provisions because that's where the votes are.

On this point, Hillary's "Ensure That I Win the 2008 Presidential Election Act" is absolutely correct: black and Latino inmates far outstrip their white counterparts as a factor of their presence in the population. As noted above, there are 1.4 million black men in the criminal justice system. The number of blacks alone equals as many people as inhabit the city of Philadelphia, the fifth largest city in America. In some cities, over 50 percent of all young minority males are under criminal or court ordered supervision.[6] Additionally, according to the Bureau of Prisons, Latinos make up 31 percent of the federal prison population.[7]

Assuming that all felons and prisoners—black and Hispanic—vote for Democrats at the same rate as the non-arrested civilian population, they constitute a huge treasure trove of votes for the Left. Furthermore, studies estimate that should a bill like Clinton's ever pass, at least a third of all felons would likely vote in the presidential election. Of those, an estimated 85 percent, or 1.2 million votes, would go to the Democrats.[8]

Now don't think that Senators Kerry and Clinton are alone. There are quite a few liberals on this bandwagon. Take a look at former Iowa governor Tom Vilsack. Not wanting to be outdone, or to lose out on a significant advantage heading into the 2008 Democratic presidential primary, dark horse candidate Tom Vilsack recently acted to give felons in Iowa the right to vote. After all, he couldn't let Clinton and Kerry bask in all the felonious glory. In his eagerness to show that his decision was merited and not as reckless as many critics might have imagined, he told the *New York Times* about studies claiming that enfranchisement deters recidivism.[9] Ah, yes! It's that "I must vote for a liberal or I'll kill again" syndrome we've all been reading so much about. You can almost feel the pre-election energy inside prison cells everywhere: "Yeah, I tell ya what . . . if they don't let me vote for Hillary Clinton, I just may have to go and murder someone—again!"

College professors who teach argument and logical fallacies should file this one under *post hoc, ergo propter hoc* (Latin for "After this, therefore because of this"). Just because it rains every time I walk outside, does not mean that me walking outside *causes* it to rain. But why should Vilsack care? He's supporting the politically correct cause and has been lauded by the *New York Times*. He's fighting against the Man (assuming, of course, that by the Man we mean logic, reason, civility, and any sense of sanity).

Liberal Democrats like Clinton, Kerry, and Vilsack never miss a chance to grandstand on race matters. They are always trying to showcase their commitment to diversity and equality, and for them this issue is no different. By couching the debate in terms of protecting numbers of criminals from being disqualified from voting, the bamboozlers contend that once a criminal has served his time and paid his debt to society (as if murderers, rapists, or molesters can ever fully repay the victim and the family of those they've harmed), it's "a matter of fairness" that they should be given their rights back. Who's giving the rape victims their dignity and security back? Who's restoring the pedophile victim's innocence? Who's giving the murder victim's life back?

But I digress.

Whether liberals' eagerness to reinstate the voting rights of criminals is just a cynical election ploy or a genuine reflection of liberals' longstanding love affair with criminals doesn't matter. One thing is certain: doing so would trigger a seismic shift in America's fifty-fifty red state vs. blue state reality. Writing in *Newsweek* magazine, George Will explained, "It is indelicate to say but indisputably true, most felons—not all; not those, for example, from Enron's executive suites—are Democrats. Or at least were they to vote, most would vote Democratic."[10]

This alone should give Americans pause. If those who maim, rape, and kill their fellow citizens overwhelmingly support liberals and the Democrats, maybe it's time to rethink how the rest of us cast our ballots. What do the felons know about Democrats that we don't? Voters should ask themselves: do we really want convicted child molesters to have a say in the punishments for child molesters? Is it wise to allow rapists to affect laws covering rape? "If you're not willing to follow the law," says Roger Clegg, vice president of the Center for Equal Opportunity, "then you shouldn't claim the right to make the law for everyone else by voting."[11]

But even beyond all this, giving convicted felons the right to vote would be nothing short of the worst form of bamboozling of minorities and the poor. Liberals would be rewarding those who terrorize minorities most: felons. And let's not forget that most of those minorities in prison have committed crimes against other minorities. This is particularly true with blacks. According to the U.S. Department of Justice, of the 559,130 crimes of violence committed against black Americans in 2004, 73.6 percent were perpetrated by blacks.[12] Furthermore, black murder victims are almost entirely killed by other blacks. According to the Bureau of Justice

Statistics, from 1976 to 2004, *94 percent* of all black murders were committed by blacks.

But liberals couldn't care less. They'd win elections. And at the end of the day, that's what's important. Yet tellingly, this is just another example of how liberals exploit minorities and the poor. The cellblock voting bloc is simply too large for liberals to ignore. So by talking in terms of racial equality and fairness, Democrats bamboozle the very law-abiding minorities whose neighborhoods are under siege. It's breathtaking to see their boldness.

Meanwhile, black and Latino Americans, whose communities are disproportionately impacted by crime, are told that their biggest problem is the law enforcement community—the very same law enforcement community that tries to save their neighborhoods every day. "Systemic racism" and poverty, liberals tell us, are the "root cause" of crime, not the individuals who commit them. Given the history of unfair implementation of laws and the unfair prosecution of minorities (largely the fault of the Democrats, as we'll see in Part 2 of this book), it's easy to see how anti-establishment rhetoric might resonate with minorities. But by giving criminals safe harbor in their neighborhoods, the bamboozled are aiding and abetting the very thugs who prey on them.

Come on now!

Growing up in Mississippi, the epicenter of the Jim Crow South, my father suffered tremendously from poverty and the inequalities of a racist society. Yet my father didn't grab a gun and join a gang. He got a degree—three of them, actually. So when I hear friends who are Democrats (and when you're black, you have a lot of them) pushing the "poverty thug" rhetoric, I tell them "what role does accountability play in these decisions? It's all about choice!" No one forces you to sell drugs, rob liquor stores, rape, or terrorize our neighborhoods. The solution is that most of these men need to get a job. I'm sick and tired of the blame game.

Only liberals would insult the poorest among us with a condescending compassion that paints poor folks as potential criminals. That's ridiculous and insulting. Some of the most decent and moral people you'll ever meet are poor. Poverty doesn't cause criminality, criminals cause criminality! Guns don't kill people, people kill people!

Let's take a look at what the Left wants minorities and the poor to believe. According to liberals, there is a racist government that forces minorities to commit crimes. Then bigoted cops, joined by racist judges and prosecutors operating in a massive conspiracy, frame and see to it that otherwise upstanding and law-abiding minority citizens are sentenced. This is their explanation for the nearly 1.4 million inmates?

Don't misunderstand, our criminal justice system is not perfect. Moreover, any reports of law enforcement malfeasance are dismaying, and whenever these events happen, the punishment should be severe. But these are the exception, not the rule. Unfortunately for the Left, this is all part of that vast right-wing conspiracy Hillary Clinton warned us about.

It was Rev. Jesse Jackson who said, "There is nothing more painful to me at this stage in my life than to walk down the street and hear footsteps and start thinking about robbery and then look around and see somebody white and feel relieved."[13]

Jackson isn't a bigot for keeping his guard up. Neither does his rare moment of candor make him a closet racist. It does make him statistically literate.

In fact, this example gives a great insight into the hypocrisy of the race-baiting tactics of the Left. When liberals engage in race-baiting about crime, their tactics may prove politically satisfying in the short run. But any gains come at the expense of primarily black and Latino neighborhoods. America cannot allow this. The overwhelming majority of minorities are law abiding, God-fearing Americans, and yet they are the ones who suffer most from criminal mayhem. No amount of rhetoric and protests by liberals will change that fact. As Bill Cosby courageously pointed out in his now-famous Pound Cake speech before the NAACP, commemorating the fiftieth anniversary of the *Brown vs. Board of Education* ruling, minorities are the ones being victimized:

> I'm talking about these people who cry when their son is standing there in an orange suit. Where were you when he was two? Where were you when he was twelve? Where were you when he was eighteen, and how come you don't know he had a pistol? And where is his father, and why don't you know where he is? And why doesn't the father show up to talk to this boy? . . . People getting shot in the back of the head over a piece of pound cake! Then we all run out and are outraged: "The cops shouldn't have shot him!" What the hell was he doing with the pound cake in his hand? I wanted a piece of pound cake just as bad as anybody else. And I looked at it and I had no money. And something called "parenting" said "if you get caught with it you're going to embarrass your mother." Not, "You're going to get your butt kicked." No. "You're going to embarrass your mother." "You're going to embarrass your family."[14]

Are there crooked cops in America? Sadly, there are. Does a fraction of the law enforcement community abuse its authority or harbor racist attitudes? Tragically, the answer is yes. And when these inexcusable violations occur, they must be prosecuted to the fullest extent of the law. Period. But victims in poor and inner-city neighborhoods know better than anyone who the real predators are. For these people, their problem consists of the hoods and thugs who often live in their neighborhoods.

Liberals don't talk about the victims, because that would underscore the twin themes of personal accountability and individual responsibility, arch enemies of liberalism. Instead, liberals prefer to stoke minority frustrations and dissatisfaction.

The result of all this, of course, is that if nothing is done about crime, minority communities are less safe. As the communities continue to decline, increasingly more of the middle class leaves them. Next, businesses flee and the vicious cycle of neighborhood decay continues. Finally, only the criminals and those with no other options are left in these ghettos. This pattern is happening over and over again in black and Latino neighborhoods across the country.

There is no doubt that the disproportionate incarceration rate for blacks and Latinos has produced devastating consequences for the children growing up with inmate fathers. Moreover, the oft-heard complaint from black women that the ballooning prison figures have limited the pool of marriageable black males in America is not without merit. When the number of college-age males in prison is at near parity with the number of men in college among blacks, empathetic minds can understand the frustration of many black women. But increasing the dating and marriage pool by being soft on crime is hardly a strategy for strengthening minority families. Playing patty-cake with criminals—whatever their race—is not the solution to addressing the consequences of high minority incarceration rates of men in the black community. Punishing criminals is the best way to end criminality or prevent it in the first place.

The numbers don't lie. The consequences of being bamboozled are all around us. We don't need to look far to see what coddling of criminals by liberals has meant for the overwhelming majority of law-abiding poor people in America, people striving to live the American dream and raise their children without the fear of stray bullets whizzing past them on their way to school. "It's very much in the interest of poorer Americans to be tough on crime policies," said Bill Kristol, editor of the *Weekly Standard*. "The poor are the victims of crime disproportionately. . . . If you are a poor mom trying to raise a couple of kids, the last thing you want is a bunch of crack dealers getting out of jail and put back in your neighborhood."[15]

These challenges are significant and real, and no one should diminish the pain involved, particularly for young boys searching to find their way into manhood without a father figure to light their path. Having spent decades working with wayward young men, my mentor and family friend, Judge Joe Brown, says that the cards are stacked against young boys growing up in homes where no strong male presence can be found:

> If you don't give the boys an adventure, they are not going to do very well in life. And you've got adventure out on the street, a lot of danger out there on the streets, so what are you going to do to give them adventure or to glamorize the adventure that is not essentially negative? See, rap glamorizes the adventure and the danger, but it does it in a negative way, but it's reflective of a reality . . . You have a total dearth in the inner city of male ritualization, man-training . . . Boys are being raised in families where for four or five generations there has been no man involved with the family. And I mean 'man,' not just male. There is a lack of understanding of what a male growing up is supposed to acquire in knowledge, a complete lack of understanding in what men are supposed to do. And that has caused a complete breakdown in social order.

Feminists are likely to balk at Brown's call for greater male ritualization and man-training and say that such efforts would only result in "patriarchal hegemony." But it was following the path of the bamboozlers that led us to where things are today. Minorities should hardly be deterred from seeking out the conservative values that for generations sustained and girded all American families. To be sure, the pathologies that a fatherless upbringing can create for young boys and girls are sobering. Indeed, study after study continues to reveal that children that grow up in homes without a father are more likely to grow up to be incarcerated themselves.[16]

The important thing is to realize that these patterns should not be seen as a justification for ignoring or weakening the laws that protect the innocent. Moreover, blaming police departments and "racist America" ignores the simple fact that no one, not even the most virulent racist, can force someone to commit murders, join gangs, or rape women and children. Much to the chagrin of liberals, human beings are responsible for their own actions.

"It's not supposed to be nice on the San Francisco [liberal] mentality to really come down on somebody and kick his butt when he doesn't do right," says Judge Joe Brown. "He's not supposed to be held accountable; he's supposed to deal with his emotions and express himself, and he does not want his creativity, nor his or her self-esteem to be slightly scrunched by dealing with reality. The liberals don't do anything to change the problem because they encourage the development of the problem."[17]

Judge Brown isn't preaching conservatism, he is promoting common sense. Instead of making inner-city neighborhoods safer, liberals often wage symbolic policy fights that inflame racial resentment. But to what end? Sure, it keeps inner-city residents angry (most of whom are black and Latino), and they continue voting for

Democrats. On the other hand, the inflamed racial tensions do nothing to keep communities of color safe. This reality is seldom discussed. The effort by Hillary Clinton and John Kerry to restore the voting rights of four million felons is hardly the dream for which Dr. Martin Luther King Jr., W. E. B. Dubois, Mary McLeod Bethune, and countless others fought and died.[18]

So here's a suggestion: why not fight to keep those who kill minorities *out* of the community, rather than fight to keep them in it? Why not organize marches to protect girls who get raped, not marching to support the rights of their rapists? How about supporting policing tactics that make communities safer? But liberals won't do these things because it would hurt, not help, Democrats in winning elections. And so, the love affair liberals have with criminals continues.

Schemes by liberals are designed to do what the bamboozlers do best: sucker Americans into believing that the Democrats have, as a party, historically fought for minorities and the poor, and that they continue do so today. As we'll see in Part 2 of this book, this claim is laughable and unsupported by the evidence. They (liberals) continue to intellectually insult us.

Specifically, liberals spend a great deal of time fomenting anger among minority voters. They do so by raising issues that largely ignore the true catalysts of crime in the inner city instead of focusing on policies that would address the dearth of present and actively engaged fathers and intact two-parent families. It is vital that black Americans whisk away liberals' time-wasting "blame whitey" arguments, says top-rated black radio host and *New York Times* best-selling author Larry Elder:

> How dare I suggest that the fate of blacks is, well, in the hands of
> blacks! Many blacks, encouraged by the so-called black leadership,

view life starkly. Us against them. Black versus white. Rich versus poor. Key is the following assumption: that whites encourage, endorse, perpetuate, welcome, are happy about, and take pride in the oppression of blacks. Challenge the traditional white-man-done-me-wrong-and-continues-to-do-so mentality, and some blacks go absolutely crazy.[19]

We need to get on with the difficult and dire task of rebuilding and restoring the role of men as integral to child rearing and the overall health of the family. Let's start by debunking liberals' racist paranoia surrounding two more issues that liberals rally around: changing the sentencing disparities between crack versus cocaine, and eliminating the so-called racist death penalty.

The moral dexterity of liberals is sometimes breathtaking. Take, for example, the debate over giving tougher sentences to users of crack versus powdered cocaine. During the late 1980s and '90s our nation's inner cities reached the height of the crack cocaine epidemic. As a consequence, today under federal law, possession of five grams of crack cocaine triggers a mandatory minimum penalty of five years in prison. Defendants convicted of selling crack cocaine receive sentences equal to those convicted of selling 100 times (500 grams) the same amount of powder cocaine. Simply put, you'd have to have nearly 100 times as much powdered cocaine to receive the same sentence you would for selling crack cocaine. This 100-to-1 ratio has been cited by some as being unfair.

Not surprisingly, because of their vastly different street values, users of crack cocaine tend to be poor and disproportionately minority, whereas powdered cocaine, preferred by the Wall Street and Hollywood jet set, tends to be bought and used by wealthier individuals.

At the time the law was adopted, however, there existed a rare moment of moral clarity. Some liberals, including members of the Congressional Black Caucus, supported significantly stiffer punishments for criminals who sold crack cocaine versus powdered cocaine. Their rationale was predicated on three justifications: First, crack is more addictive than powdered cocaine (due to its method of intake). Second, they wanted to keep this addictive drug out of black communities. And finally, and most importantly, because of its low price point and easy methods of production, black leaders wanted to avoid its potential to spread like wildfire through minority communities, leaving devastated lives in its path. Similarly, this is the reason that crystal meth (predominantly in rural white communities) is also treated so harshly by state and local governments.

So beginning in 1986, Congress enacted tougher drug laws, including mandatory minimum sentences for crack cocaine, resulting in crack cocaine use having a greater penalty than powdered cocaine. But by 2001, many political leaders recognized that the disparity had to be addressed. President George W. Bush said, "I think a lot of people are coming to the realization that maybe long minimum sentences for the first-time users may not be the best way to occupy jail space and/or heal people from their disease. And I'm willing to look at that," and encouraged that lawmakers examine "making sure the powder-cocaine and the crack-cocaine penalties are the same. I don't believe we ought to be discriminatory."[20] The ACLU interpreted this statement as a sign that the administration would support repeal of the crack cocaine sentencing measure.

The ACLU, however, misinterpreted the president's intentions. In 2002, the president's deputy attorney general, Larry D. Thompson, who happens to be black, offered testimony before the

Sentencing Commission. Thompson argued for bringing crack and powdered cocaine punishments into greater alignment, even though crack's effects on communities are far worse. He noted that crack is more psychologically addictive, results in far more emergency-room episodes, contributes "heavily to the deterioration of neighborhoods and communities," is associated with violent crime to a far greater extent (crack convictions are twice as likely to involve a firearm), and "is strongly linked to prostitution" (86.7 percent of women in one survey were not involved in prostitution the year before they started using crack). Nevertheless, Bush's deputy attorney general said it was time to narrow the gap between the two. To correct this, Thompson argued, we shouldn't reduce crack sentences. Instead he urged that punishments for powdered cocaine be increased. This would level the playing field by raising the penalties for powdered cocaine use to levels similar to that of crack cocaine.

Characteristically, the ACLU and other liberal groups were in an uproar. Raising powdered cocaine sentences they asserted "would have a disproportionate impact on Hispanics, who comprise over 50 percent of powder cocaine defendants."[21] Imagine: punishing powdered cocaine use is a conspiracy against Latinos. "This change would make the current problems even worse" and would "lead to additional racial disparities, thus increasing skepticism and distrust of the criminal justice system in minority communities," the ACLU argued.[22] This isn't a help for either the black or the Latino population—this type of advice is destructive and is reminiscent of the Jim Crow terrorism that ravaged so many blacks in the Deep South.

Reasonable people can and should debate the effectiveness of American drug policies. Indeed, many libertarians and some conservatives, including conservative William F. Buckley Jr., have long argued for reforming certain portions of drug laws and punishments. I have no problem with that. But if you're going to have laws regulating drug use, you should be allowed to recognize which types of drugs are doing the most harm.

And it is for this reason I take exception to the actions of the Congressional Black Caucus. These elected leaders originally supported tougher crack sentences, and in some cases even argued for tougher penalties than the ones that were adopted. Now they have reversed course without any admission of flip-flopping. And to add insult to injury, they use the "race card" to bamboozle minorities into believing that a policy that *they helped create* was a racist right-wing conspiracy designed to oppress blacks and Latinos. John J. DiIulio Jr., scholar and former director of White House Faith-Based Initiatives, explains:

> Liberal experts contend that the penalties for crack cocaine possession and sale are excessive compared with powder cocaine penalties. I concur. And liberals are also right that blacks are far more likely than whites to use and sell crack instead of powder cocaine. But . . . they feed the conspiratorial myth that federal anti-crack penalties were born of a white conspiracy led by right-wing Republicans. Go check the *Congressional Record:* in 1986, when the federal crack law was debated, the Congressional Black Caucus (CBC) supported it, and some CBC members pressed for even harsher penalties. A few years earlier it was CBC members and other Democrats in Congress who pushed President Reagan, against his considered judgment, to create the Office of National Drug Control Policy.[23]

As DiIulio also points out, it was President Clinton, a Democrat, not any Republican presidents, who diffidently refused to change the federal penalty structure for drug crimes. But again, one wouldn't know that from listening to critics as they spew their harsh and unfounded race-baiting rhetoric. Consider these statements by two of the most senior Black Caucus members, Congressman John Conyers and Rep. Charlie Rangel. First, Congressman John Conyers, the dean of the Congressional Black Caucus, had this to say: "We all know that these unfair sentences have exerted a terrible toll on communities of color, but many in Congress have lacked the bravery to take an issue that has been such a focus of political demagoguery."

Bravery?!

Conyers continued: "Mandatory sentencing laws disproportionately affect people of color and, because of their severity, destroy families."[24]

The *laws* are destroying families, Congressman? Or is it the crack addicts who are destroying families? Which one, Mr. Conyers? Do you really expect us to believe that families would be stronger if crack addicts were inside our homes and neighborhoods, free to inflict violence and crime on innocents?

Say it with me: *bamboozled!*

Up next is Rep. Charlie Rangel, a charismatic veteran politician from New York. Representative Rangel, who originally supported the early crack sentencing laws, wrote a letter to the Inter-American Commission on Human Rights on March 3, 2006, about the sentencing disparity. In his letter, Rangel inexplicably lashes out at Bill O'Reilly, Rush Limbaugh, and Sean Hannity—none of whom were then or have ever been elected officials—for cracking down on crack cocaine. Here's a copy of Rep. Rangel's letter:[25]

CHARLES B. RANGEL
15th Congressional District
New York

Congress of the United States
House of Representatives
Washington, DC 20515-3215

March 3, 2006

Inter-American Commission on Human Rights
OSB Building of the Organization of American States
1889 F Street N.W.
Washington, D.C. 20006

Dear Commission:

I regret that I am unable to be present at today's hearing. I have to be in New York for a previously scheduled engagement. I am extremely pleased to know that this issue will be receiving the attention it so deserves. In 2002, 81.4% of those convicted of crack cocaine offenses in federal courts were Black men. Because African Americans serve substantially more time in prison for drug offenses than their white counterparts, black communities and families are directly affected by the disparity in sentencing and the mandatory minimum sentencing guidelines of the Controlled Substance Act. I feel very strongly that the current law is unfair and must be revisited in order to bring a sense of fairness to sentencing in Crack Cocaine cases.

Amnesia is always a dangerous thing. Back in 1986, Congress was frightened by the specter of crack cocaine leaving America's inner cities and coming to the suburbs. So in an effort to protect America from the onslaught, Congress passed mandatory minimum sentences for drug possession and use. This took the discretion of sentencing out of the hands of judges. The legal minimum punishment for having powder cocaine became 100 times less than the punishment for having crack cocaine. Cocaine—crack as well as powder—did not overrun the country, but the damage was done.

That's why I continue to sponsor bills that attempt to stop mandatory minimum sentencing for crack cocaine. And that's why I'm supporting the "Cracked Justice" campaign, which launched here on Feb. 13. Several criminal justice organizations, including Families Against Mandatory Minimums and the Sentencing Project, are making sure federal mandatory drug sentences don't reach their 21st birthday.

The issue is considered such a blatant human rights violation that the campaign was recently granted an audience from the Inter-American Commission on Human Rights. The March 3rd hearing will display to the world uniquely American contradictions that seem to be willfully forgotten by the mainstream media and by the three branches of government.

No one can justify the 100-to-1 ratio. Although there are larger numbers of documented white crack cocaine users, federal drug enforcement and prosecutorial practices have resulted in the so-called "War on Drugs" being targeted at inner city communities. This has caused an overwhelming number of prosecutions and convictions coming from these communities, with African Americans disproportionately subject to the unreasonably harsh, crack cocaine penalties.

Clearly we are talking about different neighborhoods (cocaine the choice for affluent white neighborhoods and crack for Black and Latino urban centers), not different crimes. Ironically, crack and cocaine have the same level of high, so the difference is literally cosmetic. "Tough on crime" rhetoric be damned, this discrepancy is both stupid and inconsistent with a civilized country. Congress should be considering how to make sure young people stay out of jail, not keeping legislation on the books that put more of them inside. Study after study shows that it costs less to rehabilitate and treat victims of drug abuse than it is to warehouse them, but that won't sell well to Red State champions Bill O'Reilly, Rush Limbaugh or Sean Hannity.

I've been trying to do my part. I introduced my legislation on this issue—the Crack Cocaine Equitable Sentencing Act—in 1993. I introduced it again last year. It would both eliminate the mandatory five-year penalty for first-time possession of crack cocaine and equalize crack and powder cocaine offenses.

Can this battle be won under this administration and this Congress? Those of us in the thick of the fight don't have the luxury of asking this question. Like Mrs. Parks and Mrs. King, I'm marching on 'till either victory is won or I'm remembered well.

The law destroying the crack-cocaine disparity will be reality soon, and I believe with all my heart I'll be there to see it signed. Now that Black History Month has come quickly to a close, I now understand more than ever that I owe this battle to those ancestors, old and new, who had much tougher fights than mine.

Sincerely,

CHARLES B. RANGEL
Member of Congress

CBR/llm

Here's the rest of the story. Rep. Charles Rangel was a key sponsor of the original bill. In fact, he was *so* central to passing the original Anti-Drug Abuse Act of 1986 that during the bill signing ceremony, President Ronald Reagan said this: "United, together, we can see to it that there's no sanctuary for the drug criminals who are pilfering human dignity and pandering despair. There've been some real champions in the battle to get this legislation through Congress: Senators Bob Dole, Robert Byrd, and Strom Thurmond; Congressmen Bob Michel, Jim Wright, Benjamin Gilman, Charles Rangel, and Jerry Lewis."[26]

Look at it again: Rep. Charles Rangel: *A champion in the battle to get this legislation through.*

There's nothing wrong with policymakers admitting they were wrong, or even that their thinking has changed as new information or more accurate data have emerged. Honest changes in thought and heart occur. There's nothing wrong with that.

Rangel isn't the only elected official who might say one thing one day and another thing another day. It actually is the standard practice for liberal bamboozlers. I asked John McWhorter about this phenomenon and he provided some insights into why this happens so often:

> I love talking to black audiences, but my least favorite aspect of black audiences is that all you have to do is say the word "racism" and half of the room goes, 'Mom-hmm.' It's this powerful word, as if that defines our whole existence—how white people feel about us. Somebody can say "Republicans are racist" and just the sound of the two words used in the same sentence gets people excited. I wish that weren't true. I wish we could be more constructive.[27]

But all this misses the biggest and most important point: *why in the world are we wasting time on foolishness like this when there are so many real problems in America; particularly in communities of color.* If it's not crack, it will be some other drug that fills the voids in the hearts of young black and Latino teens. And if they're not selling crack, they'll be selling crystal meth, acid, or ecstasy, or engaging in binge drinking, or . . . the point is that liberals are so busy passing laws and then calling those same laws racist that they've ignored the core issue: the collapse of the family and the urgent need for male leadership in the homes and lives of their children.

David Banks, principal of the Eagle Academy in the Bronx, says that so much of what he sees in his students and ailing young black men goes straight back to the role of fathers in the home:

> I think this issue of fatherlessness, beyond the economic issues that have been written about, I believe is one of a very serious level of selfishness and irresponsibility. To a very, very large extent a lot of our men are not taking care of their children—it's not about financial issues. It's simply about that they've been allowed to be part of a culture that portrays them as victims. And my feeling is—and I know a lot of these men—it's nonsense. Nonsense.[28]

It will be up to the next generation of leaders to move beyond the race-baiting rhetoric. What plagues America is not stiff crack penalties. What plagues America is that record numbers of young men are turning to crime instead of college, building impressive criminal records instead of outstanding résumés. In early 2005, Bill Cosby noted the sheer folly of a liberal leadership that exploits black voters to win Democratic Party gains. On the misleading rhetoric of its crack versus cocaine sentencing, Cosby said of the bamboozlers: "I'm having a problem, ladies and gentlemen. OK, we even it up, let's have a big cheer for the white man doing as much time as the black man. Hooray! Anybody see any sense in this? Systemic racism, they call it, that the white man is not doing as much time as the black." What blacks should focus on, said Cosby, is getting the crack dealer to stop selling crack.[29]

Rays of hope exist for those willing to see them. In an essay titled "You're Misleading My People," Howard University honors student Tracy Hunter, writing well before Bill Cosby made his comments, challenged leaders about crack cocaine penalties: ". . . tell me what my community gains from that? More drug overdoses in the black community? More crack heads? More drugs being carried and sold to our children? Yeah, that's a whole lot to fight for! I know you think you're doing the best you can, but maybe you need to redirect your focus. Maybe instead of trying to find others on whom to place blame for the problems within our communities, we need to look at our communities themselves."[30]

When liberals aren't busy blowing smoke about crack cocaine sentencing disparities, they can be found spinning myths about the "racist" death penalty. Their agenda requires victimology and race-baiting to succeed. It's all they've got to go with. And so, liberals proclaim their love for convicted murderers, no matter what hell they've unleashed on victims and their communities.

Exhibit A: Stanley "Tookie" Williams, founder of the Crips Los Angeles street gang and the murderer responsible for the 1979 killings of a twenty-six-year-old convenience store clerk and an immigrant Chinese couple and their adult daughter. Williams has never apologized for their murders. However, in order to engender sympathy, he has written a few children's books while on death row.

And while in prison, Williams reportedly refused to aid police investigations with any information against his gang and was implicated in attacks on guards and other inmates as well as being involved in multiple escape plots.

Transcripts show that the killing of twenty-six-year-old Albert Lewis Owens at the 7-Eleven market near Whittier, California, was no accident. Williams shot out a security monitor and then killed Owens, shooting him twice in the back at point-blank range as he lay prone on the storage room floor. Once back in Los Angeles, when asked why he had shot Owens, Williams said that he "didn't want to leave any witnesses."

Williams also said he killed Owens "because he was white and he was killing all white people." And reputedly, Williams had bragged about the shooting, stating, "You should have heard the way he sounded when I shot him, it was hilarious," as he made gurgling or growling noises and laughed about Owens' death.

What attracted the Left about this case? Well, he was the founder of one of the most barbaric street gangs in U.S. history, he was convicted of murdering an innocent family in cold blood, and he was defiant in the face of overwhelming evidence—a perfect *cause célèbre* for liberals.

In December 2005, after all of his appeals had been exhausted, a thorough examination of Williams' clemency request was done by California governor Arnold Schwarzenegger. Afterwards, the governor issued an appropriately solemn and sober public statement:

> Based on the cumulative weight of the evidence, there is no reason to second-guess the jury's decision of guilt or raise significant doubts or serious reservations about Williams' convictions and death sentence. . . . There is little mention of atonement in his writings and his plea for clemency of the countless murders committed by the Crips following the lifestyle Williams once espoused. The senseless killing that has ruined many families, particularly in African-American communities, in the name of the Crips and gang warfare is a tragedy of our modern culture.[31]

And from there, the bamboozlers began their latest crusade. They rounded up a team of spinmeisters who were tasked with conning the public into seeing the episode as yet another example of the way evil conservatives and Republicans impose the racist death penalty against another black man. Their task has been made a little difficult, mind you, because according to a recent *ABC News/Washington Post* poll, 65 percent of Americans support capital punishment.[32]

First to weigh in was, not surprisingly, the Reverend Jesse Jackson, who's always willing to offer up quality alliteration for a good cause: "I feel pain by the governor's decision to choose revenge over redemption and to use Tookie Williams as a trophy in the flawed system. To kill him is a way of making politicians look tough."[33]

Next to join in was, the paragon of virtue, rapper-turned-pornographer Snoop Doggy Dogg (a.k.a. Calvin Broadus). Incidently, for more information about this, read the *New York Post* story revealing that Broadus was removed from a Muppets movie scene because of his known association with pornography production at http://www.answers.com/topic/snoop-dogg.

Stanley Tookie Williams is not just a regular guy, he's an inspiration. He inspires me, and I inspire millions, so that's a hundred-million people inspired by what he does. Through time and perseverance he's been able to turn his life around while being incarcerated. He shows people how to stop killing each other and fighting against each other and learn how to live with each other.[34]

Thanks, Snoop, for your words of wisdom. Now we're all enlightened.

"The Democrats have adopted and embraced what I call the San Francisco mentality, which is an apology for the world being what it is," says Judge Joe Brown. "In other words, you child-proof society and nobody ever grows up and nobody is ever accountable."

There is a reason that most Americans—black and white—support capital punishment. And it has nothing to do with racism. They view it as a just consequence for some of the most outrageous crimes. And the fact of the matter is, as a result of safeguards built into our system, it can't reasonably be argued that today the system is somehow anti-black.

According to the U.S. Department of Justice, between 1976 and 2004, blacks were responsible for 52.1 percent of all homicides, versus 45.9 percent for whites. Nevertheless, since the death penalty was reinstated by the Supreme Court in 1976, more than half of those sentenced to die have been white.

In 2004 alone, black offenders outnumbered white offenders seven to one.[35] Moreover, of persons under sentence of death in 2004, 1,850 were white and 1,390 were black. But when actual executions are shown, the number is startling. Of the sixty persons executed in 2005, forty-one were white and nineteen were black. Given that for over nearly three decades blacks have been responsible for 52.1 percent of all homicides in the United States, one would expect that black death row figures and/or execution rates would be at minimum numerically equal to, if not higher than, those of whites. It just isn't true that more blacks are sentenced and executed than whites.

In fact, if the death penalty is inherently racist and unfair in how it is carried out, as liberals claim, one would expect to see sentencing and executions of blacks in far larger numbers. The data shows exactly the opposite. If anything, the death penalty is disproportionately skewed against whites, not blacks.

Reasonable people on both sides can disagree over the morality of capital punishment, but arguments that the death penalty is racist are simply unfounded. Worse still, the bamboozlers' obsession with fueling animosity between whites and minorities diverts attention away from a final sober statistic: in 2004, there were 15,913 homicide victims, 7,557 of whom were black. Conversely, that same year there were only fifty-nine executions, nineteen of which were black Americans. Wouldn't it make more sense for liberals to devote their energies to developing strategies designed to save the lives of the almost 16,000 people who are murdered every year than to defend the roughly sixty murderers executed a year?

And for those liberals who claim to be so concerned about the plight of black Americans, wouldn't it be more logical to organize marches and rallies standing up for the rights and safety of the over 7,500 black citizens murdered each year, rather than doing so for the nineteen who murdered others?

It's something to consider.

The devastating consequences of illogic and misplaced priorities by liberals have diverted attention from the real source of much criminality, and that is a fatherless generation of boys growing up without an adult male to shepherd them into manhood. A host of various minority voices increasingly identify the need for more positive black male role models; namely, actively engaged fathers. In an interview with Judge Joe Brown, he spoke about the erosion of strong, positive male influences on the lives of today's youth:

Why is it that America has the largest penitentiary population in the whole world? It's because they have gotten away from this thing called accountability. It is the front of manhood to be responsible for community well-being. And what you've done is you've made man a three-letter negative word, male a four-letter cuss-word, over the last four generations. I can remember going to UCLA and all around the campuses in the '60s and the '70s when the intellectual was going around saying, "These male chauvinist pigs need to be put in check! They need to learn to control this aggressiveness. They need to learn to emote, to cry, to shout, to let it all hang out and become in touch with their softer sides." That doesn't work.[36]

Without the breaks on aggression that Brown talks about, rudderless young men are left adrift redundant, without a captain to help them chart their course. Indeed, this phenomenon, says rapper Xzibit, host of the wildly popular a popular MTV television show, *Pimp My Ride* leads to particularly poor decision making about the future among youth: "I think the biggest problem as young black men in this country is that we have become used to immediate gratification, and that will destroy you. . . . What becomes attractive with stealing is that I can enjoy the things society has, but I get it faster. It's immediate gratification. That's more attractive than going to college for five years, you're halfway done with your life before you even get to enjoy your car."[37]

Xzibit's insight into the importance of delayed gratification is right on target, even if the title and content of the program he hosts normalizes the "pimp culture" and glorifies hyper-materialism. Studies have long shown that children who learn to delay gratification early on surpass their peers educationally and professionally later in life. Therefore, building a culture in the home that nurtures and fosters long-term goals is an essential building block for future success. A parent's ability to establish within the home these kinds of attitudes, values, and predispositions, says black Harvard University professor Orlando Patterson, is essential if black males are to surmount the sizable gap between them and all other groups. In a March 2006 *New York Times* article, Patterson attributes the self-destruction of young males to what sociologists refer to as the "cool-pose culture" that many young black males seem unwilling to let go of. "For these young men, it was almost like a drug, hanging out on the street after school, shopping and dressing sharply, sexual conquests, party drugs, hip-hop music and culture, the fact that almost all the superstar athletes and a great many of the nation's best entertainers were black."[38]

Conservative black columnist Stanley Crouch, writing in a November 2006 *New York Daily News* article entitled, "Memo to Young Black Men: Please Grow Up," described how appalled he was when surrounded by black eighteen- to thirty-five-year-old men during the taping of a popular television program for black youths. "As a father with a daughter nearly thirty years old who has never been close to marrying, I was once more struck by what my offspring describes as 'a lack of suitable men.' She has complained often about the adolescent tendencies of young black men, as has just about any young black woman when the subject comes up."

Crouch then asked a black female writer in her forties who had worked for rap magazines and other publications for her take on the subject. "The way she understood it was that these young black men do not see growing up as having any advantages to it. One is either current, or old-fashioned and outdated. The only success they [young black men] think they can believe in is had by either athletes or rappers . . . So they hold on to adolescence and adolescent ways as long as they can."[39]

Will greater involvement from fathers and mentors solve all that ails America and wipe out crime? Of course not. But what serious person would argue that, all other things being equal, a strong father in the home devoted to prospering and loving and disciplining his children would be anything but beneficial? It's not a cure-all, but it's a start.

"We've lost a bit of that drive to hold high expectations for our children," says radio-talk show host Hallerin Hill. "We don't have many men staying at home and modeling for their young men and the kids that they have—'this is what it means to be a man against the odds.' We don't have many women modeling for their daughters 'this is what it means to be a great woman.' . . . They have excused themselves from excellence."[40]

Hill says that as a young black man navigating his way into manhood, "one of the greatest gifts he had was two parents who pushed him to be more than what he and the culture thought he could become."

My parents placed on me higher expectations for me to live up to. They didn't say, "Because you live in a country that sometimes can be very racist or in its history has been very racist, because you live in a society where you have to overachieve just to be credited with achieving, because you live in a society that will make judgments about you, you can use that as an excuse for mediocrity." No. They said, "'We're going to hold you to high expectations. You don't get to get a mulligan in life because it is going to be more difficult for you as a black man. . . .'" [They said,] "You are special. You are great. You have potential. We want to draw out of you that great potential." They had this fierce unconditional love for me that said, "We will not accept mediocrity from you; we expect excellence from you." And I thrived on the fact that somebody believed in me, but also put a foot in my butt and said, "Don't whine! Don't wait for somebody else to do it for you. Get up and be about it!"[41]

Just because every inmate didn't have parents like Hill's does not mean that we shouldn't strive toward that goal—quite the reverse. Liberals lambaste conservatives' emphasis on personal responsibility, self-reliance, and strong two-parent homes as unrealistic, simplistic, rigid, and outmoded. "I'm not saying marriage will cure it all, by any means," says Kay Hymowitz, author of *Marriage and Caste in America*, "but I am saying that it is an integral piece of the problem and we need to be talking about it. If that means that, at times, we have to be making statements that might hurt the feelings of people, so be it—we simply have to have this discussion at this point. Too many people have been hurt by the fact that they are growing up without their fathers."[42]

In contrast, the Left is in such a hurry to pander to the lowest common denominator of morality, the liberal message is: "Join us. We won't judge you. You're not a criminal. You're a victim! Racist cops and a racist America are the real criminals! So we'll protect and coddle you . . . and one day you'll cast your felon ballot for us!"

To date, the race baiting on issues of law and order by bamboozlers has hypnotized the inner city. This has had devastating consequences. It's time to snap out of the trance of victimhood. The core values of faith and family that have been our North Star are being undermined. And as we'll see, it has been liberals who've used black and Latino people of faith as unwitting accomplices to further their agenda of irreligion.

5

UNHOLY ALLIANCE

Liberal Faithlessness vs. Belief and Conviction

Blacks are very conservative on social moral issues, but they are not going to compromise.

—Reverend Al Sharpton

[Latinos] tend to be a very conservative culture. We live by religion, we live by our families.

—Eva Longoria, actress on the TV show *Desperate Housewives*

It has often been said that blacks and Latinos hold values of faith and family that would make them far more comfortable with white evangelicals in the Republican Party than the Hollywood secularists that make up the base of the Democratic Party. Actress Eva Longoria, better known as Gabriella Solis on the mega-hit show *Desperate Housewives,* recently found out about this phenomenon.

In 2004, Longoria, who has been dubbed "a siren voice of the American Left," acted as Democratic presidential nominee Senator John Kerry's "Hispanic ambassador." In an interview with reporter Stephen Armstrong, Longoria says her work on Kerry's behalf taught her a sobering lesson about courting the Latinos. "I went out and got

Latinos to vote," says Longoria, "but they voted for the wrong person. They voted religion." Longoria then "wearily" explained that Latinos "tend to be a very conservative culture. We live by religion, we live by our families."[1]

What Longoria is lamenting is what pollsters call the "God Gap." It's a phenomenon that reveals that, overall, the more regularly a person attends church, the less likely he or she is to vote Democratic. This schism between "the Faithful," as President Clinton's former pollster Stan Greenberg calls them, and the secularists continues to widen; we are a nation separated over values. According to a recent Pew Research report taken just two months before the 2006 midterm elections, voters said the GOP is friendlier to religion than Democrats by a nearly two-to-one margin. Even after the Democratic takeover of the House and Senate, Pew data reveal that the Mark Foley and Ted Haggard sex scandals didn't so much hurt the GOP among the Faithful as it energized Independents to show up on election day in greater numbers and support the Democrats. The God Gap is most prevalent within white evangelical protestant voters, where Republicans enjoy an almost fifty-point advantage over Democrats.

Books by angry leftist secularists have been hot sellers lately. These screeds attack church-going conservatives as irrational dolts who are screwing up America. But as even the liberal Rabbi Michael Lerner concedes in his book, *The Left Hand of God: Taking Back Our Country from the Religious Right*, "Many on the Left, to be blunt, hate and fear religion. . . . The Left's hostility to religion is one of the main reasons people who otherwise might be involved with progressive politics get turned off."[2] On the other hand, those liberal Democrats that don't "hate and fear religion" and freely espouse their faith can, according to Steven Waldman, founder and operator of BeliefNet, be attacked by secularists who "tend to think that all the religious mumbo-jumbo entails a dangerous mixing of church and state."[3]

John Gibson, host of Fox News "The Big Story" and author of *The War on Christmas*, a book that undoubtedly prompted the publication of some of the liberal books attacking Christianity, says that organized atheists and secular progressives have adopted a view that says, "We're tired of coddling you soft Christians, those Christians and those religionists who can't bring themselves to disavow this superstition of Christianity. We're tired of standing with you because then we have to put up with these Muslims, these crazy Muslims and all the nasty things they say and do in the name of their religion. So now we are disavowing you soft Christians. We're calling you out. You're just as bad as those crazy Muslims."[4]

Even so, the fault lines of faith and politics may be shifting. Hispanics are now the largest minority in America. The political ramifications of faith and family, so integral to the Latino community, are coming to the forefront, just as Eva Longoria acknowledged. Latino voting patterns break sharply along denominational lines. Close to half of all U.S. Catholics under twenty-five are Hispanic.[5] In 2004, the Pew Forum found that 63 percent of Latino protestants, the fastest growing segment of the Latino electorate, voted for President George W. Bush, versus 37 percent who voted for Senator John Kerry.[6] Latino Catholics, on the other hand, were almost perfectly reversed, with only 31 percent supporting Bush and 69 percent backing Kerry. Overall, however, Bush boosted his showing among Latinos by almost double (40 percent) during the 2004 election, an impressive achievement to be sure. Still, less than half of all eligible Hispanic voters voted during the last presidential election. And with issues like illegal immigration hanging in the balance, no one knows which way these voters will ultimately break.

But one thing is certain: whichever party can mobilize the Latino electorate will yield huge dividends.[7]

"I tell my parishioners, 'Could you take the Bible in the voting booth with you when you're going to pull that lever?'" says Bishop John Gimenez, pastor of the 5,000-member Rock Church in Virginia Beach, Virginia. "You've got the left wing and the right wing, but neither one can fly without the other. The bird doesn't fly unless it has two wings. So I'm both Democrat and Republican, but above that I'm Christian. And that's the bird that I want to see fly."[8]

Like Latinos, blacks—across all income levels—are anchored by the church. That's true even in secular sanctuaries like Hollywood, reports the *Los Angeles Times*. "The Bible in our culture has been more than just the word of God," says Louis "Buster" Brown, a Grammy-winning music producer. "It's been our hope through slavery. It's been our hope through civil rights." The talented movie actress Angela Bassett, who's worshipped in the West Angeles Cathedral for over fifteen years, agrees: "When you realize that every breath is a gift from God. When you realize how small you are, but how much he loved you. That he, Jesus, would die, the son of God himself on earth, then you . . . you just weep."[9]

Where blacks differ, of course, is that while Latino voting patterns are not unified, blacks vote as a group, with 90 percent having consistently supported Democrats over the past few decades. Most white evangelical conservatives look at those numbers and scratch their heads in wonderment. How can blacks be so religious and yet vote for a party that vigorously opposes their most sacred values? Likewise, why don't Latinos overwhelmingly side with those who defend, and are not hostile to, their faith? These are important questions that further reveal the extent to which liberals have been successful in obfuscating issues and bamboozling voters.

That said, it's important to stress that no political party—or human institution—has a lock on divine grace and mercy; God doesn't don a donkey or elephant pin. Attempts to stuff an infinite God into man-made boxes limit the power and mystery of the Almighty. No one knows what lies in another man's heart. For example, take these remarks by Congressman Jesse Jackson Jr., a committed Democrat sincere in his faith (and it's wrong to argue otherwise):

"My faith is a faith that is born of the condition that through Christ, change is possible," says Jackson. "Not that the status quo itself is reinforced, but that Saul can be Paul, that Cassius Clay can be Mohammed, that Malcolm Little can become Malcolm X, that people can change."[10]

One would hope that few Americans would besmirch the spiritual journey of a fellow believer just because he votes a different way. Yet the dramatic schism between those in so-called leadership positions within communities of color and those they represent raises fair and legitimate questions. There comes a moment in every young black person's life, sometimes in college, when he or she asks a silent but powerful question: *Why do we all vote for a party that's against almost everything that's integral to our faith? The faith that is reflected in the powerful Negro hymnals which sustained us through slavery, Jim Crow, and the civil rights movement? Are we to believe that it is no longer relevant today? Why are we so loyal to those most hostile to our faith?* It's a question many blacks ask silently. I know I did. It's a question that you want to tuck right back down where it came from. *Well,* you figure, *we can't all be wrong. There must be something I've yet to learn. There must be something I don't know that explains why we vote against our values.* Many Latinos go through the same process. But there isn't anything that explains it.

There's fear.

There's social sanction.

There's being ostracized.

And that's it. That's what keeps you shuffling along cheering for liberals, all the while praying that they don't keep partial-birth abortion legal, or further restrict public expressions of faith, or redefine marriage, or rip God out of the Pledge of Allegiance or "In God We Trust" off our coinage, or . . . you get the picture. Frances Rice, chairman of the National Black Republican Association explains it:

> When they do surveys of black Americans and ask them values questions, they are aligned almost one hundred percent with the Republican Party. But when they ask them which party they are going to vote for, almost one hundred percent say the Democratic Party. They are not voting their values. Blacks think conservative, and they're voting liberal because they don't know the true agenda of the Democratic Party. They won't tell blacks what their agenda is. They just go in and cast the Republicans in a negative light, and then they get the black ministers and leaders to get them all on a bus and vote straight Democratic, without even knowing what policies those Democrats are pushing, like gay marriage. They are against the school choice opportunity scholarships to get black kids out of failing schools. They are against saying God in the pledge. They sued the Boy Scouts because they have God in their pledge and because they will not let homosexual men be in charge of young boys. They killed welfare reform. They are against Social Security reform, even though blacks on average lose $10,000 in the system because blacks on average die five years younger. There is a wealth transfer from poor blacks to middle class whites. The Democrats are against us . . . about everything—the No Child Left Behind Act—that is designed to bring accountability in our system and allow black children to get tutoring to bring themselves up. They've got blacks saying that the No Child Left Behind Act is not fully funded when $13.1 billion has

been put in the system! President Bush has sent more money into education than any president in history.[11]

How, one wonders, did the liberal elite, a group so at odds with the sentiments of those they lead, manage to obtain the reigns of power? Moreover, what will it take to pry them loose from their suffocating clutch?

One explanation involves the emergence within the inner-city community of self-appointed spokesmen like Reverend Jesse Jackson, Reverend Al Sharpton, or Minister Louis Farrakhan, men who've been elected to absolutely nothing and yet claim to speak politically on behalf of all blacks and the poor. And as Lloyd Williams, president of the Harlem Chamber of Commerce points out, even when black leaders are elected, they sometimes forget who is representing whom: "Oft times in the black community, the elected officials perceive that they were elected to be our spokespersons as opposed to being our representatives, and there's a distinct difference."[12]

Nowhere is this clearer than in the realm of religion. The rift between the faith-based values that define Latino and black public opinion and the liberal agenda their votes support is great, yet its existence is an excellent example of the liberal exploitation machine's effectiveness in bamboozling Americans. The values chasm between people of color and limousine leftists like Nancy Pelosi, George Soros, Ted Turner, Barbra Streisand, and Michael Moore has never been wider. And nowhere is this more apparent than on the life and death issue of abortion.

It's not difficult to understand why the Zogby poll found that 62 percent of black Americans and 78 percent of Latinos are against abortion.[13] Beyond the deep religious convictions that lead people of color to protect the lives of the unborn, another reason for the prevalence of black and Latino pro-lifers is that a disproportionate number of lives are snatched from their communities every year. A recent *Washington Post* story, citing the Alan Guttmacher Institute, reported that white women get about 40 percent of all U.S. abortions, black women get 32 percent, and Hispanic women constitute 20 percent of all abortions.[14] In fact, black women are almost four times as likely as white women to have an abortion, and Latino women are 2.5 times as likely.[15] And tragically, 94 percent of all abortion offices are located in metro areas with high black populations, says Pastor Clenard Childress of the New Calvary Baptist Church in Montclair, New Jersey. This fact, according to Childress, has created a system akin to "black genocide." And when one adds the comments of Planned Parenthood founder Margaret Sanger regarding the so-called "Negro Project," the truth becomes much clearer: "The most successful educational approach to the Negro is through religious appeal. We do not want word to go out that we want to exterminate the Negro population, and the minister is the man who can straighten out that idea if it ever occurs to any of their more rebellious members."

"I'm not convinced that any of the people who have run Planned Parenthood over the years have said, 'Let's wipe out all the black people,'" Childress said. "But that's been the effect of it."[16]

A *San Francisco Chronicle* story on abortion cited Childress's provocative and attention-grabbing phrase (which also happens to be the name of his organization's website—www.blackgenocide.org) in its lead sentence.[17] But Childress is quick to point out that the term isn't original to him. In fact, it belongs to an unlikely source: Reverend Jesse Jackson. In 1977, Jackson, who is now an abortion supporter, used the term in a powerful speech challenging the hearts and minds of pro-abortion advocates. "Abortion is black genocide," Jackson said. "What happens to the mind of a person and the moral fabric of a nation that accepts the aborting of the life of a baby without a pang of conscience?"[18]

Reverend Jackson's question, even if posed over a quarter-century ago, is a good one. And, thankfully, it's one that, much to the chagrin of the bamboozlers, blacks have answered definitively. Yet the Democrats remain staunchly pro-abortion. As conservative commentator and best-selling author Ann Coulter put it, abortion has become the liberals' "holiest sacrament" and "the single most important item on the Democrats' agenda." Coulter goes on to argue that while liberals denounce soldiers dying in Iraq as unconscionable, 1.3 million aborted babies in America every year is "something to celebrate."[19]

Taking a glance at the multimillion dollar pro-abortion lobbying groups' websites, it's easy to see what she means. One can attend the Evening of Chocolate Gala at the swank Glenview Mansion, where pro-abortion activists can get their groove on while "enjoy[ing] an elegant evening of music, dancing, and fine chocolate desserts from local bakeries." Some lucky liberal will even win luxurious auction prizes, including "a weeklong vacation" and "a vintage 1966 bottle of Chateau Calon-Segur."[20] For those watching their waistlines or not in the mood for chocolate, there are the ever-popular "Pro-Choice Happy Hours." And further bolstering the case that abortion advocacy is practically a social event, the site reminds its readers, "if you know of any pro-choice friendly bars," the site states, "please contact the office."[21]

In a nation where an estimated 4,000 infants are aborted each day, this kind of cavalier party atmosphere is beyond callous. It's cruel. But liberals hardly see it that way; Christians—whether black, white, or Latino—standing up for the lives of the unborn are the callous and cruel ones. Yes, in a liberal world where Planned Parenthood sells t-shirts that proudly declare "I had an abortion," it's no wonder why so many liberals find it perfectly acceptable to mix their pro-abortion "values" with hobnobbing at chic social gatherings.[22] Liberals' celebratory attitude about an act so gruesome and tragic seems to belie the liberal line that what Democrats want is to keep abortion "safe, legal, and rare," as Bill Clinton, the so-called first black president, (newsflash, Bill: you're white!) told us. But when a leading pro-abortion voice proposes transforming the anniversary of *Roe v. Wade* into "I'm not sorry" Day, it's hard to take liberals seriously.[23] I wonder if Mr. Clinton is aware that since 1973, more than twice as many blacks have died from abortion than from heart disease, cancer, accidents, violent crimes, and AIDS *combined.*[24] But more than that, I wonder how many people of color would allow themselves to be used by liberals were that statistic more widely known and available.

"Abortion is the most tragic civil rights violation we face today," said Day Gardner, national director of Black Americans for Life. "You would think that Sharpton and Jackson, as self-proclaimed 'leaders' of the civil rights movement all these years, would sound the charge to end abortion. More and more black churches are beginning to support pro-life agendas—not because of a need to fit into a particular party, but rather to draw a line when it comes to life issues."[25]

Those in positions of black influence and authority seem not to be terribly worried about mass defections over the black genocide that occurs to the tune of a 9–11 terrorist attack against blacks every two days. In fact, black elites have become so confident in their positions of authority that in 2004, the NAACP acted in complete disregard for its members' views when it adopted a pro-abortion stance, despite the fact that a clear majority of black Americans reject abortion as anathema to their most deeply held values.[26] A search of the word "abortion" on the NAACP website further proves that officials know full well how out of step they are with the majority of blacks—only two mentions of the word pop up, and one of these is a footnote.

"Blacks are very conservative on social moral issues," Reverend Al Sharpton told me, "but they're not going to compromise."[27] Presumably he means on which party they will support.

But there are signs that this may yet change. Given the Democratic Party's penchant for taking black voters for granted, it's easy to see why liberals are so confident that those pesky conservative values that so many blacks and Latinos adhere to won't hinder the liberal exploitation agenda.

The same demeaning attitudes that secular progressives have toward Christians who oppose abortion spills over into their attitude toward the overwhelming majority of believers who oppose gay marriage. Voters continue to send a deafening message to our elected leaders: the majority of Americans do not want to redefine the centuries-old institution of marriage simply because liberals want them to. An August 2006 Pew Research survey found that by a 56 percent to 35 percent margin, Americans continue to oppose gay marriage. Not surprisingly, the "God Gap" shows up in full force. And here again, conservative values of blacks are rock solid. In fact, opposition to gay marriage is almost identical for white evangelicals (78 percent) and black protestants (74 percent).[28] Interestingly, black and Latino opposition to gay marriage exceeds white opposition.[29]

The bamboozlers view these numbers as further proof that Christians are bigots. During the 2004 presidential election, liberals were shocked when a small band of black voters in Ohio had the *audacity* to buck the party and vote the values of their faith. "We didn't see it coming this last time," Reverend Sharpton told *Newsweek*. "We didn't see them [Republicans] using the church and the morals of the church to win votes."[30]

Allowing one's morals to guide one's decisions is hardly a novel concept—it motivated abolitionists, the suffrage movement and the civil rights movement. But the irony of one of the most politically active reverends in America decrying "using the church and the morals of the church to win votes" is apparently lost on Sharpton. Moreover, liberals have been complicit in their own efforts at mixing church and state because during election cycles they willfully provide "walk-around" money to minority ministers in order to secure the vote on election. Aren't churches tax exempt?

Liberals are wise to be alarmed by the fact that overwhelming numbers of blacks and Latinos oppose gay marriage. Moreover, with many gay marriage legal actions plodding along quietly and successfully in 2006 and on into 2007, liberals fear stirring up the hornets' nest of opposition that exists among many black and Latino ministers, especially those of the so-called mega-churches that can number upwards of 10,000 parishioners. Even for many black and Latino religious leaders traditionally affiliated with Democratic causes, a willingness to break with the Democrats remains strong on these issues.

Look at the example of Bishop Eddie L. Long. He heads Atlanta's New Birth Ministry Baptist Church, whose membership stands at a massive 25,000 members. He has been strong in his support of right-to-life and traditional marriage. A November 2006 *Newsweek* article reported that Long's principled stand over the sanctity of marriage sparked "an angry exchange between him, Sharpton, Jackson, and Louis Farrakhan late last year at a conference at New Birth. Speaking from the pulpit, Jackson asked the congregation how many of them actually knew someone gay who was getting married. No one in the room raised his hand. Jackson then replied, in a reference to the Republicans: 'Is it worth sleeping with the enemy?'"[31] How desperate can you be?

The fierce liberal condemnation of the blacks and Latinos who oppose gay marriage and abortion (who represent the overwhelming majority view) demonstrates just how serious they believe the stakes are in the upcoming elections. Heading into the 2008 presidential election, liberals know what Reverend Dwight McKissic of the Cornerstone Baptist Church in Arlington, Texas, knows: "If the same-sex marriage issue is on the political landscape in the elections, more blacks will vote Republican. Blacks who voted Republican made the difference last time and they can do it again."[32] What's more, the rise of black mega-churches has begun to rob old guard black liberals like Jackson and Sharpton of their spotlight and has begun to challenge their influence and relevance. Not surprisingly, Sharpton is now concerned that these new voices and perspectives might be muddling the bamboozlers' effectiveness: "These ministers are allowing moral and social issues to become confused," warns Sharpton. "The end of the war in Iraq, higher minimum wages and affirmative action—those are our issues right now. Not same sex marriage or even abortion."[33]

Cutting and running in the war on terror, passing wage controls that destroy black jobs, and implementing policies that racially condescend to minorities and soothe white liberals is more important than ending the destruction of 1,500 black babies a day and fighting to preserve the God-ordained institution of marriage?!

Bamboozled!

But the minority community is slowly beginning to see the real designs of the liberal exploitation agenda and the Democratic Party's Far-Left agenda. As University of Utah professor Armando Solorzano points out, Latino culture is so rooted in Christianity that even its everyday language is infused with reflections of faith. "When we say *Adios! Go with God*, or *God be with you*, we are not just saying 'good-bye,' we are entrusting the other person to God's care, we are wishing God to accompany people in their journey. Our religion and spirituality are more than a way of thinking, they are a way of living."[34]

Given the conservative values and centrality of Christian faith that permeate Latino and black American culture, it's easy to understand why bamboozlers continue to ratchet up the race baiting, scare tactics, and racial bullying that is their trademark.

It's also no mistake that these attacks have only grown more intense in the wake of President George W. Bush's historic support for faith-based initiatives. The White House Faith-Based and Community Initiatives makes faith-based and community organizations (FBCOs) eligible to receive federal grant monies for those organizations that provide social services to communities. In March 2006, the White House reported that faith-based organizations received over $2.15 billion in funding.[35] Liberal critics protest that the influx of federal funds erodes the separation of church and state and diverts funds from government social programs to churches, synagogues, and mosques that may provide similar services, such as support for homeless citizens.

In September 2006, the Joint Center for Political and Economic Studies released a report that found that of 750 black churches, fewer than 3 percent, were receiving funds. Another racist plot by the evil George W. Bush? Hardly. Actually, the reason for this is pretty straightforward: only 11 percent had even applied for grants. The good news: 53 percent of black ministers expressed interest in doing so.[36] Interestingly, the study found that liberal northeastern congregations were more likely to have received funds than more conservative churches in the South. "Those people who were most worried can exhale," Robert M. Franklin, a professor of social ethics at Emory University said. "Churches have not been manipulated by Karl Rove. They have not sold out."[37]

On the other hand, whether Democrats will continue to sell out the religious values of Latinos and black Americans remains to be seen. What's more, only time will tell whether the relationships that President George W. Bush has worked hard to forge within communities of color will continue to be strained under the weight of Hurricane Katrina recovery efforts and the ongoing debate surrounding illegal immigration. And scandal influences the outcome as well. Last fall, the Mark Foley sex scandal gave Bush-friendly Christian leaders like Bishop Harry Jackson, senior pastor at the 3,000-member Hoe Christian Church in College Park, Maryland, pause and concern. "I believe that President Bush is a good man," Bishop Jackson said. "He means well. I do believe that there have been some problems of governance with the Republican Party."[38]

Yet, like Bishop Harry Jackson, Latino religious leaders like Bishop John Gimenez agree that ultimately, the political leaders who share the same Christian values as their parishioners will be the ones who will ultimately earn their support:

I think that Bush has done more in reaching out than most people . . . He has done more when you see the people he has put around him. There's an old Spanish proverb that says "tell me who you walk with, I'll tell you who you are." Mr. Bush has tried to bring forth, as much as he can, the attitude and concerns that govern our hearts and our souls and our spirits as Christians. And it's Psalm One that tells us, don't sit with the wicked, don't hang out with them, you know, we minister to them and so forth. . . . I'll tell you, '08 is going to be one of the most crucial times in our nation's history. When we go to the booth to vote, who is going to rule over us? Will it be the righteous that will bring joy to the heart of the people? Or will it be the wicked whose agenda is abortion, whose agenda is same-sex marriage—the anti-prayer, anti-Christian? So we have to make up our minds in the Christian ranks.[39]

Liberal Latina Eva Longoria may want to think twice about boosting the number of Latinos heading to the polls come 2008.

PART 2

THE HIDDEN HISTORY: KKK DEMOCRATS, CIVIL RIGHTS ZEROES, & THE VICTIMHOOD VENDORS

6

THE GOP VS. THE KKK DEMOCRATS

The Anti-Slavery Party Takes on the Democrats' "Iron Triangle"

There is no doubt that the Democratic Party is the party of the Confederacy, historically, that the Democratic Party's flag is the Confederate flag. It was our party's flag.

—Rep. Jesse Jackson, Jr.

Every right that has been bestowed upon blacks was initiated by the Republican Party.

— Mary Church Terrell, black Republican and co-founder of the NAACP

The liberal "script" never changes. The Democratic Party is the party of racial freedom and equality.

Just ask them.

"On every civil rights issue, Democrats have led the fight," reads the Democratic National Committee (DNC) website.[1] It's a statement so brazenly false that one wonders where to even begin in dismantling it. It's a statement that oozes bamboozlement. Indeed, in a stunningly candid—and I must say impressive—interview with

Congressman Jesse Jackson Jr., the young congressman showcased both his depth of historical knowledge and his intellectual honesty when he made this startling observation, a statement that refutes the DNC mantra:

> There is no doubt that the Democratic Party is the party of the Confederacy, historically, that the Democratic Party's flag is the Confederate flag. It was our party's flag. That Jefferson Davis was a Democrat; that Stonewall Jackson strongly identified with the Democratic Party; that secessionists in the South saw themselves as Democrats and were Democrats; that so much of the Democratic Party's history, since it is our nation's oldest political party, has its root in slavery.[2]

It's a statement both impressive in its historical accuracy and devastating in its implications. Congressman Jackson is an honest Democrat and should be applauded as such. Indeed, listening to him speak, it was easy to see how voters are drawn to his charismatic style. And yet his words stand in sharp contrast to the liberal line touted everywhere and shouted from the DNC website: "On every civil rights issue, Democrats have led the fight."

And that's where the bamboozlers come in.

When confronted with the inconvenient facts of the party's murderous past, the bamboozlers—whose job it is to keep blacks and other minorities voting for Democrats at all costs—have developed a shorthand way of brushing aside 150 years of history. You've probably heard it. It goes something like this: "Oh, yes, that. Well, you see, the old racist Democrats all fled our party and joined the Republicans. Yesterday's racist Democrats are all now conservative red-state Republicans."

Nice try.

This argument is woefully uninformed at best and blatantly deceitful at worst. For now, suffice it to say that the only former Klansman currently serving in the U.S. Senate is a Democrat, not a Republican. I guess Senator Robert Byrd of West Virginia didn't get the "all racists must switch to the GOP" memo. In fact, Senator Robert Byrd was once the senate majority leader, and Democrats have honored him most recently with the title of president pro tem of the United States Senate.

The liberal reply: "Oh . . . well . . . uh, the good Republicans like Lincoln died out long ago. That was a long, long time ago. Blacks shouldn't vote Republican because since the 1960s Democrats have been the pro-civil rights party." That would be fine, except it isn't true. For instance, who was Everett Dirksen, and which president actually signed the first civil rights bill? And for the sake of argument, even if the claim was true, what were Democrats doing for nearly a hundred years from 1865 to 1955?

Bamboozle me once, shame on you. Bamboozle me twice, shame on me.

The truth is that this claim is historically laughable. Moreover, it creates a serious quandary for liberals who seem to want it both ways. On the one hand, liberal Democrats want black voters to ignore, dismiss, or remain completely unaware of the Democrats' horrific history in order to keep 90 percent of blacks voting Democratic, thereby rolling up huge wins for the liberal exploitation agenda. But on the other hand, liberals want to justify racially divisive policies, such as reparations for slavery and affirmative action quotas, on the grounds that present-day inequalities are the result of slavery and state-sponsored segregation—nightmarish institutions that their party is responsible for! Liberals can't have it both ways.

"Unfortunately, black folks in America and black folks who come from other parts of the world to America are not aware of the history of black Americans. We are not," says Niger Innis. "And if we were, we would know that, yes, the KKK, a terrorist organization, was well established in the Democratic Party."[3]

Innis is correct. But it's not just black voters who've been hoodwinked. Most Americans, regardless of color, are clueless when it comes to the reign of terror Democrats inflicted on people of color throughout our nation's history. As Republican Party historian Michael Zak notes, even many Republicans remain unaware of just how sterling their party's history is when compared to the Democrats: "The Republican Party began as a civil rights movement. See, it's not just enough to say that the Republican Party advanced civil rights, the Republican Party began the civil rights movement. We, as a party, don't appreciate our heritage as much as we should. The heritage of the Republican Party is so much more honorable than that of the Democratic Party."[4]

So what is the history, and why has it remained hidden for so long? Some hypothesize that a liberal mainstream media, universities flooded with leftist professors beholden to the Democrats, and the DNC's well-coordinated disinformation campaign may account for the "historical memory loss" of most Americans. Today many universities have stripped American history as a required course for graduation. Instead, students may take a wide range of culturally diverse classes to satisfy the history requirement. And as each generation of America graduates, liberals hope that yet another generation will forget the true history of the Democrats.

"I think that the general public awareness of the nineteenth-century American history and maybe even the first half of the twentieth century is sort of blotted out or eclipsed by their awareness of what is going on in the more recent past," Pulitzer Prize-winning historian James A. McPherson said. "I find that all the time in my students, even here at Princeton, that sometimes they are a little bit surprised to find out that on many issues, and especially on the race issue, the Republican Party was, for a long time, the far more liberal party."[5]

One black person who hasn't forgotten his history is Reverend Wayne Perryman of Seattle's Mount Calvary Christian Center Church of God in Christ. In 2005, Perryman called liberals out on their hypocrisy when he re-filed a 180-page reparations lawsuit against the DNC. Rev. Perryman said he had two goals in doing so: 1) to obtain redress for the crimes committed against African Americans by the Democratic Party, and 2) to officially file a formal case against the Democratic Party as a permanent historic record.[6]

In my interview with historian James A. McPherson, retired from Princeton University and a renowned expert on Reconstruction and slavery, about the history of the two political parties, he said:

> From the beginning of the Republican Party in the middle 1850s until, oh, probably the 1950s, maybe 1960, the Republican Party was certainly the party much more strongly committed to civil rights and much more successful in getting some landmark things through, like the Thirteenth, Fourteenth, and Fifteenth Amendments and a lot of the civil rights legislation of Reconstruction being examples of that.[7]

Again, like Congressman Jackson, Professor McPherson, by no means a conservative Republican spokesman, speaks candidly and accurately about the roles each party has played in black Americans' struggle for equality and freedom. But these two are the exception, not the rule. Unfortunately, most liberals refuse to acknowledge the facts.

"Democrats tend to write the history books, and they have written it in such a way as to distort, play down the heritage, the achievements of the Republican Party," Michael Zak said. "But there isn't a whole lot to say about the Democratic Party regarding civil rights, so they just don't mention it. They act like the world began with Bill Clinton or Hubert Humphrey."[8]

For all these reasons and more, the time has come to set the record straight. Much to the dismay of the bamboozlers, all Americans, especially the 90 percent of black Americans who vote for Democrats, deserve to know the Democratic Party's hidden history. The time has come to reveal the painful, brutal, and shocking truth about the party that boldly claims: "On every civil rights issue, Democrats have led the fight."

If you want to understand the degree to which black Americans' opinions of the Republican Party have evolved, you need to observe two historical watershed events, one from the past and the other from the present. Keep both moments in your mind, side by side. Let's walk back in time and recreate them for you.

The first official Republican Party meeting took place July 6, 1854, in Jackson, Michigan. The upstart political party quickly realized that its mission of ending slavery and ensuring equality for black Americans would be met with fierce resistance. Still, in 1856, the Republicans became a national party when John C. Fremont was nominated for president under the slogan: "Free soil, free labor, free speech, free men, Fremont." Fremont received 33 percent of the vote. Four years later, Abraham Lincoln became the first Republican to win the White House.

The Civil War erupted only one month after Lincoln entered office. During the war, Lincoln signed the Emancipation Proclamation that freed the slaves. But in the years following Lincoln's triumphal 1865 stroll through Richmond, Virginia, being a Republican—black or white—in the South was an invitation to danger or death. Indeed, for decades, Democrats followed a three-pronged strategy designed to thwart Republican efforts to help blacks achieve liberty and equality: *demonize politically, terrorize physically, and rationalize intellectually.* Executing this three-part strategy required that three powerful groups work in tandem to achieve anti-black objectives: elected Democrats, the Ku Klux Klan, and Southern newspaper editors. Together, these three forces formed the Democrats' "Iron Triangle," a coalition that mounted a formidable and often lethal front against the Republican fight for black rights. This battle would last almost a century.

Now fast-forward 140 years.

We're at an NAACP (National Association for the Advancement of Colored People) event. Listen to the words of the chairman of the NAACP, Julian Bond. You may know that the NAACP is one of the nation's oldest civil rights organizations. What you may not know is that it was co-founded by black and white Republicans.[9] Speaking at Fayetteville State University in North Carolina, Chairman Julian Bond shared these thoughts about the party of Lincoln: "The Republican Party would have the American flag and the swastika flying side by side," Bond seethed. "We have to fight discrimination whenever it raises its ugly head." The renowned civil rights activist then called former attorney general John Ashcroft "J. Edgar Ashcroft" and compared President George W. Bush's judicial nominees to the Taliban.[10]

These comments were very extreme and arguably dangerous. One wonders whether Mr. Bond's words were an attempt to surpass the outrageous comments made month's earlier at a Congressional Black Caucus event. Less than a month after Hurricane Katrina had ravaged the Gulf Coast, Congressman Charlie Rangel (D-NY) would set a new low for race-baiting rhetoric. Speaking at a Congressional Black Caucus event, Rangel thundered, "George Bush is our Bull Connor." The audience erupted with wild cheering and applause. Not wanting to be outshined, Congressman Major Owens

(D-NY) added, "Bull Connor didn't even pretend that he cared about African-Americans. You have to give it to George Bush for being even more diabolical. . . . This is worse than Bull Connor." With the Connor-as-Bush talking point now firmly established, New York City councilman Charles Barron declared Rangel's statement ". . . an insult to Connor. George Bush is worse, because he has more power and he's more destructive to our people. . . . A KKK without power is not as bad as a George Bush with power." Our democracy thrives on freedom of speech—but this type of race baiting threatens the very fabric of our society. This venomous speech that engenders hatred and violence is completely unjustified and based on falsehoods. These leaders ought to be ashamed of themselves, as their actions were largely no different than the race-baiting propaganda that segregationists of the Jim Crow era engaged in.

But all this was amateur hour. The true "King of New York" had yet to speak. Reverend Al Sharpton outdid them all when he summed up a half-century of civil rights history with seven outrageous words: "We've gone from fire hoses to levees."[11]

While embarrassing and inconvenient to many Democrats, it is a fact that Theophilus Eugene "Bull" Connor, the Birmingham, Alabama, police commissioner who infamously turned dogs and fire hoses on black Americans, was a *Democrat*, not a Republican. In fact, if you've ever seen a case where a black was stoned, lynched, tarred and feathered, or prevented from voting, the person or persons who did this to them was most likely a Democrat.

The question should be: What caused this historical amnesia? How did the party that was formed to oppose slavery and liberate blacks become the party that critics and blacks equate with Hitler's Nazi Party? And finally, how have the Democrats managed to escape their scandalous past?

That's not to say all Americans are afflicted by this type of amnesia. Meet Frances Rice, a brave lifelong Republican in a long line of Republicans. Frances grew up in Atlanta under the Jim Crow laws that, as she points out, were put in place by Democrats. "Only with the Republican Party was I able to register to vote." Rice, who spent twenty years in the U.S. Army before joining President Ronald Reagan's Private Sector Initiatives Task Force, now serves as the president of the National Black Republican Association (NBRA). "My family was threatened by the Ku Klux Klan, and they [the Klan] were all Democrats," Rice said. [12]

To be sure, the Republican Party isn't perfect or without fault. In comparison to the Democrats, however, its record of support for equality and justice is sterling. For any liberal to equate Republican insensitivity to the crimes committed against thousands of innocents by Democrats is not only historically ignorant, it's morally wrong. From its founding and to this point today, Republicans have supported equality and justice. On the other hand, Democrats have literally had to be forced kicking and screaming—even to the point of a nationwide civil war—in order to support justice and equality.

It is almost impossible to overstate the frequency and ferocity with which Democrats throughout American history have opposed civil rights legislation and protections for blacks and minorities. Today, Democrats have successfully marketed themselves as the party that stands with minorities to combat the "evil Republicans." Sadly, most of my brothers and sisters remain in bondage, and unaware of the brutality and murder that Democrats inflicted on our ancestors. Most would be surprised to learn that those "evil Republicans" locked arms with our great-great grandparents and stood down the reign of terror perpetrated by the Democratic Iron Triangle. "It is out of ignorance of their own history that many blacks demean the Republican philosophy and condemn black

Republicans," writes PBS television commentator Tony Brown. "Blacks have been Republicans historically. . . . Democrats working hand in hand with the Ku Klux Klan gave us Jim Crow laws that effectively enslaved blacks."[13]

Democrats' willingness to use intimidation, demagoguery, and lethal force against black and white Republicans has been present almost from the GOP's founding. In one of the more shocking moments in U.S. Senate history, May 22, 1856, saw the "world's greatest deliberative body" turned into a combat zone. Senator Charles Sumner, the courageous antislavery Republican from Massachusetts, had addressed the Senate on the explosive issue of whether Kansas should be admitted to the Union as a slave state or a free state. In his "Crime Against Kansas" speech, Sumner identified two Democratic senators, Stephen Douglas of Illinois and Andrew Butler of South Carolina, as the principal culprits in this crime. Following Sumner's hard-hitting antislavery speech, Congressman Preston Butler, a relative of Andrew Butler and also a Democrat, snuck up behind him with a metal-topped cane and bludgeoned the Republican with a series of devastating blows. After the beating, Butler turned and walked calmly out of the Senate chamber, leaving Sumner bleeding profusely, as others rushed to carry him away. Sumner's cranial and spinal injuries were so severe that he was confined to a wheelchair for three years. Eventually, Charles Sumner would return to the Senate. His attacker, who abruptly resigned and was censured, was, astonishingly, immediately reelected! Butler's savagery quickly made him a hero among his Democratic constituents.[14]

But if elected Democrats' actions against white Republicans were unconscionable, their actions taken against black Republicans under the cover of white hoods were pure evil. Consider, for example, the story of Perry Jeffers of Warren County, Georgia, recounted in the March 24, 1870, edition of the *New York Times*. Mr. Jeffers, a black man, was a proud husband and father of five sons, one of whom was handicapped and therefore bedridden. The Jeffers family had a solid reputation. As plantation workers, their employers described them as hard working and industrious. These traits had allowed the Jeffers family to prosper financially. And perhaps for this reason, the Jeffers had caught the eye of the local Ku Klux Klan.

As University of North Carolina emeritus professor of history Allen W. Trelease wrote, during this period, "the Klan became in effect a terrorist arm of the Democratic party."[15] From the KKK's 1865 incarnation in Pulaski, Tennessee, the Republican Party had responded with legislative and judicial actions designed to stop the murderous group. But fresh from defeat in the Civil War, the KKK/Democratic reign of terror came fast and furious. Indeed, lynching deaths would hit their peak between 1865 and 1866.[16] As leftist Columbia University history professor Eric Foner notes, "Founded as a Tennessee social club, the Ku Klux Klan spread into nearly every Southern state, launching a 'reign of terror' against Republican leaders—black and white."[17] In his book, *A Short History of Reconstruction*, Foner observed that "in effect, the Klan was a military force serving the interests of the Democratic Party, the planter class, and all those who desired the restoration of white supremacy. It aimed to destroy the Republican Party's infrastructure, undermine the Reconstruction state, reestablish control of the black labor force, and restore racial subordination in every aspect of Southern life."[18]

In 1868, the Klan would become extremely active in trying to get blacks to vote Democrat or not at all.[19] This was especially true in Georgia. "Night riding," with accompanying whippings and shootings, became an almost nightly occurrence during the summer of 1868. These acts of terrorism were designed to keep blacks in their place economically, socially, and politically.[20] But when

Perry Jeffers was told he must join the local Democratic club in advance of the upcoming elections, he refused. Worse in the minds of the Klan, Jeffers, a wealthy black, had boldly announced he would not be voting for the Democratic presidential candidate, Horatio Seymour. Instead, he would vote for General Ulysses S. Grant, a Republican.

The KKK would have none of this; Democratic obeisance was mandatory for blacks. Given the large number of blacks in the South, Democrats needed blacks to vote Democrat or not at all if they were to have any chance of winning elections—not unlike today. That's where the KKK came in. Their role in the Democratic Iron Triangle was that of electoral enforcer. Any black who dared to consider voting for the Republican Party represented a direct threat to the Democrats' chances and therefore must be subjected to public ridicule, rape, castration, and in many instances death. So the Georgia Klan decided to make a lesson out of a successful black Republican like Perry Jeffers.

On the night of November 1, 1868, a posse of six Klansmen crept up to Jeffers' log cabin and started shooting inside his family's home through the cracks in the walls. To the Klansmen's surprise, Jeffers had been warned to expect them, and he and his sons were armed to the hilt. The Jeffers family's defensive gunfire hit and killed one of the Democratic Klansmen and wounded three others.

Four nights later, the Ku Klux Klan assembled a second posse, this one comprised of between fifty and a hundred hooded Democratic terrorists. Having once again anticipated an attack, Jeffers and his four able-bodied sons had hidden in the woods and watched as the Klansmen entered only to find Mrs. Jeffers and the fifth crippled, bedridden son. Jeffers had hoped the helplessness of a defenseless mother with an infirm child would protect them from attack. But the KKK proved ruthless. Mrs. Jeffers and the disabled child were dragged into the yard. The Klansmen shot the boy eleven times. After pillaging the Jeffers' home, the murderers piled the family's possessions in the front yard. The Klansmen then heaved the boy's body on the pile and struck a match. Illumined by the human bonfire, the Democratic Klansmen held the mother down, tied a length of bed cord around her neck, and hung her from a nearby tree.

Miraculously, Mrs. Jeffers survived the incident, as she was cut down soon after the Klansmen left. But the Klansmen weren't finished. Perry Jeffers and his sons decided to hop a train to escape to Augusta, Georgia. Little did they know, however, that the father of the Klansman the Jeffers' killed had boarded the same train with a double-barreled shotgun. During one of the train's stops, six men converged on Perry Jeffers and his four sons and dragged them off the train. One son escaped. The others were walked into the woods and shot. Their bodies were then thrown into a well.[21]

Had the stories like Republican senator Charles Sumner and black Republican Perry Jeffers merely been isolated incidents, one might be inclined to dismiss them as tragic anomalies of Democratic lawlessness. But they weren't. These examples merely highlight how two sides of the Iron Triangle—Democratic politicians and the Ku Klux Klan—worked in tandem to achieve the Democrats' political objective of black domination.

Even before the Civil War, blacks like Frederick Douglass, a Republican and a staunch abolitionist, had courageously spoken for the need to provide blacks with basic legal protections. But as the Civil War drew to a close, the Democrats transferred the violence of the battlefield to violence against black and white Republicans. During this period, "the Democrats were everywhere the party of white supremacy."[22]

One of the most historic Republican victories against Democrats came in the form of passage of the Thirteenth Amendment. The amendment was to officially and forever abolish slavery. But Democrats had effectively carried out their role in the Iron Triangle by defeating the amendment initially. During the next election, Republicans won a three-fourths congressional majority; they could have railroaded the amendment through without Democratic support. But Lincoln was a visionary. In an effort to heal the wounds of the nation, he wanted the historic measure to be a bipartisan achievement. So he lobbied hard for Democrats to change their votes. Yet in the end, of the eighty Democrats who voted, a paltry sixteen was all Lincoln could convince to support the historic amendment. Professor McPherson recounted:

> When the result was announced, the most tumultuous celebration in the history of Congress took place. Republican members jumped to their feet and cheered, clapped each other on the back, and shouted triumphant congratulations to their colleagues. In the galleries, black onlookers embraced each other and wept tears of joy. The House voted to take the rest of the day off "in honor of this immortal and sublime event."[23]

The Democratic Party's inability to keep blacks in bondage only fueled the party's desire to lash back at blacks and their Republican liberators. In the wake of Lincoln's assassination and throughout Reconstruction, Democrats grew even more vigorous in their determination to deny blacks full entry into American life. In effect, the Democrats were arguing that while they might have lost the Civil War and the ability to own slaves, the South could create a surrogate form of slavery by enacting so-called black codes and Jim Crow laws. These laws were designed to strip blacks of basic rights and privileges, such as employment and voting rights, and thereby rob freedmen of all personal autonomy and decision-making power in their own lives.

As soon as Democrats began enacting these unconstitutional policies, Republicans again took action. The GOP's efforts were complicated, however, by the fact that Lincoln's successor, Vice President Andrew Johnson, was a lifelong Southern Democrat and virulent racist. "In terms of damage to the country," says Michael Zak, "Andrew Johnson was the worst president in American history."[24] Lincoln and Johnson were polar opposites. For example, in reference to Frederick Douglass, whom President Lincoln had called "one of the most meritorious men in America," Johnson said: "I know that damned Douglass; he's just like any nigger."[25] Johnson would later contend that, "white men alone must manage the South. No independent government of any form has ever been successful in their [blacks'] hands. On the contrary, wherever they have been left to their own devices they have shown a constant tendency to relapse into barbarism."[26]

For his fellow Southern Democrats, Johnson proved to be the perfect Trojan horse. One of the first indications of this occurred when Johnson vetoed the Civil Rights Act of 1866, a precursor to the Civil Rights Act of 1964 (the subject of the next chapter). The measure protected freedmen from black codes and other repressive laws. Republicans overrode President Johnson's veto and passed the landmark bill.

The political side of the Iron Triangle was doing the best it could to oppress blacks, but their minority numbers made it difficult to achieve lasting results. To increase their numbers and achieve greater electoral success, the Democrats would need to lean on the second side of its Iron Triangle—the Ku Klux Klan. As GOP historian Michael Zak told me, "In most areas of the South, leadership of the Ku Klux Klan and the Democratic Party were indistinguishable, and the white supremacist Democrats used the Klan to eliminate Republican opposition, assassinating many Republican officeholders and intimidating countless others."[27] The methods they used varied throughout the South. Sometimes Klansmen in disguise rode through black neighborhoods at night and warned blacks to either vote Democrat or stay away from the polls. Other times, they would send Republican officeholders notices warning them on pain of death to resign or leave the area. Similar warnings were issued to black and white Republican voters and also teachers who taught at black schools. The Democratic terrorists would sometimes get creative and leave miniature coffins with "K.K.K." written above skulls and crossbones on Republican doorsteps.[28]

Random night beatings were another popular terror tactic of the Democrats and they were used to strike fear in the hearts of blacks who might dare to vote Republican. Generally the victims of these attacks were poor and unknown citizens. But prominent black and Republican local leaders were also sometimes singled out for special attention. One of the most famous state-level cases of this type involved the murder of State senator John W. Stephens of Caswell County, North Carolina, in 1870. Democrats had become envious of the Republican leader's strong relationship with the county's black majority. Not only did the Klansmen strangle and stab him to death, they then blamed the crime on blacks in order to drive a wedge between black voters and the Republican Party. As for avoiding prosecution, Democrats didn't need an alibi; the judges and law enforcement officials in the area were overwhelmingly Democrats. In fact, Frank Wiley, a former Democratic sheriff, had been the person tasked with luring Senator Stephens to the location where his attackers could kill him.[29]

Other parts of North Carolina were equally under siege by the Democratic Klan. In November 1868, hundreds of poor black families in Alamance and Caswell Counties were expelled from their homes and jobs because they had participated in recent elections. Again, with law enforcement and court officials almost universally being Democrats, Klan outrages went forward without interruption. For example, Joseph Harvey, a black man, had been given 150 lashes on his bare back while Klansmen clubbed his baby to death. The Moore County Klan burned down houses and barns to drive out black and white Republicans; the Democrats shot a black woman and then killed her five children, one of whom had its skull crushed under the heel of a Klansman's boot; Jacob Starling was branded in five places on his body with the letters "U.L.," which stood for Union League, a black Republican organization of which he was a member (because both the sheriff and superior court clerk were Democrat Klansmen, they did nothing to stop these actions, even though both were present).[30]

Executing the Democrats' electoral terror strategy was also made easier by the fact that virtually all Southern newspapers were run by editors who were Democrats—the third piece of the Iron Triangle. When combined with the muscle of the Ku Klux Klan and the obstructionist-elected Democrats, these influential Southern newspaper editors rounded out what became an astonishingly effective troika. Democrats worked within the political system to derail the Republican civil rights legislation, the Ku Klux Klan intimidated blacks and white Republicans into voting Democrat or not at all, and the biased Southern newspaper editors, serving as the Party's mouthpiece, slanted news coverage to cover the tracks of the Ku Klux Klan. That's assuming, of course, the newspaper was even willing to acknowledge that the KKK existed. According to historian William Randel, "some of the Democratic editors consistently denied the presence of the Klan . . . while others defended its activities, no matter how violent."[31]

Underplaying or denying the Ku Klux Klan's political purpose was also a common tactic used by politically savvy Democratic leaders. By flying under the radar, Democrats could help their state avoid federal intervention into Klan activities. Leading Democrats at the state level (whether they belonged to the Klan or not) were usually at pains to deny any connection between their party and the Klan, yet many members made no effort to hide it.

The Democratic Iron Triangle's enormity was reflected in the term Klansmen had given their organization: the Invisible Empire of the South. But it was the Klan's political effectiveness that had begun to demoralize Republicans and leave them feeling helpless, which was the Democratic strategy all along.[32] At the state level, desperate Republicans began screaming for dramatic action to help blacks and Republicans fight back:

> State senator T.M. Shoffner of Alamance [North Carolina], a Republican, introduced a bill late in 1869 authorizing the governor to suspend *habeas corpus* and to use militia to suppress lawlessness in counties such as his own where Ku Klux terrorism had overawed the civil authorities and raged out of control. Governor Holden was besieged with requests from harried Republicans around the state for military relief . . . The Klan was furious at the proposal (which eventually became law), and in late December or early January one or more of its units voted for Shoffner's assassination. . . . The Ku Klux terror was so all-encompassing that even members of the order . . . dared not speak openly against it.[33]

Helping the KKK cover its tracks throughout the state was Josiah Turner, editor of the *Raleigh Sentinel*, one of the most influential newspapers in North Carolina. In private conversations, Turner "cheered the Klan as a superb electioneering device. . . . His position was identical to that of highly placed Klansmen who wanted to use the order selectively for political purposes."[34] Indeed, in 1868, the Republican vote plunged, allowing Democrats to carry the state by 8,000 votes and seize control of the legislature. Ten of the fifteen counties that went to the Democrats had experienced significant Klan activity.[35]

By 1871, Josiah Turner's *Raleigh Sentinel* had become the chief Democratic organ in North Carolina. As a loyal partisan, Turner took a prominent role in advancing, rationalizing, and covering up the Ku Klux conspiracy throughout the state:

> The *Sentinel's* first admission that the Klan actually existed, on April 29, was coupled with a charge that the Jones County murders were really committed by the Union League; members of that order, it asked people to believe, were busy killing one another in order to blame it on the Democrats. This was too absurd to repeat indefinitely, and the *Sentinel* soon contented itself with holding the Union League responsible for calling the Klan into existence in the first place.[36]

Meanwhile, in Florida, the Iron Triangle was making decisive gains for the Democratic Party. In Columbia County, the Klan went on a killing spree and killed at least seven black Republicans. The county's state senator, Dr. E. G. Johnson, was later assassinated in 1875. Since the number of Democrats and Republicans in the legislature was evenly split, Johnson's death gave Democrats the majority in the Senate. As one Democrat put it, "death makes way for liberty." From 1868 to 1871, eight Florida counties saw an estimated 235 deaths.[37]

Even after Reconstruction, lynching deaths remained widespread. Tuskegee statistics indicate that 3,426 blacks were lynched in the United States in the period from 1882 to 1947. Of these, 1,217 were lynched between 1890 and 1900.[38] But here again, the role played by newspaper editors who were Democrats—in a manner similar to that played by liberal enablers in the media today—proved essential. Incendiary headlines like "Give Way, Carpetbaggers" and "Death to the Scoundrels," which both appeared in the Gainesville *New Era*, were not uncommon.[39] Klan apologists were often used by the pro-Democratic newspapers to advance a widely accepted thesis throughout the South: "unworthy elements eventually infiltrated the Klan, took control, and gave it a bad name."[40] But while this view might have made some Democrats feel justified in supporting the terrorist arm of their party, the ubiquity of Klan brutality throughout the South belied this notion entirely.

Still, the Iron Triangle's incredible political success was undeniable. What's more, it was beginning to set the stage for what would become a powerful, long-lasting political coalition throughout the South. Princeton University history professor James McPherson's investigation of politics in Arkansas and Georgia found that in the 1868 campaign more than 200 political murders were reported in Arkansas, including the ambush killing of a Republican congressman on October 22. While the death toll in Georgia was lower, beatings were higher. These tactics spread terror and kept thousands of Republicans from heading to the polls. McPherson found that in twenty-two Georgia counties with a total registration of more than 9,300 black voters, Ulysses S. Grant received only eighty-seven votes. Even more amazing was the fact that in eleven Georgia counties Republicans received not a single vote. But it was the Democratic Iron Triangle's ability to permanently alter voting patterns that was most astonishing of all. What had been a 7,000-vote Republican majority in the one election had morphed into a Democratic majority of 45,000 in the presidential election.[41] The lasting impact of these voting patterns has been historic. Until Sonny Perdue's victory in

2002, no Republican had been elected Georgia's governor since Reconstruction.

As successful as the Iron Triangle had been in Georgia, those results were *nothing* compared to what Democrats had achieved in Louisiana. Twenty-one parishes, who in the previous election had tallied 26,814 Republican votes, now tallied only 501 ballots for Republican presidential candidate Ulysses Grant. The Iron Triangle had wiped blacks off the electoral map. In all of Louisiana, what had in April been a 58 percent Republican majority, in seven months morphed into a 71 percent Democratic majority. Again, the impact of this shift is felt to this day. In 2000, 62 percent of Louisiana voters were registered Democrats versus only 21 percent Republicans.[42]

With the Democratic Iron Triangle wiping Republican majorities off the map in the South, the GOP knew that were its congressional majority to dissolve, Democrats would simply repeal their Civil Rights Act of 1866. So they began considering ways to permanently protect blacks from Democratic Party oppression. If Republicans could amend the Constitution to make all persons born on U.S. soil citizens, they could forever graft black rights directly into the Constitution. Thus they proposed the Fourteenth Amendment: "No State shall deprive any person of life, liberty, or property without due process of law; or deny any person within its jurisdiction the equal protection of the laws." When blacks were considered "property," Southern slave owners had a vested if cynical motivation not to kill them. With blacks becoming citizens, however, that incentive was now obsolete, and that's what Republicans feared.

When the Congress voted on passage of the Fourteenth Amendment, the House supported its passage 120 to 32. In the Senate, the margin was 33 to 11. In both chambers, every single vote in favor of the amendment belonged to a Republican, every single vote against it belonged to a Democrat. Lewis L. Gould, author of a history of the Republican Party, maintains that the passage of the Fourteenth Amendment "remains one of the most important historical legacies of the Republican Party."[43]

The Republican Party had already made monumental progress for black Americans, often while risking their own lives. But with the Democratic Iron Triangle rolling up huge wins all across the South, the Grand Old Party knew its days were numbered. Andrew Johnson had narrowly survived Republicans' failed attempt at impeachment, but Ulysses S. Grant had been elected president shortly thereafter. Republicans had hoped Johnson's departure might have quashed Democrats' hatred of blacks. But as they soon learned, Johnson had simply been one part of a hydra-headed monster. With Klan violence erupting all over the increasingly Democratic South, the GOP remained unwavering in its support and advancement of blacks. Indeed, Democrats' escalation of violence only steeled GOP resolve and gave Republicans an added sense of urgency to press on while they still had the political capital necessary to fight for black freedoms. With Andrew Johnson gone, before the end of Reconstruction in 1877, Republicans would fight for and win three major civil rights victories. Not until 1957 would America see another civil rights bill.[44]

The next Republican victory came on February 3, 1870, with the ratification of the Fifteenth Amendment. Hundreds of black Republicans were elected to various legislatures and former Union army chaplain Hiram Revels became the first black American to become a U.S. senator (in Jefferson Davis' old seat, no less). As a result the Democratic Iron Triangle accelerated its efforts to purge Republicans from the polls. Indeed, it would not be until 1935 that a black would be elected as a Democrat to the Congress; prior to then every black member of Congress had been a Republican. Still, the GOP was committed to ensconcing black voting rights in the fabric of the Constitution. Therefore, the Fifteenth Amendment stated: "The right of citizens of the United States to vote shall not be denied or abridged by the United States or by any State on account of race, color, or previous condition of servitude." But just because Republicans had outlawed voter discrimination in the Constitution, that didn't mean Democrats would honor the law. In fact, with Democrats gaining control of the House in 1875 and the Senate in 1879, it wouldn't be until the Voting Rights Act of 1965 that the Fifteenth Amendment would be fully enforced.[45] This would mean that a nearly 100-year period would lapse before the right of blacks to vote was recognized. It is ironic that today the very party that took the rights away wants credit for protecting them.

The second Republican civil rights victory was the passage of the Ku Klux Klan Act of 1871. This law gave the federal government the power to stop and prosecute terrorist organizations, of which the Ku Klux Klan was considered one. But the crowning jewel of the Republicans' myriad civil rights bills was the Civil Rights Act of 1875, the precursor to the Civil Rights Act of 1964. The bill had been the life's work of Republican senator Charles Sumner, the GOP stalwart whose powerful oratory against the pro-slavery Democrats had resulted in him being bludgeoned on the floor of the U.S. Senate.

Sumner's bill would protect the civil and legal rights of citizens and would prohibit racial discrimination in public accommodation. This meant that in facilities or services that were funded by taxpayers (the public), all individuals, regardless of race, would be guaranteed full and equal accommodation. On the day of his death, Sumner told a former attorney general: "You must take care of the civil rights bill—my bill, the civil rights bill—don't let it fail." The following year it was passed.[46]

Despite all these challenges, the Grand Old Party somehow managed to achieve enormous, historic achievements for black Americans. The Thirteenth Amendment, Fourteenth Amendment,

Fifteenth Amendment, the Civil Rights Act of 1866, the First Reconstruction Act of 1867, the Ku Klux Klan Act of 1871, and the Civil Rights Act of 1875 gave black Americans rights they had never known.

In the modern political era, Democrats' incendiary rhetoric remains as the last part of the original Democratic Iron Triangle. Moving forward, Democratic politicians retooled their political focus, the Klan reemerged and swelled in size, and the mainstream media stayed true to its Democratic roots. These developments made the twentieth century ripe for robbing Republicans of the centerpiece of their party's founding—achieving liberty and individual freedom for all.

Had the Democratic Party not been such a lethal and obstructionist force, it is conceivable that the civil rights legislation of the 1950s and 1960s would have been unnecessary. After all, Republicans had already passed nearly identical legislation a *century* ago, only to have it fall prey to the Democratic Iron Triangle.[47] Still, as the next chapter will reveal, once again it would be Republicans who would be largely responsible for the introduction and passage of these later civil rights bills. As black Republican co-founder of the National Association for the Advancement of Colored People (NAACP) Mary Church Terrell once said, "Every right that has been bestowed upon blacks was initiated by the Republican Party."

7

THE CIVIL RIGHTS SHELL GAME

How the Democratic Party Erased Its History and
Duped a Nation

*Son, when I appoint a nigger to the court, I want everyone to know
he's a nigger.*[1]

—President Lyndon Baines Johnson

*There are white niggers. I've seen a lot of white niggers in my time.
I'm going to use that word.*[2]

—Senator Robert Byrd

We've read about the murderous history of the KKK Democrats in
the nineteenth century. And most Americans, when reminded of
this past, think that since that was such a long time ago, something
dramatic must have happened in the intervening period that
explains why Democrats are so beloved today. What happened?

The KKK Democrats of the nineteenth century were followed
by the Democratic bigots and hucksters of the twenthieth century.
These modern-day Democrats were, fortunately, less murderous
but their actions were no less pernicious. Today their campaign to
rewrite history has been so successful that even questioning the

Democratic Party's commitment to civil rights defies conventional wisdom. As John McWhorter notes, "There is a sense that we're [blacks] only supposed to vote Democratic because the Republicans are supposedly racists."[3] Many Americans, especially people of color, have been duped into believing that twentieth-century Democrats are our nation's leaders on civil rights. And it is true that Democrats were the leaders . . . the leaders of the *opposition* to the Civil Rights movement! The Civil Rights movement is often thought of as beginning in the 1960s and is portrayed as the golden age of the Democratic Party. This, however, is a laughable liberal fantasy and a delusion.

"What today we refer to as the Civil Rights movement of the 1950s and 1960s, was actually the second Civil Rights movement," says Michael Zak. "The first civil rights movement was led by the Republican Party in the 1860s and 1870s. And it passed the Thirteenth Amendment banning slavery and the Fourteenth Amendment, the Fifteenth Amendment, and several civil rights acts. Those civil rights acts were thwarted by the Democratic Party and by President Andrew Johnson."[4]

Princeton University history professor James McPherson agrees: "From the 1850s to the early part of the 21st century, the Republican Party was the party of black rights for the majority of that period, a century—from 1860 to 1960. It's only been the last 45 years or, let's say, the last 40 years that that has changed and has now kind of flipped over."[5]

In the years between the end of Reconstruction and the beginning of the second civil rights movement—the period commonly referred to as Jim Crow—Democratic bigots abounded. In the early part of the 1900s, one of the most powerful of these individuals was Democrat and United States president Woodrow Wilson. Although Wilson was born in Virginia and raised in the South, he began his political career in New Jersey. (Similarly, I was born in Mississippi and began my political career in Washington, D.C., but people still consider me to be a Southerner.) At the time, Wilson was the only U.S. president to hold a PhD. He had also been president of Princeton University and was an accomplished scholar—equipping him to be a first-rate bamboozler. In 1912, the legendary black intellectual W. E. B. DuBois, the sixth black man admitted to Harvard University, shocked his readers in the pages of the NAACP magazine, *The Crisis*, when he pledged his support for Wilson as president of the United States. Blacks at the time, almost all of whom were Republicans, couldn't understand why DuBois would stand with this former Southerner. It was a critical error on DuBois' part. He trusted that Wilson meant what he said. And who can blame him? After all, who wouldn't believe a man who wrote in a letter to a black official the following, as Wilson did:

> Let me assure my fellow colored citizens the earnest wish to see justice done the colored people in every manner and not merely grudging justice, but justice executed with liberality and cordial good feeling. Should I become President of the United States they may count upon me for absolute fair dealing for everything by which I could assist in advancing their interests of the race.[6]

It could be copy from a release by the modern Democratic Party. Very convincing—and misleading.

Once elected president, Woodrow Wilson got down to business doing what Democrats throughout history have done best, disenfranchising blacks. Wilson dismissed fifteen of the seventeen black supervisors who had previously been appointed to federal jobs and replaced them with whites. Ambassadorships to Haiti and Santo Domingo, positions traditionally given to blacks, were now to be given to whites. Next on his agenda were executive orders for the Treasury Department and Postmaster General, imposing segregated departments. As Richard Wormser had written, these orders "put blacks in their place by forcing them out of positions of competence and authority and into menial jobs." Things were to move in a new direction: "Blacks could be doormen or messengers but not auditor for the navy nor recorder of deeds, two positions that had been held by blacks since Grant was president."[7]

With a bigoted Democrat now back in the White House, word spread quickly across the nation that discriminating against blacks was back in favor. In Georgia, for example, the head of the Internal Revenue Division fired all blacks. Even Wilson's wife, Ellen, got in on the racist rout. "Ellen Wilson was said to have a hand in expanding the segregation of federal employees in Washington . . . Salaries were reduced, in some cases drastically."[8]

As segregation began rolling back the gains black and white Republicans had fought and died to secure for black Americans, Democrats continued flexing their white supremacist muscles. One group of black women, for example, chose not to use special lunchrooms that had been set aside for blacks in D.C. Mrs. Archibald Hopkins, a white woman, reminded the black women that consequences for disobedience were different now: "Why do you go where you are not wanted?" she said to the black women. "Do you know that the Democrats are in power?"[9]

With Woodrow Wilson now flaunting his racist behavior, W. E. B. DuBois began eating the words of his earlier endorsement. In one article, DuBois wrote, "How long will it be before the hateful epithets of 'Nigger' and 'Jim Crow' are openly applied?" DuBois would soon get his answer. Wilson dropped his guard momentarily and showed the world what he truly was—a racist. On March 21, 1915, President Wilson held a special White House screening of a movie near and dear to the heart of every loyal KKK Democrat, *Birth of a Nation*, based on the best-selling book, *The Clansman*. After watching the pro-Ku Klux Klan propaganda, Wilson infamously said, "It is like writing history with lightning, and my only regret is that it is all so terribly true." The film became wildly popular and was used as a massive recruiting tool and national campaign that swelled KKK membership by the millions.[10] As James McPherson reminded me during our interview, "He did see that film—it was screened in the White House for him and he did endorse it. . . . I think his impact on the revival of the Klan and on the popularity of that movement, no matter what he later said, was important."[11] After nearly three decades of fighting the KKK, it took only one Democrat eight years to restore their luster and power.

In addition to being a Democratic bigot, Wilson was also a sexist. After dismissing women and the women's suffrage movement, which was dominated by Republican women like Carrie Chapman Catt and Susan B. Anthony, Wilson finally gave in to the movement's demands that he support a federal amendment for women's suffrage—but did so largely after much of the legislative work was already done. Following his League of Nations debacle, the racist Democrat finally left office having hacked away at the victories Republicans had won on behalf of black equality. Wilson had not achieved this feat alone. Fellow members of his party in the United States Senate had been successful in killing Republican supported anti-lynching laws. But after eight years of having a bigoted Democrat in the White House, Americans would elect three Republican presidents back to back— Warren G. Harding, Calvin Coolidge, and Herbert Hoover.

One of President Harding's first acts as president was to give what W.E.B. Dubois would call the famous "Birmingham Speech."[12] In this speech given in Birmingham, Alabama, during its centennial celebration, Harding stressed three themes:

1. The Negro must vote on the same terms that white folk vote.
2. The Negro must be educated.
3. The Negro must have economic justice.

President Coolidge notably advocated a national commission to address the grievances of blacks. And he regularly used Howard University (one of the nation's oldest black universities) as a forum to give public addresses advocating the plight of blacks. He even issued presidential orders and directives to undo the rollback of rights of blacks in the federal government undertaken by President Woodrow Wilson. And history records the famous GOP Convention speech that Herbert Hoover gave in which he proclaimed:

> The Whig party temporized, compromised upon the issue of freedom for the Negro. That party disappeared. It deserved to disappear. Shall the Republican Party receive or deserve any better fate if it compromises upon the issue of freedom for all men?[13]

Building on the gains of Harding and Coolidge, he encouraged his wife to use her position as First Lady to promote advocacy for blacks.

Then in 1933, the nation elected the man who would reshape the Democratic Party, beginning a new era of bamboozling blacks. Who was that man? Franklin Delano Roosevelt.

The Great Depression had been brutal on all Americans, but its effects on blacks were devastating. Low education and high poverty rates made blacks economically vulnerable. That meant the political climate was ripe for exploitation. Like most Americans, many blacks, struggling to survive, were taken in by Roosevelt's promises to use the government to take care of citizens and their needs. The alphabet soup of New Deal programs FDR set in motion were especially popular among the poor who saw they had the most to gain from government assistance. Yet FDR, the great American "savior," turned a cold shoulder to the cause of advancing black civil rights. As Professor McPherson explains, FDR's New Deal policies, while politically shrewd, had little influence on civil rights laws whatsoever:

> New Deal programs were not active in any direct way in promoting civil rights legislation. And, in fact, Democratic leaders in Congress vigorously opposed any civil rights legislation. President Franklin Delano Roosevelt, dependent on Southern political leaders, in the Senate, especially, did not push them very hard.[14]

Overlooking this callous disregard for the plight of blacks, liberals like to argue that FDR's social policies and income redistribution were advantageous to black Americans and the poor. But as Jim Powell, senior fellow at the Cato Institute and the author of *FDR's Folly*, demonstrates, the truth is exactly the opposite—FDR's New Deal policies prolonged joblessness for millions of Americans and were especially devastating for blacks:

- The New Deal's flagship National Industrial Recovery Act introduced minimum wage regulations that resulted in some 500,000 blacks, mostly in the South, losing their jobs.
- FDR's Agricultural Adjustment Act was designed to restrict production and send food prices up. Less production meant less work for thousands of poor black sharecroppers, not to mention higher food prices.
- The 1935 Wagner Act legalized labor union monopolies as part of FDR's efforts to create his infamous New Deal Coalition of support from Unions, Catholics, Jews, and blacks. But the move had the effect of excluding blacks, given that the unions had a long history of discrimination against blacks.

- New Deal spending programs sent monies flooding into communities, just not black ones. These federal dollars were often channeled away from the poorest citizens, including millions of Southern blacks, because bamboozlers knew they already had black votes and could divert resources to other constituencies with which FDR could buy more votes.[15]

FDR's economic policies had not been intentionally designed to harm black Americans, but they did. Moreover, President Franklin Delano Roosevelt's judicial nominees displayed a breathtaking degree of contempt for the rights and concerns of black Americans. One of his nominees to the Supreme Court led to a showdown in the United States Senate. That nominee was Alabama U.S. senator Hugo Black, a former Klansman who as a lawyer had defended Klansmen against murder charges. On August 17, 1937, Republicans stood together in opposing Hugo Black. Unfortunately, they were unsuccessful.

Even with this record, FDR was effective in wooing black voters for one significant reason: he had a potent weapon in Eleanor Roosevelt, whom he often used to great symbolic effect. The most famous instance of this involved the time that the Daughters of the American Revolution refused to allow Marian Anderson Black to perform in their Washington hall in 1938. Eleanor Roosevelt successfully arranged for the concert to be presented at the Lincoln Memorial. While this action did nothing substantive to advance the civil rights or economic empowerment of black Americans, the First Lady's efforts generated enormous publicity and goodwill within the black community and made many blacks reconsider their attitudes toward the party that ensured their ancestors' oppression.

Bigot Woodrow Wilson and opportunist Franklin Roosevelt—both Democrats had been successful in bamboozling blacks. But their efforts were child's play compared to the transformative civil rights shell game ushered in by presidents John F. Kennedy and Lyndon Baines Johnson—Democrats as well.

The mythology that surrounds John F. Kennedy and Lyndon Baines Johnson in the hearts and homes of most blacks is stunning. Even during our interview, I could hear the subtle cadence of hero worship in the voice of a somewhat begrudging Reverend Al Sharpton: "You had many Democrats that murdered us, that were Dixiecrats and lived to fight against us. And then the Kennedys and the Lyndon Johnsons came in and stood over a period of time of being beat down by the movement and turned around and repudiated that and turned the party to a pro-civil rights party." I then asked Sharpton why he thought that a vicious racist like LBJ supported the Civil Rights Act of 1964, a bill that would have been entirely unnecessary to pass had Democrats over one hundred years prior not knocked down Republican-led civil rights legislation: "I don't know why they [Kennedy and LBJ] did it, but they did it and the Republicans haven't done it. So if somebody said to me, 'George Bush just said that we've got to fight racism, we've got to stand for affirmative action, no justice/no peace,' I wouldn't care why he did it. I would just care that he did it."[16]

Other blacks give LBJ glowing credit for advancing the cause of civil rights. "I happen to think that Lyndon Baines Johnson was the greatest president in our nation's history, short of Abraham Lincoln," Congressman Jesse Jackson Jr. told me. This is curious logic, to be sure. If you hate blacks all your life and then do the right thing, you're a hero. But if you fight for justice and equality all your life, but happen to be a Republican, such as Senator Everett Dirksen of Illinois, the real hero of the Civil Rights Act of 1964, you're undeserving of praise and support?

That doesn't wash. But today that's what passes for a consensus.

To show just how dramatically liberals have rewritten history, I want to briefly take you inside the historic battle to pass the landmark Civil Rights Act of 1964. The bill pushed by Kennedy was a weaker version of an earlier bill that the Republican Party had proposed.

When President John F. Kennedy sent his civil rights bill to Congress in 1963, the measure forced Southern Democrats to choose between partisan loyalty to their president, and loyalty to their party's racist history. These Democrats chose the latter.

To build support for the bill's passage, Dr. Martin Luther King Jr. and other members of the Civil Rights Movement organized the August 28, 1963, March on Washington, which would culminate in the magisterial delivery of Dr. King's epic "I Have a Dream" speech. But when Kennedy and Johnson got wind of the plans for the rally, they were unsupportive. Were violence to erupt and be broadcast to the nation, the administration feared that support for his reelection would diminish. King said that Kennedy had a "schizophrenic tendency" when it came to civil rights. Indeed, according to BBC reporter and author Nick Bryant, prior to the historic March on Washington, Kennedy "spoke scornfully of how the black demonstrators who were arriving in the capital might 'shit' on the Washington monument."[17] These attitudes and concerns were just part of an overall mindset of indifference and political expediency when it came to Kennedy's handling of blacks as part of his electoral coalition.

But if Kennedy could be detached and callous toward the black struggle for equality, Lyndon Baines Johnson was downright hostile. According to acclaimed LBJ biographer Robert Caro, prior to 1957, Johnson "had never supported civil rights legislation—any civil rights legislation. In the Senate and House alike, his record was an unbroken one of votes against every civil rights bill that had ever come to a vote: against voting rights bills; against bills that would have struck at job discrimination and at segregation in other areas of American life; even against bills that would have protected blacks from lynching."[18]

Those who worked closely with Johnson reported that his private behavior toward blacks could be downright malicious. Robert Parker, Johnson's longtime black employee and limousine chauffeur, states in his autobiography that Johnson "called me 'boy,' 'nigger,' or 'chief,' never by my name . . . Whenever I was late, no matter what the reason, Johnson called me a lazy, good-for-nothing nigger. . . . I was afraid of him because of the pain and humiliation he could inflict at a moment's notice."[19]

Following Kennedy's assassination, the bill was now left to Johnson to get signed into law. But there were several hurdles in the way, and most of them were Democrats. Among the biggest and most powerful of these was former Klansman Robert C. Byrd (D-WV). Byrd delivered a record-setting Senate filibuster designed to defeat the bill. Moreover, he helped to galvanize a third of all Senate Democrats to oppose the bill.

Today, Byrd still serves proudly on the floor of the U.S. Senate and is widely praised by his fellow Democrats. Massachusetts senator Ted Kennedy says Byrd is "what our Founding Fathers were thinking about when they were thinking about a United States Senate. He brings the kind of qualities that the Founding Fathers believed were so important for service to the Nation."[20]

Byrd's racism runs deep. As he once wrote in a letter, "The Klan is needed today as never before and I am anxious to see its rebirth here in West Virginia . . . and in every state in the Union."[21] In another letter, the former Klansman wrote that he would refuse to ever fight in the Armed Forces "with a Negro by my side. Rather I should die a thousand times, and see Old Glory trampled in the dirt never to rise again, than to see this beloved land of ours become degraded by race mongrels, a throwback to the blackest specimen from the wilds."[22] He voted against the Civil Rights Act of 1964 and the Voting Rights Act of 1965.[23] Then in 2001, Byrd, appearing on Fox News, told then-host Tony Snow: "There are white niggers. I've seen a lot of white niggers in my time. I'm going to use that word. We just need to work together to make our country a better country, and I'd just as soon quit talking about it so much."[24]

Notwithstanding his past opposition, Johnson had made the decision to support Kennedy's civil rights bill. Passing the legislation should have been easy for Democrats. As Republican Senate minority leader Everett Dirksen noted:

> First, let me point out that in this Senate are 67 members bearing the Democrat label. It takes only a majority to enact the Administration bill, namely 51. It takes 67 to impose cloture if cloture is needed. I say to the President, that his Party has enough members to do both jobs. If as he has said to me, the job cannot be done without Republicans, perhaps he should turn the reins of government over to Republicans. With such a top-heavy majority, we should not find it necessary to turn to his Party for results.[25]

For Johnson to have any shot of passing the bill, he'd need Republicans to, once again, do the heavy lifting. Forget what you think you know about the vote for the Civil Rights Act of 1964. In the House, Republicans had supported the bill 138 votes to 34—a ratio of 4 to 1 in favor. Democrats, however, had been more divided, voting 152 for and 96 against passing the civil rights law—barely 1.5 to 1. Former Klansman Byrd, who today is referred to as the "conscience of the Senate," was loaded for bear and prepared to block the bill in the Senate.

On purely philosophical grounds, Republican presidential candidate Barry Goldwater and five other Republicans would side with the twenty-two Democrats who were against the bill. What were Goldwater's objections? Goldwater believed that the 1957 civil rights bill and earlier Republican versions of the civil rights bill that he had supported—but which had been filibustered by the Democrats—protected the rights of individual owners while also securing civil rights for blacks. This new bill in his view went one step too far by covering private property owners rather than just local, state, and federal governments, which in his view were the real problem. Note, however, that for the Democrats it was precisely the provisions covering local and state governments that they opposed.

President George W. Bush's Secretary of Housing and Urban Development (HUD), Alphonso Jackson, is a black man who knows a thing or two about the fight for civil rights:

> Goldwater didn't help it any, OK? But Goldwater was a fair man. See, Goldwater actually was right—and this is actually what most people don't understand. Goldwater said we didn't need the 1964 Civil Rights Act. He was right—we didn't need it, because we had the Thirteenth, Fourteenth, and Fifteenth Amendments . . . Goldwater was a purist, he believed in the Constitution and he said why do we have to pass the 1964 Civil Rights Act if we've got the Thirteenth, Fourteenth, Fifteenth Amendment that says we can't discriminate? Blacks are human beings, the same as everybody else. If you legitimately look at it, he was right, constitutionally—we shouldn't need the Civil Rights Act. We got it because it satisfied the needs of liberals and some blacks who said that unless we have this act, we're not going to be able to really deal with all of the discrimination that occurs in this country.

But Byrd and the Democrats were already on a path to kill the bill by filibustering it. For the bill to have any chance, LBJ would have to convince Everett Dirksen to gather his tiny band of Republicans to save the bill.

"Now you know this bill can't pass unless you get Ev Dirksen," Johnson told Hubert Humphrey. "You and I are going to get him. You make up your mind now that you've got to spend time with Ev Dirksen. You've got to let him have a piece of the action. He's got to look good all the time."[26]

LBJ needed Dirksen to convince a majority of Senate Republicans to support the bill for it to have any chance of overcoming the Byrd filibuster. As Frances Rice notes:

The Democrats were fighting every piece of civil rights legislation that was put forth by the Republicans in the 1960s. It was a Republican, Everett Dirksen from Illinois, who pushed the civil rights laws of the 1950s, 1964, 1965, and 1968. Had it not been for Republicans, those laws would not have been passed because some Democrats were busy filibustering those laws. They're the ones who passed the black codes and Jim Crow laws. It was the Republicans who started the NAACP and historically black colleges.[27]

Minutes before the vote was to be taken, Senator Everett Dirksen delivered a floor speech calling for cloture—the suspension of a filibuster—that is regarded by some scholars as one of the great Republican orations in history.[28] When the final votes were taken, over four-fifths of Senate Republicans voted for the bill, thereby handing LBJ the legislative win of the century, and once again fighting for black rights, even if there was to be little political benefit from black bamboozled voters. Contrary to what most Americans believe, "the civil rights legislation of the 1960s was, in fact, supported by most Republicans in Congress," Princeton University professor of history James McPherson said.[29]

There are at least four reasons why Democrats have been successful in running their shell game of civil rights on Americans in general and blacks in particular. The first reason is that, rightly or wrongly, American presidents get the credit and the blame for major events that occur during their term(s) in office. We remember presidents before we remember senators. LBJ, therefore, walks away the great hero of civil rights, even while muttering the N-word under his breath. It's not fair. It's not right. But that's the way the American political system works.

Second, black Americans during the Kennedy era fell in love with JFK when he did one very simple, very symbolic thing: he placed a phone call to Dr. Martin Luther King, Jr., when King was imprisoned in Birmingham, Alabama, the site from which Dr. King would draft his famous "Letter from a Birmingham Jail." This highly symbolic gesture, combined with Robert Kennedy's support for civil rights legislation, ingratiated the Kennedy clan to the King family (specifically to Martin Luther King Sr., a lifelong Republican). The gesture wasn't so much designed to swing support to Kennedy as it was to keep Martin Luther King Jr. neutral in the election. But when Barry Goldwater, who had voted against the act, was tapped in 1964 as the GOP nominee, LBJ was handed an easy issue on which to contrast himself against the Republican candidate—civil rights.

Third, even when voters are informed about the murderous, hate-filled history of the Democrats, liberals erase their party's entire history with a blanket statement that claims, over the last forty years, there has been a migration of the racists out of the Democratic Party and into the GOP. Secretary Jackson says that's hardly true. "Now the Democrats came back with a unique argument and they said that they all became Republicans. Only one of them became a Republican, and that was Strom Thurmond. The rest of them stayed Democrats until the day they died—they didn't change parties. . . . Fulbright and Albert Gore, Sr. (father of former vice president Al Gore), et cetera."

And even for Strom Thurmond, one must remember that when he set the record for the longest filibuster in the history of the United States Senate, it was not as a Republican. It was not in 1964; it was in 1957 in opposition to the Civil Rights Act of 1957. Southern senators, who had agreed as part of a compromise not to filibuster this bill, were upset with Thurmond because they thought his solo filibuster made them look bad to their constituents.[30]

On September 16, 1964, Thurmond, increasingly at odds with the national Democratic Party over racial integration, switched his party affiliation, becoming a Republican. In South Carolina and other states of the Deep South, white segregationists supported Goldwater in 1964 instead of Johnson, whose support of the Civil Rights Act of 1964 and integration rankled the segregationists.

Thurmond played an important role in South Carolina's support for Republican presidential candidates Barry Goldwater in 1964 and Richard Nixon in 1968.[31] Indeed, as Ann Coulter has pointed out, "In 1948, Thurmond did not run as a Dixiecan, he ran as a Dixiecrat—his party was an offshoot of the Democratic Party. And when he lost, he went right back to being a Democrat."[32]

Moreover, Americans should never forget that it was as recently as 1967 that Southern Democrats filibustered federal anti-lynching legislation. *Lynching! In 1967!* The same year the Green Bay Packers beat the Kansas City Chiefs in the first Super Bowl; the same year the first issue of *Rolling Stone* magazine was published; the same year *The Graduate* and *Bonnie and Clyde* were hits at the box office. Democrats were still trying to stop minorities from being full citizens.

Finally, Democrats have been successful in cowing the Republican National Committee into apologizing for the so-called Southern Strategy used in the 1970s by Richard Nixon to pry the South away from Democrats. By using race as a wedge issue, on such racially polarizing topics as busing and crime, Democrats contend that Republicans engaged in racial insensitivity and innuendo-laden imagery and words designed to subtly trigger racial voting. This "stealth bigotry," liberals argue, is evidence that the GOP is the party of racists. Former RNC chairman Ken Mehlman, speaking before the NAACP, said, "Some Republicans gave up on winning the African-American vote, looking the other way or trying to benefit politically from racial polarization. I am here today as the Republican chairman to tell you we were wrong."[33]

Conservative commentator Bill Kristol says the criticism over a GOP Southern Strategy is overstated: "Republicans, I think unfairly in large ways, were tagged as having a Southern strategy and not caring about civil rights and they made some mistakes as well . . . Most people in the Nixon White House were not in any way racially bigoted."

Moreover, how is it that the NAACP—an organization that has run ads blaming then Governor George Bush for the brutal dragging death of James Byrd—claimed that if blacks don't vote, Republicans will take money from children, and black churches will burn. How can this have any claim to the moral high ground? And above all that, how in the world is it that the GOP, the party founded to free slaves from racist Democrats, is the only one saying "sorry" here?! Maybe I missed it, but when are Nancy Pelosi, Harry Reid, and Howard Dean going to atone for their party's murderous history of oppression?

Secretary Alphonso Jackson knows about the brutality of Democrats firsthand. He was there that fateful day in March 1965 when he and fifty other black civil rights marchers were headed to join Dr. Martin Luther King, Jr. to register voters and were blocked from crossing the Pettus Bridge by two hundred state troopers armed with whips, nightsticks, tear gas, dogs, and electric cattle prods. That day, known historically as "Bloody Sunday," left Secretary Jackson with both emotional and physical scars. And his impassioned portrayal of this event brought tears to my eyes:

> Who stood at the schoolhouse door in Little Rock, Arkansas? It was a Democratic governor—it wasn't a Republican governor, and Eisenhower sent the troops in there to integrate Little Rock. Who stood at the door in Alabama? It wasn't a Republican governor, it was a Democratic governor who stood at the door. Who, when I was standing on the Pettus Bridge that Sunday morning, March 1965, who was standing before us? Al Lingo, who was a Democratic sheriff. Who said we couldn't vote? It was Goldsmith and Smithfield, the mayor of Selma, Alabama. See, we don't have a sense of what our history is about . . . I was there on Bloody Sunday—I have the dog bite on my left leg to this day, I carry it.[34]

It is often said that those who do not know their history are doomed to repeat it. In the context of the Democratic Party's past practice of exploiting blacks for political gain, many people have wrongly assumed the practice has ended. But that's not true, because the phenomenon manifested itself again as recently as in the 2006 election. It happened in the race for the United States Senate in Maryland. Kweisi Mfume ran in the Maryland Democratic primary for Senate against Ben Cardin. With Mfume having dutifully served his role and fulfilled his purpose as a charismatic spokesman for the cause, who would have guessed that he'd be callously pushed aside in favor of Ben Cardin. But that's exactly what the Democrats did, even though Mfume had helped with the national campaign for the Democrats in 1992, 1996, and 2000. He had held elected office as a congressman and had served as president of the NAACP. None of these things counted. Throughout this time he towed the Democratic line and supported practically every initiative the party put forward. Still the Democrats endorsed the white candidate.

Even black Republicans, such as Secretary Alphonso Jackson, found the move alarmingly disloyal: "It's the most amazing thing that the chairman of the Democratic Party, Howard Dean, said that we don't endorse people in the primary when we have Democrats running against each other. Well, the national party and the state Democratic Party in Maryland endorsed Cardin over Kweisi Mfume. Now, my position is, if you don't endorse anybody, why did that happen? . . . They were supposed to fight it out themselves. The national party raised money for Cardin against a black man."[35]

As State senator Nathaniel Exum put it, "They don't take us serious. We're the most loyal constituency, and they don't take us serious. They have never done anything, and they pay us lip service."[36]

One could almost feel sorry for Democrats like Mfume who got chewed up, spit out, and tossed aside by Democrats. Indeed, in the end, it seems the bamboozler was the one who got bamboozled.

That most Americans don't carry that same knowledge of history and scandalous record of disregard of minorities is one of the reasons that Democrats have had such success in hiding their murderous history. Citizens owe it to all those who bear the scars and paid the price of freedom to learn and to never forget the truth.

8

THE RISE OF THE VICTIMHOOD VENDORS

Teddy, Jesse, Julian

We've gone from Jim Crow to James Crow, Jr., Esq. They are a little more shrewd or more polished, but the results are the same.

—Reverend Al Sharpton

A lot of those people got caught up in the thrills of sticking it to the white man. Again, it was because of insecurity. I honestly believe that deep down inside, Jesse Jackson, Al Sharpton, Julian Bond, and Maxine Waters do not like themselves very much. They grew up black in a time when it would have been very hard not to feel inferior. They're getting a sense of pride and accomplishment out of complaining.

—John McWhorter

Sometimes, crises create leaders; sometimes great pressure makes diamonds.

Sometimes . . .

On August 29, 2005, leaders at all levels of government had the opportunity of a lifetime to showcase stellar leadership, but most failed to do so. Hurricane Katrina hit the region where I grew up with a vengeance and claimed the lives of 1,500 Americans. The massive storm ripped homes and families in half. As almost everyone agrees, the rescue and recovery efforts were far too slow in coming. President Bush failed. Louisiana governor Kathleen Blanco failed. New Orleans mayor Ray Nagin failed. None of these failures were acceptable. All could and should have done more.

Yet federal, state, and local executives weren't the only ones who failed the people of the Gulf Coast region. Another form of moral failure came from those who preyed upon the grief, poverty, and brokenness of a people. I'm not talking about the looters, or even the over $1 billion in hurricane relief fraud that the Government Accounting Office now estimates likely occurred.[1] No, I'm talking about something much more valuable than possessions or money. I'm talking about the political exploitation of poor people victimized by one of the worst hurricanes in recorded history. I'm talking about the kinds of paranoid "blame America first" rhetoric that gushed from the mouths of race hucksters like Spike Lee, Nancy Pelosi, and Louis Farrakhan. Out of extreme tragedy, these so-called leaders chose conspiracy over calm, hostility over hope.

"I heard from a very reliable source who saw a twenty-five-foot-deep crater under the levee breach," said Nation of Islam leader and minister Louis Farrakhan. "It may have been blown up to destroy the black part of town and keep the white part dry," he said. "These explosives are from the government side," Farrakhan explained during a press conference. Later, the spiritual leader declared that if these charges were true, "somebody is guilty, then, not only of mass destruction of property, but of mass murder."[2] Fox News' David Asman caught up with Farrakhan and probed his earlier comments. Following a recitation of a vision he received while riding inside a UFO (no, I'm not joking), Minister Farrakhan explained: "Now, here we are in 2005. Many, many people in the Ninth Ward, black and white, believe that what happened in 1927 happened again, but this time, race and class were used. Now, I don't know whether it did or did not happen, but when people believe something like that, it is the duty of those who can search out a rumor and prove its truth or its falsehood [to] do that to either dispel the rumor or prove its truth. So those who are culpable may be brought to justice. . . . All of the evidence is not in, sir, unless an investigation is carried out to prove that is only a rumor."[3]

Farrakhan's reference to the 1927 dynamiting of levees, he said, came from the book by John Barry, *Rising Tide: The Great Mississippi Flood and How it Changed America.* So David Asman interviewed Barry to ask him whether the government blew up levees in 1927 to rid the city of blacks and save white communities. Quite the contrary, Barry explained, "In 1927, the city of New Orleans, to protect itself, did dynamite, using the governor's authority and things like that, a levee outside the city. But that was an entirely white community. There were very, very few if any blacks in that community. That was about money, it wasn't about race."[4]

Yet the facts matter little to the victimhood vendors, the liberal bamboozlers who, at almost every turn, strain to make anything and everything about race—a celebration of black misery and failure administered at the hands of sinister—often invisible—"structural" forces of white supremacy. "We must be the only group in human history who have been taught to spend so much time looking back and talking about the obstacles, instead of standing up and trying our best to get past them," John McWhorter said.[5]

Never mind that just two weeks after the massive storm pummeled the Gulf Coast, private donations from "racist America" skyrocketed to a record $700 million, a pace that according to *USA Today* exceeded levels of giving in the wake of the September 11 terrorist attacks. In just two weeks, the American Red Cross received

$503 million, almost the same amount as it had received two *months* after September 11.[6] But these hopeful acts of American compassion are of little use to the victimhood vendors; they are, in fact, a nuisance, something to be brushed aside, because they don't fit their pre-written "script" of victimhood.

And so, it's hardly surprising that residents, understandably demoralized after having endured the hellish ravages of Hurricane Katrina, would go before the United States Congress to testify that the levees were blown up, just as Minister Farrakhan and later Hollywood director Spike Lee, creator of the documentary, *When the Levees Broke*, alleged. Speaking before the House Select Committee, black New Orleans resident and community activist "Mama D," or Dyan French, swore under oath that the levees were bombed: "I was on my front porch. I have witnesses that they bombed the walls of the levee, boom, boom! Mister, I'll never forget it." Another resident, Leah Hodges, agreed with French's assessment. "Certainly appears to me to be an act of genocide and of ethnic cleansing," Hodges told the House committee.[7]

Terrorized citizens could perhaps be excused for buying into such impossible conspiracy theories. But reporter Lisa Myers wanted to investigate further, so she interviewed Harvard University professor Alvin Pouissant about why individuals are sometimes persuaded by fantastical conspiracy theories. In her report, Myers explained that "such conspiracy theories are fueled by years of government neglect and discrimination against blacks: slavery, segregation, and the Tuskegee experiments, during which poor blacks were used to test the effects of syphilis." As Pouissant explained to Myers, "If you're angry and you've been discriminated against, then your mind is open to many ideas about persecution, abandonment, feelings of rejection."[8]

Fair enough. But maybe there's another explanation. Maybe years of race-baiting rhetoric from liberals like Senator Ted Kennedy, Minister Louis Farrakhan, Reverend Jesse Jackson, Senator John Kerry, Speaker Nancy Pelosi, and Julian Bond, in part, explain the phenomenon. Perhaps the endless diet of victimhood, racial paranoia, and liberal policies explain, in part, why so many people of color have been bamboozled. The exploitation agenda by liberals hinges on the continued stranglehold of Democratic Party support among minorities. To maintain their grip, Democrats rely on the victimhood vendors—shakedown artists and hustlers—men and women whose job it is to ensure minority voters continue to blindly follow the party. They often inflict social and cultural punishment on any minority who would dare to exercise a modicum of intellectual independence or contemplate voting for a candidate other than the pre-approved Democratic Party selection.

"Jesse Jackson and Julian Bond. See, that's a racket—they have got to keep this information from being disseminated. They have to, if they are going to stay in place," Secretary Alphonso Jackson said. "That's what most black people don't understand. The civil rights movement is unlike what Reverend King talked about—it's a business now. So the business is to keep us uninformed—that's the business. Isn't it amazing that Condoleezza Rice, Colin Powell, and Rod Paige have never been on the cover of *Jet, Ebony*, or *Essence,* or *Black Enterprise* magazine? Isn't it amazing?"[9]

Secretary Jackson's observation is an important one. Indeed, the first rule among the victimhood vendors is to give as little public credit to conservatives or Republicans as possible. Name calling and attacks, not praise, are to be hurled at those who challenge the liberal exploitation agenda. The victimhood vendors avoid doing or saying anything that might give black voters a positive impression about the GOP or conservatism. The script could have come straight out of a fairy tale: the victimhood vendor hath been sent to slay the evil conservative dragon. It's that childish and ridiculous. But such is what passes for liberalism these days.

"I think people who are good at making excuses, for their failed policies and actions are often good at doing nothing else and perhaps the only exception is name-calling," says former Ohio secretary of state Ken Blackwell. "I try to look for win-win situations while all too frequently Reverend Jackson and others look for ways to create zero-sum gains because that is where they shine."[10]

And so, when you chat with the likes of a Reverend Al Sharpton, for example, he says things like: "We've gone from Jim Crow to James Crow, Jr., Esq. They are a little more shrewd or more polished, but the results are the same."[11] There's no denying that Sharpton is a master at crafting sound-bite-friendly spin, and few are more entertaining to listen to than he. But as Secretary Alphonso Jackson points out, Sharpton's blurring of history only serves to bolster the victimhood vendors' code:

> I like Al, but I disagree with him. Al said something at the Democratic National Convention that I thought was important. He said, "Mr. President, Mr. Bush—we didn't stand on the Pettus Bridge and get beaten to give up our rights." Well, I did stand on the bridge. He wasn't there. I was there, all right! And the two people I saw across from me were both Democrats, not Republicans.[12]

One of the clearest examples of the victimhood vendors' willingness to discard truth to prop up Democrats and tear down Republicans involves liberals' starkly different responses to Bill Clinton and George W. Bush's handling of policies pertaining to the continent of Africa. Bill Clinton, the champion of black America— indeed, "the first black president,"[13] as his flaks boastfully declare— sat, watched, and did nothing as one million Tutsis were butchered by Hutu rebels in Rwanda, often by the blood-soaked blade of a machete. Clinton's "Africa Matters" rhetoric may have soothed black souls, but his actions (or lack thereof) spoke volumes. But don't take my word for it. Here's what liberal *Nation* magazine writer David Corn wrote about Clinton's inaction on the tenth anniversary of the Rwandan genocide:

> The Clinton administration dithered for weeks over whether to use the G-word [genocide], for doing so would have compelled the administration, under international law, to take direct steps to stop the killings. But after the disaster in Somalia, Clinton had no stomach for becoming involved in another messy conflict in Africa. In public, he had more to say about the caning of a young American in Singapore than the murders of hundreds of thousands in Rwanda.[14]

In a devastating article titled "Bystanders to Genocide" published in *The Atlantic* magazine, the reporter revealed that the Clinton administration, infamous for its verbal gymnastics and parsing of phrases, went to great lengths to quash the use of the word "genocide," even going so far as to initially refer to the slaughtered Africans as mere "casualties."[15] Clinton's moratorium of the word "genocide," however, would soon fall under the crushing weight of the hundreds of thousands of African corpses piled up during the genocidal holocaust.

In the aftermath, Clinton did what Clinton does best: he spun black folks, both in Africa and America, and let the victimhood vendors and his liberal buddies in the media clean up his mess. In March 1998, the same month Kathleen Wiley testified before the grand jury in the Monica Lewinsky sex scandal, Jesse Jackson, Clinton's special envoy to Africa and "spiritual advisor," orchestrated a ten-day trip for Clinton to take a break from bamboozling

Americans to extend the favor to Africans. There, Clinton delivered a pathetic excuse camouflaged as yet another one of his lip-biting apologies. Standing in Kigali, Rwanda, at the airport, Clinton said, "Scholars of these sorts of events say the killers, armed mostly with machetes and clubs, nonetheless did their work five times as fast as the mechanized gas chambers used by the Nazis." The first black president continued, "All over the world there were people like me sitting in offices, day after day, who did not fully appreciate the depth and the speed with which you were being engulfed in this unimaginable terror." For emphasis, Clinton intoned, "Never again."

Translation: "Don't blame me, black folks. I didn't know what was going on during those three months as hundreds of thousands of black bodies were being mutilated. After all, I'm Bill Clinton. The first black president of the United States." Despite the overwhelming coverage of these events as they were occurring and his access to classified intelligence briefings, he claimed that he didn't know about them. Was he held accountable for this? No, none of this deterred the victimhood vendors from sidling up to Clinton. Nor did it stop Clinton's support in the media. This crowd of fawning flaks who posed as serious journalists heaped mounds of Monica-distracting praise on the compassionate Clinton during the time he was traveling to the mother continent. Here's a taste of the sugary sweet media coverage one CNN reporter heaped on President Clinton for his "historic" trip to Africa:

> For the first time a continent appears willing to trust and believe in the words of support from an American president. This does not mean that relations have been transformed in a matter of eleven days; Africa has been betrayed by politicians too many times before. But there was little doubt about the sincerity of President Clinton's concluding remarks on the continent: "If we face the future together

it will be a future that is better for Africa and better for America."
On a sunny Senegalese day, with the sun on my back, I believed Bill
Clinton, and I think Africa did as well.[16]

Boy, talk about hard-hitting journalism! Attack dogs, those CNN
reporters! I predict, however, that the sequel to Clinton's greatest
hits is just around the corner. Come 2008 when Hill and Bill are jet-
ting around the nation, there by their side will be the loyal victimhood vendors signaling to the bamboozled masses that Hillary will
become—drum roll, please—"the first black female president!"

Clinton's inaction in Rwanda notwithstanding, Clinton's record
on AIDS in Africa was equally lacking. As Armstrong Williams wrote,
"President Clinton shut his eyes to AIDS. Despite the ballooning toll
in human life and suffering in Africa, the U.S. budget for nonmilitary
aid remained woefully static during the Clinton administration."[17]

Contrast that against President George W. Bush's truly historic
commitment to combat AIDS in Africa. Over the objections of some
in his own party who felt his proposal too generous, Bush pushed for
and got a $15 billion AIDS assistance bill through the Congress. So
unprecedented was Bush's proposal that Melvin Foote, executive
director of the nonpartisan Constituency for Africa organization,
said Bush's "$15 billion commitment is unparalleled. *Clinton offered
$300 million, parking-meter money, even though he knew it was a
tremendous challenge* [emphasis mine]. Clinton opened the door and
broke some new ground when he went to Africa. But in terms of the
content, there wasn't much delivered. . . . When you say Africa matters, you've got to beef up the team, and he didn't do that. The Bush
team looked at the continent, understood what they needed to do
and did it. I mean, that's Bush's hallmark; he sizes the situation up
and then he's ready to move. He's handled it a lot more substantively.
Clinton gave us a bone, and Bush put some meat on the bone."[18]

Noted liberal AIDS activist and Live Aid founder Bob Geldof agrees. "Clinton talked the talk and did diddly squat, whereas Bush doesn't talk but does deliver. You'll think I'm off my trolley when I say this, but the Bush administration is the most radical, in a positive sense, in their approach to Africa since Kennedy," said Geldof.[19] However, what really blew Clinton's lid was when liberal Hollywood actor Richard Gere, who apparently missed that day's DNC talking points memo, blasted Clinton from the podium at a Hillary Clinton fund-raiser: "Senator Clinton, I'm sorry, your husband did nothing for AIDS for eight years." Clinton characteristically pulled off the gloves and punched back. "I don't blame Richard Gere, because he's an actor," said Clinton dismissively. "He doesn't know. I think that somebody told Richard Gere something because they were trying to score a few political points."[20]

After Clinton left office, writer Jill Nelson, writing for *Savoy* magazine, published an article titled, "We've Been Bill-Boozled." In it, Nelson writes, "For eight years we have embraced Bill Clinton as an honorary soul brother. The puzzling thing is, we looked the other way as he hung us out to dry. We shout that we love him and cheer as if he's actually done something for us besides, as James Brown puts it, talking loud and saying nothing."[21]

One would be hard-pressed to think of a better summation of the Clinton legacy: "talking loud and saying nothing."

In addition to backing a Democrat whose policies have sold minorities, the victimhood vendors never tire in their readiness to play the race card, or race bait. Everything—and I mean *everything*—is to be yet another example of racist America, oppressive poverty, and white supremacy.

So why do it? Why must the victimhood vendors race bait? Answer: because the liberal exploitation agenda demands that people of color, particularly blacks, vote for Democrats—or else.

Thus, the race brokers are dispatched like racial S.W.A.T. teams to do the Donkey Party's dirty work. Sometimes this work involves holding high-profile press conferences that will be widely covered by their friends in the liberal mainstream media—many of whom are never too tired to give conservatives a black eye. Other times it may involve scamming corporations by threatening race-driven protests unless certain "actions" are taken to atone for the company's wicked and insensitive ways. "Jesse Jackson is a shakedown artist," says Frances Rice. "He goes to corporations and says, if you don't give me money, I will call you a racist."[22]

Indeed, Kenneth Timmerman's *New York Times* best-selling book, *Shakedown: Exposing the Real Jesse Jackson*, and Reverend Jesse Lee Peterson's book, *Scam: How the Black Leadership Exploits America*, chronicle in devastating fashion the inner workings and intricacies of the victimhood vendors' pressure machines. These authors persuasively argue that the victimhood vendors frequently use intimidation and coercion to achieve their ends.[23] Furthermore, because these phony leaders are beholden to the Democrats and their liberal agenda, they have paralyzed minority voters' ability to make both parties compete for their support, thus making minorities and blacks in particular the dupes of the Democratic Party. Free-thinking black leaders—even those who consistently vote Democratic—see this as a troubling trend that atrophies black voter influence. As Lloyd Williams, the Greater Harlem Chamber of Commerce president sees it, blacks' automatic support for Democrats and knee-jerk condemnation of all things Republican is unproductive and wrongheaded. He believes that blacks need to find ways of not condemning leaders simply because they're from another party. "I think that we are too disproportionately Democratic," Williams says. "I would like to see us be able to balance our vote and be more of a swing factor at different points in time."[24]

Easier said than done, says Bill O'Reilly:

It's more profitable for the black leadership to say to the 13 percent of Americans who are African-American, look, you're getting screwed; I'm going to help you, so give me money, support my organization, because I'll help you, and those white guys aren't going to do it. That resonates among many blacks. So if you're a black leader and you say, why don't you give the Republican a shot, why don't you listen, they're going to go, what's in it for them?[25]

That black Americans have allowed themselves to be bamboozled by a bunch of unelected, angry, self-appointed "race-hustling poverty pimps," as former black Republican congressman J.C. Watts once famously called them, is unacceptable.[26] *All* Americans can do better. That we've allowed ourselves to be taken for granted by a left-wing party whose beliefs are diametrically opposed to our values is truly remarkable. Bill Clinton may have blathered endlessly about his commitment to multiculturalism and a government that "looked like America," but it was the party of George W. Bush that respected people of color enough to put them in positions of real authority and influence: both the first and second black secretary of state, the first black National Security Advisor, the first Latino attorney general, the first women appointed to the Supreme Court, the first Asian-American woman in U.S. history appointed to a president's cabinet . . . were all appointed by Republicans.

And yet, minorities still stubbornly support liberals and the Democrats. Having hidden the real history of black Americans' long climb to overcome the Democrats' racist mountain of opposition to justice and equality for blacks, the victimhood vendors have successfully managed their flock—getting them to obediently follow their every command. "If you already own somebody, then you don't have to buy them," says Secretary Alphonso Jackson. "The Democrats own us, so they don't have to buy us because we are already owned."[27]

Liberalism's "you're not responsible for yourself" and "if it feels good do it" message resonates with many Americans because it offers absolution from personal accountability. It is especially intoxicating to our community because it provides a mechanism by which all that ails America in the inner city—rampant out-of-wedlock birthrates, soaring incarceration rates, disappointing educational attainment, a gangsta rap culture that promotes hyper-sexuality and degradation of women—can be wiped clean by liberals' victimhood thesis. Liberalism, then, functions for many as a sort of "get out of responsibility free" card that offers solace and the ability of liberals to condescendingly sympathize about governmental action to save the second-class citizens from themselves. The long arm of slavery and Jim Crow oppression, Democrats tell us, explains all that plagues our community. Wisely, they leave out that unfortunate part about their party being the primary cause of the plague. Today, they sponsor government-fostered pathologies that have in the past and continue today to slow the advancement of women and people of color. The thing that matters most, the liberal exploitation agenda tells minorities, is that we stay angry and aware of our victim status at all times. *Never forget*, the bamboozler's creed whispers, *you aren't responsible for your own success, Uncle Sam is. The Man owes you one. After all, he's yo' baby daddy. Government, not individuals, determines human prosperity.*

This disastrous message has metastasized through the American psyche like a cancer and diminished too many people of color's capacity and drive for greatness. Professor McWhorter reminds us:

A lot of people have the sense that the most important thing about being black is to be part of a grand story of victimhood in the past and the present. The cult of victimology means that for way too many of us, we use the whole racism thing as a way of feeling like we matter instead of having some private or positive way of feeling like we matter. . . . It's an insecurity based on 350 years of being treated like an animal. It's an inferiority complex left over from the bad old days. . . . There is a kind of pride that we need to get back. The funniest thing about black America right now is that for a lot of us, we derive a sense of pride from talking about why we can't do things. You watch people like Sharpton or even black college professors smiling as they talk about the obstacles, like the victory is in saying why you can't do it. . . . There is no group in history who has gotten ahead in a perfect world. Therefore, it's not going to happen to us. If anybody thinks there is supposed to be an exception for black people because we were brought here as slaves, they need to wake up and forget it. There is not going to be an exception. It's not fair—get past it. . . . A lot of those people got caught up in the thrills of sticking it to the white man. Again, it was because of insecurity. I honestly believe that deep down inside, Jesse Jackson, Al Sharpton, Julian Bond, and Maxine Waters do not like themselves very much. They grew up black in a time when it would have been very hard not to feel inferior. They're getting a sense of pride and accomplishment out of complaining.[28]

The third tactic the victimhood vendors employ is that of social and communal sanction for any black or Latino American bold or daring enough to break loose from the chains of liberal exploitation and Party dominion. When this happens, the victimhood vendors kick into their seek and destroy mode. After all, if black and Latino voters are given an alternative way of thinking, or an opinion that doesn't parrot the bamboozler mantra, then that voice must be silenced, discredited, shown to be something less than authentic.

Black conservatives, therefore, must be made out to be "Uncle Toms," and "Oreos." Liberals boast endlessly about their love of diversity and tolerance, but when push comes to shove, the bamboozlers reveal their hypocrisy in strident and bigoted colors.

Take, for example, former NAACP chairman and congressman Kweisi Mfume, demonizing black conservatives before the NAACP membership: "When the ultraconservative right-wing attacker has run out of attack strategy, he goes and gets someone that looks like you and me to continue the attacks." Mimicking a line from an earlier speech by Julian Bond, Mfume said, "And like the ventriloquist's dummies, they sit there in the puppet master's voice, but we can see whose lips are moving, and we can hear his money talk."[29] Some, like Armstrong Williams, found Mfume's comments almost amusing in their hypocrisy: "The NAACP should know about funding from big groups, because it is funded by liberal white organizations," Williams told the *Washington Times*. "It gets money and backing from the NEA [National Education Association], the AFL-CIO, and look at who is sponsoring its convention." Interestingly, the sponsors include some of the very companies liberals love to hate most, such as Wal-Mart, Shell Oil, and General Motors, each of whom chipped in anywhere from $100,000 to $250,000 for past NAACP conventions.[30]

Take a look at what the bamboozlers did to Republican Michael Steele after they ran Mfume out of the Maryland United States Senate race. Michael Steele defied the edict of the victimhood vendors and ran as a pro-life, pro-family, pro-free market Republican. Liberal bigotry was on display for all to see, although Michael Steele's party stood strongly behind him. And yet he was subjected to the vilest of treatment by Democratic Party activists. Fearing a mass black exodus to the Republican Party, liberal Democrats stopped at nothing to defeat Steele.

Once, when Steele appeared on stage to speak at a campaign event at a historically black college, Democrats in the audience pelted him with Oreo cookies. The cookies were meant to symbolize Steele's betrayal of his blackness: like an Oreo, Steele was black on the outside but white on the inside. But they were just getting warmed up. The *Boston Globe* reported that on one popular liberal news website, "Steele's picture was grotesquely doctored, making him look like a minstrel-show caricature. 'I's Simple Sambo and I's Running for the Big House,' read the insulting headline accompanying the picture."[31]

I asked former lt. governor Steele about his brush with bigotry:

My credit report was stolen by the Democratic Senatorial Committee. Two of the committee's political operatives in the research department—a director and assistant director—got my social security number from court documents in Prince Georges County and used my social security number online and got my credit report. . . . (Democrat Senator Charles Schumer) publicly did not apologize to me. He publicly has not admitted to this day that he was wrong. Imagine if this was Senator George Allen, two years ago, when he was heading up the Republican Senatorial Committee . . . If he or someone under his watch had stolen Barrack Obama's credit report while he was running for the United States Senate . . . Can you imagine the headlines? We would still be hearing about it today. . . . I think there was clearly an effort. Why would you bring Oreo cookies to a debate? There's a little bit of forethought there. After the debate was over and I started to leave, these folks started tossing these cookies and they land at my feet. I ignored them and I turned to a buddy of mine and said, "Got milk?" We joked about it. But the reality of it is, there's a lot of insidious callousness and I consider somewhat hateful racist attitudes as well as actions that have been taken by a number of folks in the Democratic Party who are absolutely scared to death of having a black Republican of any stature. They have had such a control over the black voters for the past forty years that they're afraid to let go. They figure that without the black vote, where do they win elections? How do they win?[32]

The liberal mainstream media's double standard on such incidents is unacceptable. Steele is correct in noting the relative ho-hum attitude the liberal media often take in reporting episodes of bigotry by the Left. But Steele is merely one in a long line of black conservatives who wear their liberal lashes like badges of honor. Sadly, this remains the price of ideological emancipation, a price that many like-minded blacks are understandably unwilling to pay. Thankfully, however, Americans have several beacons who have begun to light the way. Senator Mel Martinez, Congressman J.C. Watts, Supreme Court Justice Clarence Thomas, D.C. Circuit Judge Janice Rogers Brown, Attorney General Alberto Gonzales, Secretary of Education Rod Paige, Secretary of Housing and Urban Development Alphonso Jackson, Secretary of Labor Elaine Chao, Secretary of State Colin Powell, Secretary of State Condoleezza Rice—all are Republicans with true power and national and international influence, not hollow symbolic nods to diversity. And yet each remains a target for any number of racially-tinged attacks by bamboozlers.

Consider, for example, the attack by syndicated cartoonist Ted Rall, who, according to nationally syndicated columnist Ruben Navarrette Jr., "tried to paint Gonzales as Attila the Hun with a law degree, an advocate of torture, someone inspired by Nazis, 'one of the most twisted minds the American legal system has ever produced'"; or what about white Wisconsin radio talk-show host John Sylvester who called Secretary Condoleezza Rice an "Aunt Jemima" and General Colin Powell an "Uncle Tom"; or how about liberal syndicated cartoonist Jeff Danziger who published a cartoon showing Condoleezza Rice as a black mammy cradling an aluminum tube, baby bottle in hand, with the caption: "I don't know nuthin' about aluminum tubes."[33] When the controversy erupted over Danziger's racist cartoon, he issued the obligatory press release. Still, the scribbler of cartoons couldn't resist taking a final swipe at Rice, whom he said was a "political operative, out of her depth."

The *Wall Street Journal* wisely pointed out that Danziger's dart had the unintended consequence of revealing the lengths to which liberals will go when blacks and Latinos refuse to submit to the exploitation agenda: "The illustration is certainly revealing. For liberals, Condi Rice's real crime is bucking Democratic orthodoxy and working for a conservative president. This makes her fair game for race-based attacks even when the issue at hand has absolutely nothing to do with race. She is a black woman who, in Mr. Danziger's view, has wandered off the liberal plantation. And this is his way of putting Ms. Rice and other black conservatives in their place."[34]

"It is unbelievable that the black community has not rallied behind the Republican Party," says radio talk-show host Hallerin Hill. "During the Clinton years, he said he wanted a cabinet that looked like America. It was pure symbolism and empty rhetoric. He just wants to make sure he got the right colors reflected in the rainbow. In the Bush administration, you have a situation where blacks are given real authority in the most powerful positions in government in the world, because of the primacy of the United States."[35]

The attacks and calumnies by bamboozlers are all standard operating procedure. For a party that would otherwise go bust without nine out of ten blacks voting for them, liberal Democrats likely view such tactics as merely the cost of doing business, a necessary evil. Sadly, though, it's blacks and Latinos and inner-city Americans who continue to suffer most at the hands of the failed Democratic leadership. "I don't think that the Democratic Party has a love for black people. I don't," says Hallerin Hill. "This may get me in a lot of trouble, maybe it won't . . . I think that to the extent that black people help the franchise, they are valuable. When they don't seem to help the franchise, if you are a black person and you don't play along, you get punished, period."[36]

Hill is exactly right. Given a complicit liberal mainstream media that often panders to the Left, raising awareness and knowledge about Democrats' hidden history is made doubly hard. Honestly, that's part of the reason I wrote this book: to offer a message that could be disseminated far and wide.

The liberal mainstream media's love affair with the Democratic Party should be exposed. There's no doubt about that. Today's mainstream media is reminiscent in a lot of ways of the pro-segregation papers from the Jim Crow era.

But there's enough blame to go around on all levels, and that's something that all Americans should be aware of and concerned about, says Bill O'Reilly. He says that just as Republicans have made the mistake of writing off black voters as a possible constituency, so too has the liberal media failed at covering and reporting stories that affect blacks and Latinos:

Media bias appears in all forms, and unfortunately the underclass in America is not covered by the elite media, the underclass being poor, disenfranchised people who don't vote, people who have no power. They come in all colors, so that when you have a horrific crime in a poor ghetto neighborhood, whether it's black, Hispanic, white, that crime will be barely mentioned. Yet if a wealthy white child is killed, then it'll be page one. Why? Because most people identify with the wealthy white child, not with the disenfranchised black person. And so, therefore, the media knows that. They know that they have to make money. They know that by featuring stories that everybody's going to be galvanized—"Gee, that could be my daughter, but my daughter would never be in the 'hood, never be in the ghetto, never be dealing crack, so I don't really identify with that, and I don't feel sorry for those people." So the media goes for the stories that they feel the most readership will buy, and that's why the stories among the underclass get ignored.[37]

O'Reilly mentioned the news media, but I would add the entertainment industry also is complicit in promoting the exploitation agenda. The multi-billion dollar business that is gangsta rap culture dominates and defines much of today's youth market. While there are certainly positive notable exceptions, taken en masse, its overall influence has had a toxic and corrosive effect on young whites' perceptions of people of color, and also on the attitudes that people of color have about themselves. As is often pointed out, the overwhelming majority of hip-hop and rap albums bought today are purchased by white males. The music and imagery, however, reinforce every conceivable racist stereotype. In a December 2006 *New York Daily News* column by cultural critic Stanley Crouch, he lamented the "cultural crisis" that pervades so much of gangsta rap culture. He says America is ensnared in a crisis "in which young black men adorn themselves with surface trappings and take on the obnoxious vulgarity of thugs." Crouch then says:

Added to this low-lying mix are the supposedly sympathetic liberals, who are more than happy to submit gutlessly to the black middle class. These white liberals have been intellectually hustled into believing that the inarticulate thug and the freelance slut are young black people in their natural state. The black middle class, terrified of being defined as a group that kowtows to "white values," does not tend to have the nerve to stand up to this crabbed vision of life or "ethnic authenticity". . . . The tragic losers are those black kids who believe that their true identity is achieved through illiteracy, thuggish behavior, dropping out of school, and psychologically ingesting the subterranean attitudes toward women that are espoused by pimps. They are sloughing through a spiritual sewer, incapable of knowing just how much it stinks.[38]

This is not "The Dream" for which Dr. Martin Luther King, Jr. lived and died. This is hardly "The Dream" of which he spoke. In our victimhood vendor culture, we've failed to take personal responsibility for ourselves. We have failed to be accountable for the cultural images we participate in and produce. That goes for corporate America as well. It's a sad statement when individuals exhibit no moral compunction about dumping musical gasoline on a cultural bonfire that currently exists in the perverted mainstream liberal media. All this after having bought into the code of cultural relativism that liberal corporate "leaders" have done nothing to prevent. In fact, they often are responsible for producing and distributing so much that degrades and demoralizes communities of color. All they see are the dollar signs—the Benjamins. "Mo money, Mo money," and more corruption.

Publications like *Essence* magazine have taken an important and brave first step in self-policing and challenging the images and depictions that gangsta rap often promotes. In 2005, *Essence* launched the Take Back the Music campaign to challenge the hip-hop generation to think critically and responsibly about the potent messages urban music promotes. Playing devil's advocate, Juan Williams, author of the book *Enough*, asks, "If rap is so crippling to young black people, why is the same music with the same lyrics nothing more than a diversion to young white people, a majority of its patrons?" He adds, "Rap's die-hard defenders say white girls like Paris Hilton and the babes in the popular 'Girls Gone Wild' videos are doing the same thing that black girls are doing in rap videos." Williams explains that the fundamental weaknesses of such arguments are that they fail to recognize the gaping chasm that exists between black and white youth discussed in part one of this book. As Williams points out, "Paris Hilton, for one, is an heiress. If she appears in a sex video or behaves like a goof, it actually gets her publicity and advances her career. Even the white girls in 'Girls Gone Wild' appear to be on spring break from college. Many are on their way to getting a college degree."[39]

Indeed, while more black women are attending college today than ever before, the gulf between white and black still looms large. Add to that an increasing out-of-wedlock birthrate, the attending higher poverty rates that come with it, and the greater welfare dependency, and the racially lopsided effects of a gangsta rap culture become painfully apparent.

The Democratic Party continues its use of emotionally charged rhetoric, racially condescending policies, and racist smears against conservatives to divert attention away from the truth. It's mind boggling as to how Democrats have gotten away with not owning up to their party's unthinkable past.

Are Republicans blameless, pure political lambs of racial innocence? Of course not. But again, the balance of history isn't even close. Where Republicans have committed sins of disinterest and insensitivity, Democrats' historical hatred for minorities ignited lethal actions and have been followed by catastrophic policies camouflaged as contrition.

The installation of the victimhood vendors serves a mechanism of electoral control. It patronizes people of color even as it politically enslaves and isolates them. But the bamboozlers are wise to fear the truth; they are right to worry about what America might do if they peeked behind the curtain that shrouds the Democratic

Party's hidden history. For if Americans knew the truth, then the truth might set them free. Crouch reminds us to *"not forget that Harriet Tubman said that she could have gotten many more slaves off of the plantation if she could have convinced them that they WERE slaves."*[40] (Emphasis mine.)

That remains the fundamental challenge confronting America today: to realize that we've shackled ourselves to a failed ideology led by victimhood vendors who resist, at every turn, failing to tell us the truth about our past and the best path toward maximizing our future. A grievance culture of victimology won't change the hearts and minds of men. Only the Almighty can do that.

But the good news is that the capacity for human achievement and moral flourishing resides within individuals, not government agencies.

Harriet Tubman believed that.

Sojourner Truth believed that.

Frederick Douglass believed that.

Which political party in America believes that?

PART 3

BUILDING A BAMBOOZLE-FREE FUTURE

9

LATINOS IN LIMBO

The Fate of Conservatism

This amendment is racist. I think it's directed basically to people who speak Spanish.[1]

—Democratic majority leader Senator Harry Reid race baiting on an amendment to make English the national language

How long do we want to support a Democratic Party that won't let us fix our failing schools, that wants to tax our small businesses out of existence, and for decades wanted to keep us on welfare? Latinos who follow the Democratic Party blindly do so at their peril.

—Leslie Sachez, entreprenuer and political strategist

Say what you want about liberal majority leader Senator Harry Reid, but one thing is certain: liberals *sure* know how to pick a bamboozler as their fearless leader. Apparently, when you're the senior liberal senator from the gambling capital of the world, you quickly learn how to deal the race card from the bottom of the deck. Let's review the record and see him deal the race-baiter's royal flush:

- 2006: While debating an amendment to make English the national language—something that 84 percent of all

Americans and 77 percent of all Latinos support—Reid fired this one off on the Senate floor: "This amendment is racist. I think it's directed basically to people who speak Spanish."[2]

Now let's go back to the Clinton administration (which did practically nothing about the immigration issue). At that time, Senator Reid took a slightly different position on illegal immigration:

- 1993: "Our federal wallet is stretched to the limit by illegal aliens getting welfare, food stamps, medical care, and other benefits without paying taxes." He added, "These programs were not meant to entice freeloaders and scam artists from around the world." In 2006, Reid apologized for his tough rhetoric. He stated that his stance "mostly lasted about a week or two" before his wife straightened him out and taught him to be the compassionate liberal he is today.[3]

There's just one problem with the good senator's story. The next year, Reid said this:

- 1994: "We must reduce the annual admissions of legal immigrants to more moderate levels in order to provide for a better country—both environmentally and socially— in the years to come."[4]

Sadly, this is what America can expect from liberals for the next few decades to come. It's often said that "demography is destiny." Perhaps that should be changed to "demagoguery is destiny." The Democratic Party is somewhat of a one-trick political pony; if they're not pitting one racial group against another they can't compete. As America's Latino population explosion continues, the largest minority in the nation is set to expand rapidly over the next half-century. As it does, it will determine the fate of conservatism. The battle lines have been drawn. As John B. Judis and Ruy Teixeira wrote in their insightful book, *The Emerging Democratic Majority*, "Hispanic support is a crucial part of a new Democratic majority. Hispanics are the minority group that is growing the most in terms of both absolute numbers and percentage of the population."[5] If the exploitation agenda, led by race-baiting hucksters like Harry Reid, Nancy Pelosi, and Hillary Clinton, is successful in doing to Latinos what it has done to blacks, the consequences for all Americans will be dire. Following the 2006 midterm elections, the early signs aren't promising. Consider the facts:

- In just eight years, President George W. Bush and Karl Rove successfully doubled Latino Republican support from the 21 percent Senator Bob Dole received in 1996 to the impressive 44 percent George W. Bush received in 2004.[6]
- However, in the 2006 midterm election, Latino GOP support plunged, with 70 percent voting for the Democrats and an anemic 29 percent supporting Republicans.[7]
- If current trends continue, the U.S. Census Bureau projects that from 2000 to 2050, the U.S. Hispanic population is projected to grow from 35.6 million to 102.6 million, an increase of 188 percent. If this occurs as projected, the Hispanic share of the nation's population would nearly double, from 12.6 percent to 24.4 percent.[8] This projection does not take into account how a possible amnesty bill for illegal immigrants might alter Hispanic populations in America.

With the black American population projected to increase a minuscule 1.9 percent by 2050, the liberal exploitation agenda is well aware that to remain politically viable, it will need to find a new host to grab on to. "I would argue that black Democrats are on their last leg of being able to put pressure on white Democrats," argues Lee H. Walker, president of the New Coalition for Economic and Social Change. Walker, also a senior fellow of the Heartland Institute, went on to say, "They don't need you now; they got the Hispanics and Asians."[9]

Liberals, such as former president Clinton's chief political pollster Stanley Greenberg, have already begun to salivate at the prospects of a whole new class of voters to exploit:

> Hispanics have all the trappings of a loyalist group. . . . As with African-Americans, Hispanics are, for some pretty hardheaded reasons apart from civil rights, closely aligned with the Democrats. For one thing, Hispanics are among the most economically vulnerable in the country. They are three times less likely than non-Hispanics to graduate from high school and they continue to fill the lowest-paid jobs in the lowest-wage sections of the service sector.[10]

As we've seen, the exploitation agenda's future success hinges on its ability to create a grievance culture of victimhood and dependency. This culture is marked by a "blame America first" attitude—which you may recall was dubbed by the late, great former U.N. ambassador Jeane Kirkpatrick. Through the creation of a labyrinth of government programs, bureaucracies, the mainsteam media, and the hip-hop industry's glorification of the gansta life, liberals have successfully oppressed women, the poor, and people of color. They have essentially sapped their drive for self-reliance by creating a dependency-inducing welfare culture. It's often said that the Democrats fight "for the little guy." That's true: liberals fight to make sure the little guy stays little! Think about it. What if all the little guys were to prosper and become big guys? Then what? Who would liberals pretend to fight for? If the bamboozlers fight for anything, it's to ensure that the little guy stays angry at those nasty conservatives who are holding him down.

It is a travesty that blacks and Latinos remain in this grip considering the fact that we are manipulated by a political party that just so happens to be our oppressors.

Latinos remain politically in limbo because conservatives still have a chance, a window of opportunity, to garner support from this community. Prior to 1994, Democrats enjoyed a forty-year lock on the House of Representatives. Nothing says history can't repeat itself. Gaining the support and trust of Latinos will be a challenge. It will require conservatives to think and speak wisely. What's more, it will demand that conservatives challenge, at every turn, the bamboozlers who are creative at spinning the message with smoke and mirrors. Whether the Democrats can replicate the success with Latinos that they had with blacks remains to be seen. On issues critical to Latinos—faith, family values, home ownership, and enterprise—the Republican Party lines up well with Latino voters. However, one thing is certain: the decisions conservatives and Republicans make in the next several years will shape the political landscape for generations to come.

The first and most pressing issue conservatives face is, of course, illegal immigration. Liberals hope that this will become the issue that is finally capable of splitting the Republican base in half. In the wake of the recent Democratic takeover of both the House and Senate, the bamboozlers have wasted no time in trying to rewrite history. They would have us believe that the anti-immigrant rhetoric and a hard-line stance against a comprehensive immigration reform bill were large causes of the Republican defeat. The data, however, seems to suggest otherwise. According to Gabriel Escobar, associate director of the Pew Hispanic Center, the conventional wisdom is flawed: "It is important to note that immigration in the Latino population is never a top-tier issue."[11] Rosemary Jenks, director of government relations for NumbersUSA, makes a stronger case. "The election had absolutely nothing to do with immigration," Jenks said. "It was about George W. Bush and the war in Iraq."[12]

While it may come as a surprise to some, a sizable number of Latinos support enforcing the law and protecting our borders. They support a fair and controlled *legal* immigration policy. This is hardly astonishing, considering the fact that the Latino community is often the most adversely impacted from illegal immigration. Just ask former congressman Henry Bonilla, the Texas Republican grandson of a migrant Mexican farm worker whose district has been flooded by cross-border drug gang violence. "This is not an ethnic issue," Congressman Bonilla said. "This is a national security issue." Bonilla says he frequently hears from his constituents waiting for their citizenship rights. Many of these individuals have grown frustrated with the tidal wave of aliens that enter the country illegally every day. "I've already heard from some of them who are resentful of anybody being moved up in the line."[13] But in December 2006, the seven-term Republican Latino legislator was defeated in a runoff election against former Hispanic Caucus chairman and Democratic congressman Ciro Rodriguez. And that, more than anything, should remind conservatives that in politics, perception often trumps reality. If conservatives allow liberals to paint them in anti-Latino hues (and as sell-outs), liberals will own Latino voters just as they presently own black voters.

Republicans have long been "split between those who 'get it' and those who don't," writes Tamar Jacoby, a Manhattan Institute fellow. "President Bush was the most prominent Republican who got it, though he was hardly alone. Arnold Schwarzenegger, Rudy Giuliani,

George Pataki, and others have long understood the GOP's inherent appeal for the fastest-growing voting bloc in the country. . . . The issue isn't just with immigration . . . but with the offensive portrayal of the hard-liners' stance, even to Latinos who agree with them about the need for a secure border."[14]

As Jacoby attests, the notion that Latinos oppose strong border enforcement and immigration laws "across the board" is inaccurate. For example, when Arizonans voted on Proposition 200 (a bill requiring that welfare recipients first show proof of citizenship), 47 percent of Hispanics voted for the measure.[15] The Latino Coalition released its National Latino Survey in January 2006. It revealed that almost half of all registered Latino voters supported increasing the number of United States Border Patrol agents.[16] "We are so diverse in the Latino community, being from Venezuela, Uruguay to Cuba, Puerto Rico, and we tend to sort of go in different directions on that," says Bishop John Gimenez. "For instance, those of us who were born here—I was born in Spanish Harlem—don't have a big problem as far as immigration. We understand law is law, and what is good for the goose is good for the gander. So while we may feel compassion and so forth, we still know that once you start the breaking of any law, you either got to change it or it has no effect."[17]

Others saw rhetoric against illegal immigration as too strident and biting, especially as it was depicted in hard-hitting television ads that ran in states where illegal immigration remains a pressing problem. "The stereotypes and dark imagery that they lent to immigrants was disturbing," said voter Jeff Martinez of Denver. He said the ads "impact how you vote as a Latino proud of your heritage." However, Martinez says his decision to switch from Republican to Independent ultimately had more to do with general unhappiness with the GOP's inability to "do anything to help middle America" than about illegal immigration.[18]

Even though immigration was not the number one factor that motivated Latino voters in the midterm elections, the bamboozlers still were able to push their claim that Republicans are racists. Simon Rosenberg, president of the New Democrat Network, seemed hardly able to contain his glee at what he saw as early signs of a permanent divorce between Latinos and the GOP. "I think you have to look at the Republican effort on immigration as a catastrophic mistake," Rosenberg breathlessly asserted. "They now know that the Republican Party is hostile to Hispanics, which is something they didn't know two years ago. That's a big burden for them to overcome."[19]

Latino immigration activists with a stake in the debate, such as Edward Juarez, president of the International Immigrants Foundation, are just as strong in their position as Rosenberg:

Well, the truth is that the Republicans have actually aligned themselves to the—and with all respect I'm saying this—to the people that have the least knowledge, I would say, or understand the needs of America as a nation, as a people, as one people. And I'm saying this because of the fact this radical movement of closing, of building walls, of deporting immigrants and all that. That is out of touch with the reality of the needs of the nation, what the nation needs to be. I mean, you cannot take immigrants away, not because I say so. It's because the country cannot and will not. And I'm not just saying this, but the economy . . . the concern that economists have is the lack of workers to be able to continue . . . There is no other choice but to welcome these immigrants.[20]

Ed Clancy, CEO of TrueLatino, a consultancy focused on networking relationships for companies targeting Hispanic consumers, stresses the oft-cited theme that echoes President Bush's famous line that "family values don't stop at the Rio Grande."

"Jose wants to make money, support his family, and work," Clancy said. "[Latinos] have Democratic ideals. When they come to this country, they become more Republican by way of being conservatives, taking care of their own . . . I like what Reagan did in the Amnesty Act. It did a lot of good for the community and encouraging new business and immigrants to come and settle down and to follow a dream, of sorts."[21]

Clancy's sentiments are a perfect reflection of the internal tug o' war going on inside conservative circles. Indeed, in a December 2006 article for *Human Events* titled "Reagan Would Not Repeat Amnesty Mistake," President Reagan's former attorney general, Ed Meese, argued that "the lesson from the 1986 experience is that such an amnesty did not solve the problem. There was extensive document fraud, and the number of people applying for amnesty far exceeded projections." Nevertheless, Meese said, "we should remember Reagan's commitment to the idea that America must remain open and welcoming to those yearning for freedom."[22]

There's no question that illegal immigration remains an intra-party squabble within the Republican Party. But it will be the resolution of this internal dispute that will have an important impact on whether conservatives can build a bamboozle-free future. Latinos do not universally support lax immigration laws. Still, in the wake of the massive pro-illegal immigration rallies that took place throughout the nation in 2006, where marchers, many of whom were illegal immigrants, took to the streets waving Mexican flags and demanding their *rights*, it would be foolish to deny that liberals stand poised and ready to exploit the issue. It was during these rallies, let us not forget, that the U.S. Senate's "Liberal White Lion," Ted Kennedy, demonstrated his deft powers of racial bamboozlement. As BBC reporter Nick Bryant has written, "The

Kennedy administration taught Washington an ugly political lesson: that politicians could win black support through grand symbolic gestures, which obviated the need for truly substantive reforms."[23] Thus, in an effort to conflate Dr. Martin Luther King, Jr.'s civil rights legacy with Mexicans breaking into the country, Ted Kennedy telegraphed the liberal playbook for the decade to come: "More than four decades ago, near this place, Martin Luther King called on the nation to let freedom ring. It is time for Americans to lift their voices now, in pride for our immigrant past and in pride for our *immigrant future.*" (Emphasis mine.)

Sorry, Senator Kennedy, but just because your family members wiretapped Martin Luther King, it doesn't qualify you to speak for him. Moreover, by comparing our people's struggle against our Democratic oppressors to people breaking our nation's law is ignorant and insulting, sir.

Nevertheless, strong and differing views about how best to remedy the problem of illegal immigration exist between some leading conservatives. Republican congressman Tom Tancredo and former Republican congressman J.D. Hayworth have written books and spoken forcefully about the need to build a 2,000-mile border fence, impose a moratorium on immigration, achieve "attrition through enforcement," end dual citizenship, and restrict illegal aliens' access to taxpayer-funded social welfare programs.[24] Other Republicans, such as Senator John McCain, former New York City mayor and 2008 presidential hopeful Rudolph Giuliani, and *Weekly Standard* editor Bill Kristol believe that proposals by some to deport nearly twelve million illegal aliens would be impractical: "You just can't take the position that they are illegal and let's punish them," says Kristol. "Most of them are pretty hard working and pretty patriotic, a lot of them volunteer to fight in the Armed Services."[25]

Conservatives may be tempted to sidestep this "family disagreement" and instead point the finger at Clinton or George W. Bush for inaction. But the truth is that both Democrats and Republicans have been negligent in addressing the serious security threats posed by our inadequately protected borders. Moreover, as the nearly twelve million illegal immigrants already here continue to increase in size, state budgets will continue to bow under the weight of increased expenditures. What's more, some so-called Rockefeller Republicans—Republicans with strong ties to and interests in the corporate community—have willfully turned a blind eye toward the issue because immigrants represent cheap labor for many corporate and agricultural interests.

"I think that there's been a lack of courage on the part of a lot of people," Frank Gomez, former member of the Congressional Hispanic Caucus Institute and the Hispanic Council on International Relations, told me in an interview. He added, "Perhaps President Bush has shown more courage, at least in articulating and standing for a position that represents some kind of reform. The so-called amnesty that nobody wants to call an amnesty. But there's no other responsible way to deal with this. We cannot kick out of the country twelve million people. Not only would businesses crumble, but there's just no practical way to manage the exile, the deportation of twelve million people."[26]

For Democrats, the flood of illegal aliens into the country is seen as a golden opportunity. They believe the issue is a two-for-one special: not only does it allow Democrats to race bait Latino voters by making Republicans look like racial boogeyman, it also allows Democrats to gain the lion's share of votes from the twelve million illegal aliens with the passage of an amnesty bill.

"There are people who believe that the election laws are essentially unfair, that any person in the country who has come here, and is working, and has a family should be allowed to vote," says Fox

News host John Gibson. "They [liberals] really do think that all of those twelve million illegals here should vote. And they feel entitled to go out and register them to vote and to give them the vote. . . . These activist groups think that the injustices of this country are so profound that it's okay to cheat and bend these rules in order to get these people to vote."[27]

Investigations following the pro-illegal immigration rallies revealed that many of the supporters and backers of these demonstrations represented groups with longstanding hostilities toward U.S. interests.[28] Liberals may be hostile to Latinos' values of faith and family, but they are more than glad to bamboozle these voters to keep the exploitation engine chugging along. "When Bill Clinton was in office he never addressed the issue of immigration reform," said Robert de Posada, president of the Latino Coalition. "He never did anything to reform the immigration laws of this country. When they had an opportunity, they didn't do it. Now they are, like they always do, making a political issue in saying, 'You have to vote for me because I'm pro-immigrant,' yet they don't plan to do anything for immigration. . . . There is a movement away from the Democratic Party towards the Independent column and not necessarily towards the Republican."[29] Put another way, Latinos are in political limbo.

Can a nation of immigrants protect its borders, stimulate economic growth, and build a strong future that will continue to be a magnet for those who wish to legally enter the United States? Yes, assuming it has the will to do so. The political question conservatives must answer is: what must be done to galvanize the conservative base as well as regain and solidify the 44 percent of Latinos who stood with them in 2004, and the millions more who are "hardwired" to live and vote by their most deeply held conservative values?

The answer is simple: conservatives must challenge the Left's exploitation tactics and misinformation campaigns. Conservatives cannot allow Democrats to do to Latinos what they have done to black Americans. That's clearly their objective. Fortunately, wise voices are emerging within the Latino community that understand that any group that becomes entirely beholden to one political party lends itself to being manipulated and taken for granted. But so far, says Robert de Posada, Republicans have been outmaneuvered by liberals. "Where I think conservatives have missed the ball here is that instead of making this a very clear-cut case of reforming a broken system on immigration, particularly, they have allowed the Democrats to make Republicans look like they are just targeting someone that is a racial minority."

Republicans made a wise decision to appoint Florida senator Mel Martinez as the new Republican National chairman. This decision was smart not just because Martinez is, himself, a Cuban immigrant and a widely respected leader within the Latino community, but because Martinez is a savvy and effective leader. As the Republicans and conservatives prepare to do battle with liberals over comprehensive immigration reform (that puts the nation's interests first) they must have respect for those who wish to become Americans, just as President Reagan stressed. In the legislative process, they must stay true to core conservative principles that includes respect for the law, personal responsibility, and national security. This will be at the heart of the 2008 presidential election. As Frank Gomez clearly stated, many Latino voters are watching with open minds and independent electoral instincts:

I think both parties are guilty of looking at the Hispanic vote every four years instead of looking at the Hispanic vote as something that needs to be cultivated, and understood, and addressed, and researched on a regular basis, just like everybody else. If you look at

Kerry's campaign, and I criticize my Hispanic friends on the Democratic side who jumped and marched in lockstep once he got the nomination, Kerry had never been there for any Hispanics. He had never been to any conferences. And I challenged them. I said, well, here you are supporting Kerry as if he had been your friend all your life, and yet he only discovered you when he decided to run for the presidency. And that happens time and time again. On the other hand, John McCain from Arizona, he's not a native Arizonan, but he's gone over and above, and for many, many years, to understand the Latino voter. George Bush has done that, too, as a Texan. He grew up around Hispanic workers.[30]

Regardless of the ultimate policy reforms the federal government establishes to address the problem of illegal immigration, the fact remains that issues relevant to most Latino Americans are policies that impact faith and family, jobs, safe neighborhoods, high quality education, and access to capitol and national security. The success of liberals, however, hinges on transforming any and all policy debates into a contest over who can appear most devoid of racism or bigotry. Which policies best serve Latinos and the nation they love is largely irrelevant to many in the Democratic Party, says Robert de Posada:

We have been hearing about the immigration debate, and the Democrats have been making a big fuss about how the Democratic Party represents the interests of Hispanics. Well, when the Democratic Party in the House of Representatives developed their agenda or their contract for America for themselves and they take over, the word immigrant or immigration was not mentioned. . . . We see the same attitude, which is "yes, we want your support" Yes, you want us to vote for you—to be blindly loyal.[31]

What liberals care most about is morphing public debates into a game of racial brinksmanship. The people hurt most in this liberal game are, of course, Latinos.

Take, for example, the great debate over bilingual education. The president of the Heritage Foundation, Dr. Edwin J. Feulner, and coauthor Doug Wilson write that "The greatest mistake we have made in recent years was the vogue for bilingual education, which arose as a natural consequence of cultural relativism and the cult of diversity."[32] Liberal educators and administrators claimed that English immersion was ineffective and culturally insensitive to newly immigrated children or children who had been born in the United States to illegal immigrant parents. So, bilingual education, which allows children to be taught all classes except English in their native tongue, "began in the 1980s and reached an estimated 3,768,653 children at the start of the twenty-first century."[33]

Liberal "compassion" and "multicultural sensitivity," it turns out, produced catastrophic results. By effectively segregating school children based on language, bilingual education policies stunted children's assimilation in America. So eager to showcase their cultural sensitivity, liberals turned a blind eye to the overwhelming evidence that this policy was harmful to immigrant children.[34]

Children are not the only ones hurt by the bilingual programs. Adults are affected as well. Adults who grow up linguistically isolated face economic and social disenfranchisement. In a new Harvard University study, Thomas Sander, director of the Saguaro Seminar on Civic Engagement in America at Harvard's Kennedy School of Government, found that Latin American immigrants who mastered English were more engaged in their communities and were able to expand their social networks more broadly than non-English speakers. "The research doesn't suggest we should become an English-only country, but it does suggest that for immigrants, learning English is a really important skill to integrate into your own community and the broader community," Sander said. "This ought to be high on our national agenda, to get the resources so more immigrants can participate both civically and socially."[35]

Sadly, for a generation of new Americans who were the guinea pigs of the failed experiment, the liberals' anti-assimilation stance appears to have taken root among some within the Latino community. When the Pew Hispanic Center asked Latinos whether learning English was essential in order to assimilate into American culture, a startling 41 percent said they did not think it necessary.[36] This finding is hardly surprising. If the U.S. educational system didn't think mastery of English was important enough to require of its students, why would these individuals? They wouldn't.

But thankfully, 57 percent of Latinos do believe that learning English is an essential part of assimilation. "They feel there is no need to learn English because everything should be given to them in Spanish—period, that's it," says Carmen Morales, a Puerto Rican from Woodbridge, New Jersey. "They want us to change our language to accommodate them, instead of them learning English to succeed in this country." Morales adds, "If they have the time to go to the bars and watch soccer games on Spanish TV, then they have the time to learn English."[37]

And many are doing just that. Enrollments in English as a Second Language (ESL) classes nationwide are robust and growing. Had the nation's public schools, so dominated as they are by the liberal teachers' unions, not sacrificed sound teaching practices on the altar of political expediency, perhaps things would be different. But charges of xenophobia and cultural insensitivity by liberals won the day, and now a generation of immigrant children will be the ones who suffer most.

"If you want to get ahead in this country, you have to study its language," says Guatemala-born Luis Gonzales, a construction worker who takes English classes in a crowded ESL classroom in Long Island.[38] Gonzales, and millions more like him, get it; they understand that speaking English is an essential tool to making it in America. And they're right. Immigrants who improve their English skills from "not well" to "very well" have been found to increase their earnings by over 20 percent. In a study by the Federal Reserve Bank of New York, immigrants in New York City were shown to have a strong correlation between low median incomes and low levels of English fluency. In fact, after living in America several years, immigrants who speak English "very well" earn 67 percent more than those who speak English poorly. Finally, a 2003 survey by the U.S. Bureau of Labor Statistics made the alarming revelation that workplace fatalities were 13 percent higher for Latinos than for the average worker.[39]

And liberals think requiring children to master English is an affront to their culture?

For these reasons, conservatives and Republicans championed legislation to establish English as the official language of the nation. With a whopping 84 percent of Americans and 77 percent of Latinos supporting such a move, the issue might seem a no-brainer. According to a 2005 census survey, an estimated fifty-two million people in America speak a language other than English in their homes, an increase of five million individuals since 2000.[40] To be sure, speaking a language other than English in the home is not an automatic indicator of a failure to assimilate. Moreover, multilingual citizens stand to benefit the nation on a host of levels, ranging from corporate interests to providing linguistic support in the global war on terrorism. But when one considers the facts buried inside that 52 million figure, a clearer picture for the need to increase English fluency emerges: 45 percent said they speak

English "less than very well"; Spanish was the most prevalent, which was spoken by 62 percent, almost half of which said they were not proficient in English.[41]

Looking at the data, it's not hard to see why such huge majorities of Americans believe it makes good common sense to promote English among its citizens. This is true so that all Americans can experience the positive gains English fluency brings. But liberals hardly see it that way. In a 2006 editorial titled "English as Official Language Insulting," professor emeritus David McGrath of the College of DuPage, dismissed the views of the 84 percent of the nation who supports the measure when he offered this erudite comparison:

> Imagine the U.S. Senate proposing a law which mandated that all people receiving services from the government must have a white face. Wouldn't that be the ultimate racist act? The amendment in the recent Senate immigration bill that declares English the national language might not seem to resemble the above "white face" example. . . . But anthropologists, linguists, and English professors like myself are acutely aware that language is race.[42]

The good professor then goes on to explain to all of us red-state dummies that such a law would make non-English speakers fear "that you are threatening cultural genocide, a fear which is not without some validity in this country."[43]

Cultural genocide? Wow! It's pretty amazing to think that the 77 percent of Latinos support cultural genocide against their own culture!

In the minds of many liberals, the debate of our national language is yet another way to drive home their tired, worn-out message: America is evil, and conservatives are xenophobic bigots. And so it shouldn't surprise us that the leader of the Democrats in the Senate would stand and declare: "This amendment is racist. I think it's directed basically to people who speak Spanish." By Reid's account, then, 66 members of the United States Senate are bigots who support racist legislation. Moreover, using Reid's poor logic, the 77 percent of Latinos who supported such a measure are racist against . . . um, "people who speak Spanish"?

Harry Reid is no stranger to playing the race card, and he's proven his commitment to diversity by bamboozling both Latino *and* black Americans. Suffice it to say that when you're a liberal Democrat, and the Congressional Black Caucus sends you a letter rebuking you for making racial comments that have crossed the line, you *know* you've got a problem, especially when the individual the CBC is sticking up for is Supreme Court Justice Clarence Thomas! I'm, of course, referring to Senator Reid's comments ridiculing Thomas's intellect and writing abilities. "He has been an embarrassment to the Supreme Court," Reid said in a CNN interview. "I think that his opinions are poorly written." When later asked to cite an example, Reid replied, "Oh sure, that's easy to do. You take the *Hillside Dairy* case. In that case you had a dissent written by Scalia and a dissent written by Thomas. There—it's like looking at an eighth-grade dissertation compared to somebody who just graduated from Harvard."[44]

There was just one problem: Scalia never *wrote* a dissent in that case, and the one Thomas wrote was one paragraph long—and a well-written paragraph at that! To his credit, Yale University Law School graduate, House Judiciary Committee member, and former Congressional Black Caucus chairman Mel Watt reprimanded Reid: "We wrote a letter to Sen. Reid cautioning him about his comments," Watt said. "I think all of us ought to focus more on substance and less on stereotypes and caricatures."[45] The *Wall Street*

Journal's James Taranto summed it up best when he wrote: "If the Democrats retain Reid, it will tell us something about the party's commitment to racial equality."[46]

It does tell us something about the Democratic Party. It tells us that the exploitation agenda's success is above all else.

There is nothing wrong with political parties fighting hard to win voter support. Furthermore, there is nothing wrong with political parties tailoring their messages to address the top concerns of different communities and constituencies. That's healthy. That's democracy. And when it comes to building support among Latinos, a group that at the moment remains politically in limbo, both Republicans and Democrats are well within the rules of fair play to actively and aggressively court Latino support. The trouble comes when those objectives reign so supreme that party leaders are willing to turn almost any policy disagreement into a racial blood sport. And that's the problem with liberal bamboozlers. They can't accept that reasonable people can disagree on a policy issue for fundamental philosophical reasons. To liberals, virtually every issue is a chance to score racial points:

- If an individual believes that well-protected borders and adherence to the law should be the guiding principles in addressing the problem of illegal immigration, it can't be because they think it's unfair to the legions of individuals who have waited patiently in line and abided by the nation's laws to become a citizen; it must be because they are xenophobes who hate immigrants.
- If a person is familiar with the disappointing results of many bilingual education programs and opposes them, it can't be because they want to see Latino children flourish educationally; it must be because they are

cultural imperialists who live to torture children who have yet to learn to speak English.

- If an individual supports making English the national language, it can't be because he or she wants to see non-native speakers assimilate into the American family; it must be because they are racist and against "people who speak Spanish."

This is what it means to say that the exploitation agenda is based on bamboozling voters. The liberals can't win any other way, unless it runs more conservative candidates. But this would defeat their purpose.

They must stoke racial fears, because they don't have good alternatives. What else are they going to do, tell Latino voters the truth? Tell them that they reject and belittle their religious faith? Or that they despise their strong pro-life position on abortion? Or that they mock their decision to proudly serve in the military? Or that they find Latinos' strong commitment to family values silly and outmoded? Or that they would rather benefit their teacher union friends than to give Latino parents a choice about where and how their children get educated? Or that the truth is that Latino home ownership has skyrocketed to record levels under President George W. Bush?

Of course not. Liberals can't say these things. So they don't. Instead, liberals like Harry Reid race bait, pander, and obfuscate the truth about conservative intentions and results. Robert de Posada says that while Republicans have a long way to go, the leadership they've shown under President Bush has benefited Latinos:

Without a doubt, George W. Bush has been the most important president addressing Hispanic issues. This man, I mean, the employment of the attorney general and the Secretary of Commerce clearly brought Hispanics to a new height in terms of involvement in the federal government. He has appointed more Hispanics to government than any other person before him. And, at the same time, he has had the guts to address the issues that directly confront Hispanics.

The best thing Bush has done is that he has talked to Hispanics like intelligent voters. He hasn't just been focused on the immigration issue or the values; he has talked to them about taxes. He has talked to them about health care issues; he has talked about issues that directly affect their pocketbooks. And that is why you saw such a huge increase in the number of Hispanics that supported him in the past presidential election. Fifty percent of Hispanics who voted for the first time voted for George Bush.[47]

According to U.S. Secretary of Labor Elaine Chao, "President George W. Bush has appointed more Americans of Hispanic heritage to top positions in the federal government than any other president in history." And not just Attorney General Alberto Gonzales; other Latinos receive less of the media spotlight, such as Hector Barreto, administrator of the Small Business Administration; Cari Dominguez, chairman of the Equal Employment Opportunity Commission; Alicia Castaneda, chairman of the Federal Housing Finance Board; Ronnye Vargas Stidvent, assistant Secretary for Policy at the U.S. Department of Labor . . . the list of Latinos in the Bush administration is long.[48]

But as Bush enters his final years in office, the question moving forward will be: how will conservatives respond to the coming wave of liberal Latino bamboozlement? The answer to this question will have profound and lasting political consequences. The exploitation agenda worked when used on black voters; they hope it will do the same with Latinos. How Republicans respond will be the key, says Ed Clancy, president of TrueLatino: "You cannot say—'Hey, you're

Hispanic, I'm going to make you Republican.' Hispanics make their own choices . . . you can't go in and say that I'm going to do this for you, because it's a very self-sufficient society."[49]

That fact, more than any other, should excite and animate conservatives. Self-sufficiency, after all, is at the core of what it means to be a conservative. Conservatives must make that message clear. The prospects for a bamboozle-free future depend on it.

BEYOND SOCCER AND SECURITY MOMS

What Women Really Want

The things that make women anxious are exactly the same. It doesn't matter what stripe you wear in terms of party. Women care about the same things. It's just a question of how they approach the solution to the issues.

—Irene Natividad, summit president, Global Summit of Women

Women are less likely to vote for another woman. . . . On anything involving leadership, there really is a gender gap. . . . They actually will not go and vote for a woman unless she has a specific reason to vote for her.

—Robin Read, president and CEO of the National Foundation of Women Legislators

Rush Limbaugh comes across as a fairly confident guy, someone who is sufficiently aware that the things he says hold the power to influence national debate. But even Limbaugh, it's safe to say, might be surprised at how much credit some leading feminists give him for changing the women's movement. When I interviewed my liberal friend Kim Gandy, president of the National Organization for women (NOW), here's what she had to say about the power of Rush and his influence on feminism:

> **Kim Gandy:** If you go back to a certain period of time, pre-Rush Limbaugh, most women identify themselves as feminists. I mean, really most women—by large numbers. And I am frequently surprised now when I speak with women of a certain age, I'm 52, so my age and a little older who I think of as sort of conservative. And they say, "Oh, I'm a feminist." Well, of course, how can you not be a feminist? And it's because they came of age during a time when feminism had its real definition. They came of age in the '70s when there was nobody named Rush Limbaugh out there saying that feminism was a bad idea.
>
> **Angela McGlowan:** Do you believe that he's that powerful? Enough to sway opinion?
>
> **Kim Gandy:** He was, he was. The word "liberal"—people stopped using that for the most part. They don't say liberal, they say progressive.[1]

Indeed, other feminists like Katha Pollitt, an author and writer for *The Nation*, contend that mean, old conservatives are to blame for swiping linguistic toys of feminists and hauling them back into the national sandbox with new and twisted meanings: "I think that conservatives have really done an amazing job of taking away from us all the good words like 'liberty' and 'freedom' and demonizing the words that are left. Like 'feminism' and 'choice.' And 'liberal.'"[2] These are curious words of concession and defeat from such self-avowedly strong and liberated women warriors. But give Gandy and Pollitt credit: they get it. Rush's ubiquitous "Feminazi" forced the rhetorical hands of the bamboozlers.

Equally ubiquitous is the question that pops up every six months or so in articles, books, and television news segments: "Is Feminism Dead?" The truth is the feminist movement's relevance has been increasingly questioned and in decline for some time. "Now that feminism has achieved its goals," writes Naomi Schaeffer Riley for the *Wall Street Journal*, "the freedom to act like Paris Hilton seems to be all that's left . . . Today's young girls don't have to worry about whether they'll be allowed to pursue their dreams; they can go back to focusing on cute clothes. Not that today's feminists would complain. The feminist message for tweens and teens is all about dressing provocatively and having no-strings sex."[3]

Riley's cheeky words highlight the growing chorus of voices who argue that, with much of the heavy lifting of gender equality having been completed, feminism has lost its saliency. And the backlash against the movement, especially in its more radical forms, has been brutal—lethal even. "Feminism is not simply suffering from a P.R. problem," says Kay Hymowitz, Manhattan Institute scholar and author, "it's just over. As in *finished*. Supporters will smile and reply that the movement has been read its last rites often during its lifetime. What's different now, though, is that feminism appears not so much dead as obsolete."[4]

Even those skeptical of such definitive declarations would concede the enormous gains women have made that have led to the tremendous success they enjoy in today's society. If, as radical feminists alarmingly contend, America's patriarchal culture oppresses women, the oppressors appear to be slacking. According to the U.S. Census, female high school graduation rates continue to surpass males. And in the 2005–06 school year, women were projected to earn 59 percent of the bachelor's and 60 percent of the master's degrees awarded.[5] When people today talk about the gender gap, they are more likely to be referring to the rate at which female students outpace males than they are presidential voting patterns.

Large state universities across the nation are beginning to see trends like these. For example, at the University of California, women outnumber men in all the professional schools except dentistry, which is at an even fifty-fifty split.[6]

Male oppressors have also been derelict in their duty of holding women back in the professional world as well. The U.S. Census reports that between 1997 and 2002 the number of female-owned businesses spiked 20 percent, producing in 2002, a record-smashing $940.8 billion in annual receipts for women-owned businesses.[7] I had an opportunity to discuss this with Secretary of Labor Elaine Chao. Chao is herself the first Asian-American woman ever named to the cabinet. She told me that women entrepreneurs now account for more than ten million small businesses, a growth rate twice that of businesses owned by men.[8] While it will take some time yet for this new breed of women entrepreneurs to catch up to their male CEO counterparts, the Bureau of Labor Statistics reports that one out of four wives now earns more than her husband.[9]

And don't forget about politics; women continue to climb here, too. Congresswoman Nancy Pelosi, the first woman to be Speaker of the House, and Senator Hillary Clinton, the Democratic Party front-runner for the 2008 Democrat presidential nomination, are both poised to dominate the national political scene. This is also true for women at the state level. Women are making waves. "In the midterm elections we had 2,231 women running for just the state legislature alone, which is a record number," Robin Read, president and CEO of the National Foundation for Women Legislators, told me. "In the midterm elections we also had 1,363 Democrats running as opposed to 859 Republicans running, seven Independents, and two Progressives."[10]

For all these strides, however, it would be naïve to suggest that inequalities no longer exist. Clearly they do. As a female business owner myself, I have seen the sometimes silly antics competitors and rivals resort to; however, that does not make me waiver or play the victim. It's about getting the job done for your client with the utmost integrity and work ethic. For example, the fact that someone had dubbed me the "Black Barbie" of political professionals, a reference maybe to my former days as Miss District of Columbia and a print model, didn't mean a hill of beans to me. It's only noise. Yet men are hardly immune to jibes about their physical appearance. Their height, weight, strength, skin color (our affirmative action hiree), and hair (or lack thereof) are all prime targets for teasing, or worse.

Inappropriate behavior has no place in a professional setting or corporate America. However, in my opinion, you cannot equate a manager's high expectations of subordinates as being tough or gender-related. Unfortunately, some subordinates, male or female, confuse these actions as gender-related. Even some feminists concede that unfair or unequal treatment can come from female bosses as well. "Women bosses are sometimes less flexible with other women," NOW president Kim Gandy said. "Not because they want to be less flexible, but because it's demanded of them by the higher-ups, who watch them like hawks to see if they are tough enough."[11] So that knife cuts both ways.

Bonnie Erbe, columnist and host of PBS's *To the Contrary*'s adds that some women are less committed to gender solidarity than some men. "I don't think women have the same gender-based affinity that men do," Erbe explained. "Men grew up playing team sports . . . men will stick up for men, and women will frequently— let me emphasize—not all women, but as a group, women don't tend to have that locker room, team sport kind of bonding that men do."[12]

Bottom line: men and women are distinct. And these differences undoubtedly influence male and female political perceptions as well. When I spoke with Republican pollster Kellyane Fitzpatrick Conway, she elaborated on this point. "There is naturally a difference between the way men and women regard politics, and they take that view of politics directly to the ballot box." These differences, Conway says, are part of what explains the much discussed gender gap in voting. Overall, men tend to vote more Republican, and women tend to vote a little more Democrat. But Conway says that what drives the gender gap isn't abortion or so-called women's issues; instead she asserts that women "tend to look at the government more as a safety net."[13] This is especially true for unmarried women with children, low-income females, or women with post-graduate degrees. In reference to the latter, Clinton pollster Stanley Greenberg, husband of Congresswoman Rosa DeLauro, puts it in stark and startling terms:

> The revolt against established family and gender norms, nearly as dramatic as the revolt against established racial norms, allowed the emergence of modern educated women. That has produced a full-fledged political realignment among the growing group of college-educated women. The super-educated women are strongly pro-choice, but more than that, they hate symbols of faith.[14]

Ah, yes. The anti-family, anti-life, anti-faith strain that runs through so much of radical feminism that sees marriage and religion as instruments of male oppression, or "patriarchal hegemony," as they like to call it. As Clinton's pollster confesses, this radical group of bamboozlers represents a core element of the Democratic Party base. Legendary radical feminist Andrea Dworkin, who died in 2005, advanced the family and religion as patriarchy thesis, notes author Daniel J. Flynn:

A more jaundiced view of the status of women emanates from domestic feminists. Angry Andrea Dworkin labels Western women "the ultimate house-niggers, ass-licking, bowing, scraping, shuffling fools." Women's "minds are aborted in their development by sexist education," the feminist academic writes. "[O]ur bodies are violated by oppressive grooming imperatives," the disheveled Dworkin complains, and "the police function against us in cases of rape and assault." Her rant continues, "the media, schools, and churches conspire to deny us dignity and freedom . . . the nuclear family and ritualized sexual behavior imprison us in roles . . . which are degrading to us."[15]

Call me crazy, but I'm guessing that one probably didn't focus group so well.

So, instead, the bamboozlers cloak their vitriol against traditional family values and men in more palatable phrases. Still, says *National Review* Washington editor Kate O'Beirne, the thrust of their message remains clear: "They talk 'freedom of choice,' but feminists are too contemptuous of dissenting women to allow them to choose freely how to live their lives without ridicule and disdain."[16]

The much touted "Mommy Wars"—the debate over whether mothers who opt for a career are shortchanging their children—has deepened the rift between hardcore feminists and women professionals who decide to ditch their corporate jobs and severely tailored Prada suits to invest in their children and husbands as opposed to their 401Ks. But some radical feminists, like Linda Hirshman, aren't smiling. In 2006, Hirshman's book, *Get to Work: A Manifesto For Women of the World*, hit like a lightning bolt. Hirshman skewered female elites for their sizable exodus from the corridors of corporate power. Hirshman was aghast when her research revealed that 85 percent of the high-powered women she studied had either left their jobs completely or were working only part-time. So severe was

Hirshman's scolding that the *Chicago Sun-Times* review of her book said it was "appropriate that Hirshman's pocket-size book is red because it reads much like a communist manifesto, calling on women to live by strict codes for the betterment of society and for the advancement of feminism overall. Individual concerns, desires and the pursuit of happiness have no place in Hirshman's scheme."[17]

For some women, the decision whether to work and hire a nanny or stay home is no decision at all; a single mother may not be able to afford such luxuries, even though the data on the perils of day-care are widely known. But perhaps the most devastating dimension of feminism is that it commands women to drop the Baby Einstein books and strap on their corporate heels. It also requires that they completely ignore the *other* woman upon whose back feminists walk as they attempt to shatter "the glass ceiling"—and that's the nanny. Caitlin Flanagan, author of *To Hell With All That: Loving and Loathing Our Inner Housewife*, says that the fact that the gains feminists boast they've made for women "have been bought at the expense of poor women, often of poor brown-skinned women, is a bitter irony that very few feminists will discuss directly, other than to murmur something vague about 'universal day care' and then, on reflex, blame the Republicans." Because children can't raise themselves, Flanagan's argument proves lethal and lays bare the bamboozler's desire to erode the traditional institutions like marriage, faith and family that anchor American life.[18] It's an argument that the bamboozlers must be forced to address.

One woman who knows all sides of the arguments surrounding women's advocacy is Irene Natividad. She has been in charge of three different women's organizations, including the Global Summit of Women for the last sixteen years, the National Women's Political Caucus for two years, and the National Commission on Working Women for nine years. Natividad considers herself a "dyed in the wool Democrat," but during our interview, she says she feels strongly that there is value in women holding a spectrum of opinions:

> There's no reason why we shouldn't have a conservative group and one that is more progressive in its outlook. I mean, that's what makes this country special. You can create a group or belong to one that you feel comfortable with whose ideals are similar to yours. Men always bring up the cat fight business when they want to belittle us, but the point is that this is a diverse country with diverse interests. You can't paint all the women in one color. What makes me special is different from what makes you special.[19]

Natividad's is a view few would disagree with. And in my interview with NOW president Kim Gandy, she, too, embraces a big tent approach to reaching out to women. The problem, of course, is in the tactics feminists often use to build the large tent. As several conservative female scholars and organizations have demonstrated, radical feminists have not always been so straightforward and truthful in their arguments and motives. Many have engaged in egregious misinformation campaigns designed to paint men as sexual predators lying in wait.

In her book *The War Against Boys*, Dr. Christina Hoff Sommers shatters many of the myths propagated by leftist feminists. One brazen example of this involves the statement by Katherine Hanson, director of the Women's Educational Equity Act (WEEA) Publishing Center, which is "the primary vehicle by which the U.S. Department of Education promotes gender equity." Sommers writes that Hanson claimed males were to blame for the following shocking atrocities: four million women being beaten to death annually; violence becoming the leading cause of death among women; being beaten by a man at home becoming the leading cause of injury among women;

and a 59 percent increase in rapes in a single year (1990–1991). But none of it was true. Not even close.

For starters, it would have been hard for four million women to have been killed in one year, since "the total number of annual female deaths in the entire country from all causes combined is approximately one million." But according to the FBI, the total number of women who died by any and all types of murder in 1996 was 3,631, not four million as Hanson alleged. Second, the leading cause of death among women is heart disease (370,000 per year), not homicides (3,600). Sommers revealed that the injury to women and rape claims were equally outrageous. Only "1 percent of women's injuries are caused by male partners," Sommers wrote, and "between 1990 and 1991 rapes increased by 4 percent, not 59 percent."[20]

Feminists who peddle in such blatant misinformation campaigns hurt women and men. How, you might ask? By trivializing real acts of sexual misconduct and encouraging individuals to meet actual dangers or threats with skepticism. But that hardly seems to have slowed feminists from spreading false information. Indeed, shoddy statistics and scare tactics are the primary tools in the radical feminist toolbox.

One of the most persistent claims made by feminists involves the "wage gap." This myth, based on data from the U.S. Census Bureau, claims women earn only 77 cents for every dollar that men earn. This, feminists claim, is yet another example of the gender discrimination that dominates America's sexist culture. But before we dismantle this deception, let's see how much feminists have invested in its existence.

As with all the other scams, this one involves making female workers angry at an apparent injustice perpetrated against women. Also, the way this conspiracy is alleged to work is that it requires an invisible control so powerful that it has managed to surreptitiously grip the gears of an entire system. That's why liberals love boogey-man villains that can't be seen or shot or incarcerated, such as the Man or "systemic sexism" or "systemic racism." Liberals love lucid forces that they can claim sneak up on unwitting *victims*—ah, the cherished word of the bamboozler—and rob them of social justice or equality. For added effect, liberals explain that this phantom menace is so sinister that only through consciousness raising and activism can the conservative chimera be caged.

That's what's so effective about the wage gap myth: it purports to affect all women on an issue that is at once a symbolic statement of one's relative value (although a superficial one) and that directly affects a woman's standard of living. In many ways it's the perfect con. Maybe that explains why feminists from Nancy Pelosi to Hillary Clinton have made it a centerpiece of the exploitation agenda, even going to so far as to create Equal Pay Day. Citizens can even log on to the National Committee on Pay Equity's website to learn about "Justice You Can Bank On." Lest one think this a fly-by-night operation, the National Committee on Pay Equity (NCPE) was founded in 1979 by feminist groups, labor unions, state and local pay equity coalitions, and professional groups.

In preparation for "Equal Pay Day," you'll want to also be sure to purchase red clothing. As the website explains, "Wear red on Equal Pay Day to symbolize how far women and minorities are 'in the red' with their pay!" There's even an Equal Pay Day Kit, complete with the following: press releases, sample letters to send to col-leagues, sample op-eds, Pay Day proclamations . . . there's even an information packet on how to start your own WAGE club, which is an acronym for the wonderfully defiant Women Are Getting Equal. But this is respectable militancy; the WAGE Project's board of advi-sors includes former Democratic vice presidential nominee Geraldine Ferraro, Eleanor Smeal, Kim Gandy, and Pat Schroeder.[21]

Funding support also comes from the Women's Studies Research Center at Brandeis University and the Law, Culture, and Difference Program at Northeastern University School of Law.[22]

Some feminists have argued that to atone for the nation's blatant sex discrimination masquerading as a wage gap that America should institute something called "comparable worth." Bonnie Erbe explains the concept of comparable worth as "a much-maligned concept in which economists try to even out the pay gap between nurse's aides and truck drivers (or other male- and female-dominated fields)."[23]

But lest one worry that full-scale socialistic tinkering with wage rates is fast upon us, have no fear, Senator Hillary Clinton is here!

Lucky for us, Hillary has found a way to rectify the phony, man-ufactured injustice: the Paycheck Fairness Act.[24] The bill would remedy nonexistent sex discrimination by:

- Prohibiting employers from punishing employees who share their salary information with their co-workers. (Sharing salary information is often essential for understanding that discrimination exists and addressing it.) *Smart bamboozler strategy to endorse something that is already protected while also helping your lawyer buddies boost their billable hours. Double play!*
- Toughening the penalties associated with violating the Equal Pay Act. *Yes, because the current penalties are clearly not tough enough to stop sexist bosses. But remember we must oppose tougher penalties on drugs like crack cocaine because that's racist.*
- Teaching women and girls negotiation skills. (Women are eight times less likely to negotiate their starting salaries than men, and if a woman with a starting salary of $25,000 fails to negotiate for $5,000 more a year, she stands to lose more than

$568,000 by age sixty.) *This isn't a bad idea; who couldn't use help learning better negotiating skills? But there's something a little suspicious, even offensive, here. It seems that Clinton is suggesting that the VICTIM of sex discrimination is somehow responsible for being paid less! But, pay no mind. That can't be what she's saying, because everyone knows that liberalism and personal responsibility don't go together.*

• Rewarding model employers and strengthening the ability of the Equal Employment Opportunity Commission to crack down on equal pay violations. *What kind of reward do I get if I'm a model employer? A free membership in my local WAGE club? Or is it a shirt that says: "I fought the Wage Gap, but all I got was this lousy t-shirt"?*

OK, enough fun—time to end the liberal delirium. Here are the implications. As my colleagues at the Independent Women's Forum explain, the statistic the bamboozler's cite from the U.S. Census Bureau is accurate. That is, when you total all wages, across all sectors of the economy, you get a figure that works out to 77 cents banked by women for every dollar made by men. However, this figure has next to nothing to do with some invisible force field of sex discrimination. Rather, it has to do with a little word that frequently is heard by feminists: "choices."

The first choice involves the amount of uninterrupted time one chooses to work at a given job. Long spans of unbroken years working in a position, not surprisingly, correlate with higher wages. As Arrah Nielsen of the Independent Women's Forum points out, "Women are fifty times more likely than men to take time out of the workforce, for care-giving and other reasons." So, for example, when a woman leaves the workforce for, say, five years to be a stay-at-home mother until her child starts kindergarten, that's five years of lost work experience/seniority on her résumé. When, however, males and females in the same occupation, who possess similar years of experience and qualifications, are examined, the difference is virtually nonexistent. In fact, when economist June O'Neill, a former director of the nonpartisan Congressional Budget Office, conducted a definitive study on the wage gap, it was found that when controlling for variables such as experience, education, and years on the job, women earn 98 percent of what men do.[25] Nevertheless, as Kate O'Beirne points out in her book *Women Who Make the World Worse*, the myth continues:

> The persistent fable that women are denied equal pay for equal work has been a never-empty tank of gas that fuels feminism. A sympathetic public is largely unaware that the claim that women face widespread wage discrimination is a myth aggressively advanced by feminists. Disparities in wages exist between women with children and men and single women. This is not sex discrimination, but if that were better understood feminists would have to get real jobs.[26]

But wait. There's more.

Warren Farrell has been a board member of the National Organization of Women's New York chapter on three occasions. He argues that another major reason men out-earn women is that men take jobs that pay more than the jobs women take. For example, Farrell points out that men are far more likely to take "death and exposure" jobs, such as being a firefighter, truck driver, or logger, which are 95 percent dominated by men. "Conversely," Arrah Nielsen says, "low-risk jobs like secretarial work and childcare are more than 95 percent female."[27]

Farrell offers a helpful suggestion to anyone wanting to boost their wages: "Among jobs requiring little education, those that expose you to the sleet and heat pay more than those that are indoors and neat."[28]

The feminist movement insists it exists to protect a woman's right to choose her own path. But it doesn't. From abortion to gay marriage, to faith and careers, feminists support a woman's decision only when it coincides with the liberal agenda. That's not what women want.

So what *do* women want?

For starters, they don't want to be confined by boxes and pollsters' labels, like Soccer and Security Moms. Those might make for nice alliterative demographic descriptors, but they are too constraining, too limiting. Women are different. They're individuals. And the groupthink that liberals are striving to impose on Latinos is unlikely to work on women. Why? There are too many of us for us to all agree on a single vision.

But if feminism is defined as the belief that men and women should be treated equally under the law, then who isn't a feminist? The steely Republican women of a bygone era who fought for the rights we all too often take for granted were the true pioneers who paved the way for equality. The trouble with today's feminist movement, says Caitlin Flanagan, is that "it refuses to acknowledge a truth as old as civilization: that a woman's ambition to be a wife and mother can be just as powerful as her ambition to become a respected member of the labor force."[29]

What women want most is a sense of control and security over their lives. They also want that for those they love. Many are caregivers by nature. And in a post-9–11 world where threats abound and markets are easily rattled, women are looking for leaders who are graceful under fire, a vision that embodies both strength and flexibility. As out-of-wedlock birthrates soar and threats to national security gather, what women want most right now, says Robin Read, is a sense of control, in all its varied forms:

> They want control of their time. They want control of their lives, control of drugs. Interestingly enough, control of the borders, control of crime, control of spending. And they want peace—not world peace. They want peace of mind, knowing that it will be happening, that it'll be taken care of, or that they have some control over their choices. They want choices, but not very many choices. . . They are spiritual. They are the guardians of the faith, but they don't want to wear it on their sleeves . . . National security is a major issue. I'd say that's probably at the top of their political agenda. If they're marginally compromised, it might be housing, or economics, or jobs . . . But control and peace of mind are the clear things right now.[30]

Similarly, Irene Natividad says that party labels and ideologies often mask the fact that the driving impulse and desires that animate both sides remain the same:

> If you're a Republican, you figure that the way to address economic issues is by pulling yourself up by your bootstraps, by pushing for entrepreneurship, which is individual people creating their own businesses. If you're a Democrat, you talk about creating a safety net for people who don't have the resources, giving them training so that they can enter the workforce better equipped and providing them with the supports, like child care or training, that will make them much more marketable. . . . Because women have children, they worry about security all the time. Even whether their sons are going to war or not, they worry about the welfare of the entire family when there is a framework of war against which they see their future. . . . But the things that make women anxious are exactly the

same. It doesn't matter what stripe you wear in terms of party. Women care about the same things. It's just a question of how they approach the solution to the issues.[31]

It's safe to say that security, broadly defined, is a gender-neutral desire. Maybe that's why the base of Maslow's famous pyramid diagram, known as the Hierarchy of Needs, focuses on the physiological essentials like food and water, followed by physical safety. But data shows that women seem less willing to trust a woman leader to provide them with the security all humans desire. Much to the chagrin of feminists, studies reveal that women tend to judge female politicians more critically and skeptically than male politicians. Robin Read, head of the nonpartisan National Foundation for Women Legislators, is someone who understands this better than most:

> Women are less likely to vote for another woman . . . they don't see them as symbols of strength, and security is a major issue. And that's the reason the veterans of the nation are supported by women . . . But on anything involving leadership, there really is a gender gap to whom people look, and women voters look to male symbols of strength to endorse females in politics . . . They actually will not go and vote for a woman unless she has a specific reason to vote for her.[32]

If what Read says is true—and it is—Hillary better get busy bamboozling women in time for 2008.

THE FUTURE IS ALMOST HERE

"Today, we have a grand opportunity to create a new generation of women, Latino, and black leaders who can emerge within the Republican Party who are conservative and who can speak to the human experience in a way that all Americans can relate. Now Republicans have the chance to reestablish these relationships in communities of color and open new doors for all."

—Angela McGlowan

People often ask what I think the future holds for women, Latinos, and blacks. I believe there's a new rhythm for minority leadership taking shape. It's a strong and upbeat tempo that transcends partisanship and ideology. It's a cadence based on self-empowerment, not on self-pity or the reliance on the largess of traditional power bases. It has more hope and harmony than heat. You can hear and feel this new rhythm when you listen to today's leaders such as Secretary of State Condoleezza Rice, Secretary of Housing and Urban Development Alphonso Jackson, and Attorney General Alberto Gonzales, just to name a few. These leaders have moved to create a better America, a better nation, and policies that will positively impact our future and our world. These leaders have moved to the "right side," are qualified, and happen to be women and/or persons of color. You can hear and feel their confidence and courage.

Throughout *Bamboozled*, I have illustrated how one can be comfortable in his or her own skin and effectively strive for a more fulfilling life by exercising a choice, by knowing our history and how we came to the place we are today. The attainment of self-awareness and self-empowerment does not happen overnight. *Bamboozled* recapitulates our history as a nation, as women, and as a people of color. It demonstrates and speaks to the need for the development of self knowledge. *Bamboozled* shouts the urgency for us as a people to investigate, to examine, and to scrutinize the rhetoric preached to us by the traditional leaders in our community. It is up to us to choose our leaders as our forefathers intended, to know why we vote for who we vote for, to exercise our rights, and not to vote for leaders on symbolic gestures and empty promises, but to vote for the most qualified person who will help create a better society, not hold us in chains for their own advancement. *Bamboozled* opens our eyes which have been shut for so long. This book gives us the opportunity to have a brighter future, a better America. It is now up to us to make the choice to be free.

However, the challenge for conservative Republicans is not only to reach out to women and communities of color but to blend history and technology, and create understanding in order to assist young Americans. The Internet is a matrix of brilliance and buffoonery for this generation; conservative Republicans have to be the beacon of light at the end of the tunnel. I'm not talking about glitzy public-relations campaigns, I'm talking about old-fashioned grass roots campaigns and face-to-face outreach; I'm talking about conservative Republicans who are committed enough to meet young people—of all races and all genders—on their own turf (the Internet) and show them a new way of seeing their world around them.

Every young person has a defining moment—a moment when he or she has a life-changing experience or someone shares with them a life-changing piece of wisdom. Young people today—of every race—are technologically savvy and sophisticated consumers of information. They're also entrepreneurial in ways we can't imagine. This is the first generation of young people who have the ability to instantly fact-check presidential debates *as they are happening* in real-time. That means they're wary of spin—from both sides.

This generation has choices and they know it. What we conservative Republicans need to understand is that this is the most information-empowered generation in American history, and that both increases and decreases the opportunities for bamboozlement. The key is igniting their interest and passion for conservative ideas and principles. The challenge will be finding ways to spark young minds to ask big questions.

—ANGELA MCGLOWAN

ACKNOWLEDGMENTS

I am grateful for many things in my life, but none more so than God's grace and love in affording me the opportunity to write this book. Without Him, nothing is possible.

Many individuals made this book possible through the giving of their time and talents, each of whom I wish to thank. I am grateful for my Fox News family. Their unyielding support is more than fair and balanced. Specifically, I want to thank my mentor and beacon, Roger Ailes. Every second spent with Roger is an education and privilege. I also wish to thank Bill O'Reilly, Sean Hannity, John Gibson, and Bill Kristol, each of whom gave generously of their time in granting me interviews and who never fail to make me smile. Grateful thanks also goes to Juan Williams and Ellis Henican for their insights and friendship.

Members of President George W. Bush's cabinet took time out from their busy schedules to sit down with me to share their thoughts and ideas. I extend my sincerest appreciation to Secretary of Labor Elaine Chao, Secretary of Housing and Urban Development Alphonso Jackson, and former Secretary of Education Rod Paige.

Three individuals took a time out on the campaign trail to field my questions, former Maryland Lieutenant Governor Michael Steele, former Ohio Secretary of State Ken Blackwell, and NFL Hall of Famer, the great Lynn Swann. Thank you for paving the path with humility and integrity. Your insight was enormous in helping me pull back the curtain on the bamboozlers and the liberal agenda.

I would also like to thank the many smart and impressive women who assisted me in sifting through and analyzing data on issues that impact our gender. I wish to thank Leslie Sanchez, Frances Rice, Bonnie Erbe, Irene Natividad, Kellyanne Fitzpatrick Conway, Julianne Malveaux, Robin Read, Carol Jean Jordan, Debra Johnson, Kay Hymowitz, Kim Gandy, Karen Czarnecki, Cathy Areu, Sasha Burns, Julie Roginsky, and Jessie Jane Duff.

Several individuals were kind enough to walk me through their personal thoughts on political philosophy and policy. I am so grateful to Congressman Jessie Jackson Jr. for taking the time out of his congressional schedule to sit with me and to be so candid on his point of view. I am also thankful for my time spent with a true American hero and a man who was a strong advocate of diversity before it was popular, and that is 1996 Republican presidential candidate and former Majority Leader Senator Robert Dole. I am grateful for the insights of the Reverend Al Sharpton, Judge Joe Brown, Russell Simmons, Dwayne Ashley, Ed Clancy, Frank Gomez, Frank Mercado-Valdez, Professor James McPherson, Professor John Hope Franklin, Paul T. Williams, Michael Zak, Edward Juarez, Hallerin Hill, Dr. David Banks, John McWhorter, Lloyd Williams, Keith Beauchamp, Niger Innis, Roy Innis, and Robert de Posada.

I am also thankful for my tenure as host of Fox 5's WNYW public affairs show, *Good Day Street Talk*, where I had the privilege of interviewing a multitude of great leaders. I want to give special thanks to the guests who participated in my "New York City Education Special": Lillian Rodriguez, Councilwoman Eva Moskowitz, Councilman Robert Jackson, and Councilman Gifford Miller. Their insights and experience assisted in the education chapter.

The man who taught me "how to debate and never take the bait," media and executive coach Jon Kraushar, is the consummate professional. The same is true for Ron Jenson, my political advisor. I'm pleased to count them both as friends and mentors.

When I first moved to Washington, DC, Jerry Boykin, my attorney for over a decade, shepherded me through the maze. He is the perfect blend of expert and friend. My literary agent, Joseph Brendan Vallely, took on this first-time author, I'm grateful for their kindness and expertise.

At Thomas Nelson, a team of sagacious and patient professionals gave generously of their talents and time. Publisher David Dunham loves to laugh almost as much as I do. I appreciate his leadership and devotion to this book. Editors Alice Sullivan and Joel Miller applied their skilled editing scalpels in sculpting my prose. Brian Mitchell, Chris Roslan, and David Schroeder built an ambitious marketing and publicity strategy. Thank you for keeping me super busy.

Special thanks and appreciation go to Wynton Hall, accomplished author, historian, and speechwriter, for collaborating with and assisting me throughout the writing of this book. Wynton helped me make this book—my dream—come through to fruition. Thank you.

Special thanks and appreciation also goes to my brilliant researchers and interns: Tyler Rogers, Ann Kenny, Marisa Kronenberg, Jessie Wendt, Lindsey Levick, Albin Soares, Brandon Hamilton, and Nya Johnson. You guys were wonderful and you have a great future in front of you. Thank you for your enthusiastic participation.

My mother, Alberta, and my four siblings—Debra, Brenda, Carolyn, and James—always taught me that I could be anything, do anything, and achieve any goal through hard work, integrity, tenacity, and through keeping God first. They are my conscience, my counselors, and my support. Each of them is a living reaffirmation of the lessons my father taught us before his passing. I love each of you more than you'll ever know.

Lastly but certainly not least, I wish to thank my loving husband, John, for being my Rock of Gibraltar, my best friend, my counselor, and soul-mate. Thank you for all that you are to me, my love.

NOTES

Introduction:
1. Angela McGlowan, interview with Ohio Secretary of State Ken Blackwell.
2. Senator Zell Miller, "How Democrats Lost the South" *Washington Times*, November 3, 2003.
3. www.gop.com/About/AboutRead.aspx?AboutType=3.
4. Robert V. Remini, *The Legacy of Andrew Jackson* (Louisiana State University Press, 1988). Also see generally Robert V. Remini, *Andrew Jackson and his Indian Wars* (Penguin Publishing, 2001), wherein the author recounts the brutal mistreatment of Indians based on Jackson's fears that they would intermarry with whites.
5. DNA test results were released in November 1998, by the Thomas Jefferson Foundation, which formed a research committee consisting of nine members of the foundation staff, including four with Ph.D.s. After review, the committee reported its finding that the weight of all known evidence—from the DNA study, original documents, written and oral historical accounts, and statistical data— indicated a high probability that Thomas Jefferson was the father of Eston Hemings, and that he was perhaps the father of all six of Sally Hemings's children listed in Monticello records—Harriet (born 1795; died in infancy); Beverly (born 1798); an unnamed daughter (born 1799; died in infancy); Harriet (born 1801); Madison (born 1805); and Eston (born 1808).
6. Nick Bryant, *The Bystander* (Basic Books, 2006), 469.
7. Pianin, Eric. "A Senator's Shame: Byrd, in His New Book, Again Confronts Early Ties to KKK," *Washington Post*, 2005-06-19, pp. A01.
8. www.historicaldocuments.com/19thAmendment.htm.
9. *Plessy v. Ferguson*, 163 U.S. 537 (1896).
10. Paul Waldman, *Being Right Is Not Enough: What Progressives Must Learn from Conservative Success* (Wiley Books, 2006).
11. Nick Bryant, *The Bystander: John F. Kennedy and the Struggle for Black Equality* (Basic Books, 2006), 472.
12. Myrna Blyth, *Spin Sisters: How the Women of the Media Sell Unhappiness—and Liberalism—to the Women of America* (St. Martin's Press, 2004), 268.

Chapter One
1. Lynn Harris, "Who's Your Baby Daddy?" *Salon.com*, February 24, 2005.
2. Donna Britt, "In Another Era, Teen Mom was a Cautionary Tale," *Washington Post*, April 15, 2005; See also Donna Britt, "A Chorus of Empathy for Baby Mamas," *Washington Post*, April 1, 2005, B01.
3. William Raspberry, "Why Our Black Families Are Failing," *Washington Post*, July 25, 2005, A19.
4. Angela McGlowan, interview with Lt. Governor Michael Steele.
5. Kay S. Hymowitz, "The Black Family: 40 Years of Lies," *City Journal*, Summer 2005.
6. Thomas B. Edsall, *Building Red America: The New Conservative Coalition and the Drive for Permanent Power* (New York: Basic Books, 2006). In his review of

Edsall's book, George Will called this passage "astonishing" and said those seeking the real reason for the rise of Red America should simply "read that paragraph again." George Will, "Blue America, In More Ways Than One," *Washington Post*, September 17, 2006, B07.

7. Patrick F. Fagan, Robert E. Rector, and Lauren R. Noyes, "Why Congress Should Ignore Radical Feminist Opposition to Marriage" Heritage Foundation Backgrounder #1662, June 16, 2003.www.heritage.org/Research/Family/bg1662.cfm.

8. Angela McGlowan, interview with Judge Joe Brown.

9. Ibid.

10. Eugene Rivers.

11. Mark Mellman,"Mind the Marriage Gap," The Hill, December 8, 2004. www.hillnews.com/thehill/export/TheHill/Comment/Pollsters/ MarkMellman/120804.html.

12. Ibid.

13. Stanley B. Greenberg, *The Two Americas: Our Current Political Deadlock and How to Break It* (Thomas Dunne Books, 2004), 98.

14. McGlowan, Steele interview.

15. Angela McGlowan, interview with John McWhorter.

16. The Honorable Mike Leavitt, "Marriage and the Welfare of America: The Tenth Anniversary of Welfare Reform," The Heritage Lectures, No. 947, June 20, 2006.

17. Angela McGlowan, interview with Juan Williams; Juan Williams, *Enough* (Crown Publishers, 2006), 215.

18. Ibid.

19. Angela McGlowan, interview with Robert de Posada.

20. Angela McGlowan, interview with Niger Innis.

21. *Atlantic Monthly*.

22. McGlowan, de Posada interview.

23. "A Sad Day for Poor Children," (editorial), *New York Times*, August 1, 1996.

24. "Mission Unaccomplished," (editorial) *New York Times*, August 24, 2006.

Chapter Two

1. www.forbes.com/facesscan/2007/01/02/oprah-winfrey-education-facecx_cn_0102 autofacescan02.html?partner=rss.

2. Stephen M. Silverman with Susan Mandel, "Oprah Winfrey: Wealth is 'A Good Thing,'" *People*, April 11, 2006. people.aol.com/people/ article/0,26334,1182572,00.html.

3. Ibid.

4. www.evancarmichael.com/Famous-Entrepreneurs/619/Lesson-1-Give-It-All-Youve-Got.html.

5. Angela McGlowan interview with Hallerin Hill.

6. Shelby Steele, *White Guilt: How Blacks & Whites Together Destroyed the Promise of the Civil Rights Era* (HarperCollins, 2006), 126.

7. United Nations Environment Programme, "African Lakes Atlas Launched at World Lakes Event," Press Release. October 31, 2005.

8. www.census.gov/Press-Release/www/releases/archives/income_wealth/005647.html.

9. Ibid.

10. www.cis.org/articles/2001/hispanicmc/reexamining.html.

11. www.timewarner.com/corp/newsroom/pr/0,20812,667967,00.html.

12. "Increasingly Affluent African American Market Set to Reach $981 Billion by 2010," PR Newswire, February 22, 2006.

13. www.hispanicbusiness.com/news/newsbyid.asp?id=16041.
14. Angela McGlowan, interview with Julianne Malveaux.
15. Dahna M. Chandler, Derek T. Dingle, Alan Hughes, "Downfall of a Black Syndication Kingpin," *Black Enterprise*, April 2005, 70–75.
16. www.nytimes.com/2005/05/16/business/media/16simmons.html?ex=1273896000&en=077da91097413bf2&ei=5090&partner=rssuserland&emc=rss.
17. Angela McGlowan, interview with Ohio Secretary of State Ken Blackwell.
18. Angela McGlowan, interview with Congressman Jesse Jackson, Jr.
19. pewresearch.org/assets/obdeck/pdf/18.pdf
20. Rep. Maxine Waters (D-CA), "Estate Tax and Extension of Tax Relief Act of 2006: Regarding the Minimum Wage," Floor Statement, July 28, 2006.
21. Angela McGlowan, interview with Frances Rice.
22. "Characteristics of minimum wage workers: 2004," www.bls.gov/cps/minwage2004.htm.
23. Ibid.
24. www.yaf.com/minwage.shtml
25. Thomas Sowell, "Minimum Wage Not a Remedy for Jobs," *Baltimore Sun*, August 10, 2006, 17A.
26. Patrik Jonsson, "If Minimum Wage is Raised, Who Benefits?" *Christian Science Monitor,* June 22, 2006. www.csmonitor.com/2006/0622/p01s03-usec.html.
27. Thomas J. Donohue, "Living Wage Laws Kill Jobs," U.S. Chamber of Commerce, August 1, 2006, www.uschamber.com/publications/weekly/commentary/060801.htm.
28. Sowell, "Minimum Wage Not a Remedy for Jobs."
29. National Association of Bilingual Education www.nabe.org/research/demography.html.
30. Angela McGlowan, interview with Lt. Gov. Michael Steele.
31. Angela McGlowan, interview with Lynn Swann; see also Marc Levy, "Rendell's Ad on Black Radio 'Divisive,' Swann Says, Associated Press, November 3, 2006.
32. "Interview with Reverend Jesse Jackson," (transcript), FOX *Hannity & Colmes*, November 8, 2006.
33. For a balanced history of the subject, see, Terry H. Anderson, *The Pursuit of Fairness: A History of Affirmative Action* (Oxford University Press, 2004), 276.
34. John Stossel, "White Guilt Doesn't Help Blacks," Creators Syndicate, November 15, 2006.
35. Angela McGlowan, interview with Rev. Al Sharpton.
36. http://links.jstor.org/sici?sici=1077-3711(199722)16%3C112%3AJMATIO%3E2.0.CO%3B2-V.
37. www.cbsnews.com/stories/2006/06/01/politics/main1673345.shtml.
38. "Blacks Prospered Under Reagan," NewsMax.com, June 10, 2004. www.newsmax.com/archives/ic/2004/6/10/110117.shtml.
39. Ibid.
40. Michael Novak, "Reagan and the Poor," National Review Online, June 23, 2004. www.nationalreview.com/novak/novak200406230845.asp.
41. McGlowan, Blackwell interview.
42. Angela McGlowan, interview with Lloyd Williams.
43. McGlowan, Jackson interview.
44. Angela McGlowan, interview with Secretary of Housing and Urban Development Alphonso Jackson.
45. Angela McGlowan, interview with Robert de Posada.
46. Richard Miniter, "Why is America's Black Middle Class Strangely Fragile?"

American Enterprise Online, November/December 1998.
www.taemag.com/issues/articleid.17104/article_detail.asp.

47. Jerry Bowyer, "The Bush Boom is Color Blind: The Black Unemployment Rate Keeps on Falling," *National Review Online,* February 10, 2006.
48. www.bls.gov/cps/wlf-table1-2006.pdf
49. Sam Roberts, "Black Incomes Surpass Whites in Queens," *New York Times,* October 2006.
50. www.hispanicbusiness.com/news/newsbyid.asp?id=27903
51. As cited in "Single Black Female, in Her Own House," *Economist,* November 20, 2004, vol. 373, 35.
52. Angela McGlowan interview with Bonnie Erbe.
53. Peter Schweizer, "Party of the Rich," *National Review Online,* October 30, 2006 article.nationalreview.com/?q=NmE4NWY3Yjc4YmJmMDJmOGU0Zm QwNGE0MjNlMDJiZTY=.

Chapter Three
1. Mary Beth Marklein, "Advanced Placement on Upswing: Minority Performance, Representation Still Troubling," *USA Today,* February 8, 2006, 8D.
2. Jia-Rui Chong, "Morphing Outrage Into Idea," *Los Angeles Times,* October 12, 2005, A1.
3. Deroy Murdock, "Dems Need a Houseclean," *National Review Online,* January 6, 2003.
4. Angela McGlowan interview with Julianne Malveaux.
5. National Center for Education Statistics (NCES), "Comparative Indicators of Education in the United States and Other G8 Countries: 2004." nces.ed.gov/pubs2005/2005021.pdf.
6. John Stossel, "Stupid in America," ABC News, January 13, 2006. Also see: Jay Greene, *Education Myths* (Littlefield and Rowman, 2005).
7. U.S. Department of Education, "Digest of Education Statistics 2003," Tables 134 and 166, www.nces.ed.gov/programs/digest.
8. Greg Forster, "Florida's Opinion on K-12 Public Education Spending," Rose and Milton Friedman Foundation/James Madison Institute/Collins Center for Public Policy Poll, January 24, 2006. www.friedmanfoundation.org/FloridaPoll.pdf.
9. U.S. Census Bureau News, Press Release, March 17, 2005, www.census.gov/ Press-Release/www/releases/archives/governments/004118.html.
10. Angela McGlowan interview with Niger Ennis.
11. Edward Wyatt, "Success of City School Pupils Isn't Simply a Money Matter," *New York Times,* June 14, 2000, 1.
12. "African American, Hispanics Less Optimistic Than Whites about Local Public Schools," The Joint Center for Political and Economic Studies, May 14, 2003. www.jointcenter.org/pressroom1/PressReleasesDetail.php?recordID=16.
13. John Stossel, "Stupid in America."
14. Angela McGlowan interview with U.S. Secretary of Education Rod Paige.
15. "Focus on Blacks: 2004-2005,"National Education Association, www.nea.org/ teachexperience/images/blacksfocus05.pdf.
16. Michael Dobbs, "School Achievement Gap Narrowing," *Washington Post* July 15, 2005.
17. Abigail Thernstrom and Stephan Thernstrom, *No Excuses,* 200.
18. Debra J. Saunders, "Those Who Can't Sue," *Weekly Standard,* March 4, 1996.
19. McGlowan, Innis interview.
20. Thernstrom, *No Excuses,* 189.
21. Ibid., 199.

22. Angela McGlowan interview with Ohio Secretary of State Ken Blackwell.
23. La Shawn Barber, "Courting Black Vote a Bad Idea," *Washington Times*, January 11, 2004.
24. "The Widening Racial Scoring Gap on the SAT College Admissions Test," *The Journal of Blacks in Higher Education*, Autumn 2005, www.jbhe.com/features/49_college_admissions-test.html.
25. John Tierney, "Let Your People Stay," *New York Times*, February 21, 2006.
26. Ibid.
27. Glenn Thrush, "Clinton Raps Vouchers," *Newsday*, February 22, 2006. www.newsday.com/news/nationworld/nation/ny-ushill224636775feb22,0,1447657.story.
28. Ibid.
29. *USA Today*, "Teachers Give Public Schools a Revealing Report Card," October 4, 2004. www.usatoday.com/news/opinion/editorials/2004-10-04-our-view_x.htm.
30. John Stossel, "Stupid in America."
31. Paul Magnusson, "The Split Over School Vouchers," *BusinessWeek*, October 13, 2003.
32. Angela McGlowan, interview with Bill O'Reilly.
33. Angela McGlowan, interview with David Banks.
34. Ibid.
35. Jeanne Allen and Anna Varghese Marcucio, *Charter School Laws Across the States*, Center for Education Reform, Washington, D.C., 2004.
36. Michael A. Fletcher, "GOP Plans More Outreach to Blacks, Mehlman Says," *Washington Post*, August 7, 2005, A05.
37. John Tierney, "Let Your People Stay."
38. Thomas Sowell, *Black Rednecks and White Liberals* (Encounter Books, 2005), 204.
39. Ibid.
40. Jia-Rui Chong, "Morphing Outrage Into Idea."
41. Karen Hill, "No Academic Abyss: Decatur Schools Try to Close Racial Gap in Achievement," *The Atlanta Journal-Constitution*, November 13, 2005, 1E.
42. Angela McGlowan, interview with John McWhorter.
43. McGlowan, O'Reilly interview.
44. Abigail and Stephan Thernstrom, *The San Diego Union-Tribune*, November 13, 2005, G-5.

Chapter Four
1. U.S. Senator Hillary Clinton, Press Release, July 19, 2006. clinton.senate.gov/news/statements/details.cfm?id=258916.
2. S.450 "Count Every Vote Act of 2005": Title VII—Civic Participation by Ex-Offenders SEC. 701. Voting Rights of Individuals Convicted of Criminal Offenses.
3. www.aclu.org/images/asset_upload_file825_25663.pdf.
4. S.450 "Count Every Vote Act of 2005": Title VII—Civic Participation by Ex-Offenders SEC. 701. Voting Rights of Individuals Convicted of Criminal Offenses.
5. www.bop.gov/news/quick.jsp.
6. George F. Will, "Give Ballots to Felons?" *Newsweek*, March 14, 2005, 64.
7. www.bop.gov/news/quick.jsp.
8. "Felons and Democratic Politicking," *Washington Times*, March 8, 2005, A18.
9. "Extending Democracy to Ex-Offenders," *New York Times*, June 22, 2005.

10. Will, "Give Ballots to Felons?" www.msnbc.msn.com/id/7102435/site/newsweek/
11. Malia Rulon, "Momentum for Felony Voting."
12. U.S. Department of Justice,
    www.ojp.usdoj.gov/bjs/pub/pdf/cvus/current/cv0442.pdf.
13. As quoted in Doug Bandow, "Private Prejudice, Private Remedy," CATO
    Institute, www.cato.org/research/articles/bandow-reader.html.
14. Bill Cosby, "Pound Cake Speech," Address at the NAACP's Gala to
    Commemorate the 50th Anniversary of *Brown v. Board of Education*, May 17,
    2004, www.americanrhetoric.com/speeches/billcosbypoundcakespeech.htm.
15. Angela McGlowan interview with Bill Kristol.
16. As the National Fatherhood Initiative notes, even after controlling for income,
    youths in father-absent households still had significantly higher odds of incar-
    ceration than those in mother-father families. Youths who never had a father in
    the household experienced the highest odds. See Cynthia C. Harper and Sara S.
    McLanahan, "Father Absence and Youth Incarceration," *Journal of Research on
    Adolescence* 14 (2004): 369–397.
17. Angela McGlowan interview with Judge Joe Brown.
18. www.wsws.org/articles/2000/nov2000/vote-n08.shtml.
19. Larry Elder, *The Ten Things You Can't Say in America* (St. Martin's Press, 2000), 2.
20. www.aclu.org/drugpolicy/sentencing/10724leg20020404.html.
21. Stephanie Hausner "Bill Seeks to Cut Disparity in Cocaine Case Sentences," *The
    Washington Times* July 26, 2006.
22. www.aclu.org/drugpolicy/sentencing/10724leg20020404.html.
23. John J. DiIulio Jr., "My Black Crime Problem, and Ours," *City Journal*, Spring
    1996. For a conservative perspective on the failure of drug policies, see Joel
    Miller, *Bad Trip: How the War Against Drugs is Destroying America* (Nelson
    Current, 2004).
24. Congressman John Conyers, Jr., "Conyers Commends Biden on Introduction of
    the 'Cocaine Penalty Reform Act of 2002,'" Press Release, May 22, 2002.
25. www.cjpf.org/IACHR_CharlesRangel.pdf.
26. President Ronald Reagan, "Remarks on Signing the Anti-Drug Act of 1986,"
    October 27, 1986, presidential papers. Available at:
    www.reagan.utexas.edu/archives/speeches/1986/102786c.htm.
27. Angela McGlowan interview with John McWhorter.
28. Angela McGlowan interview with David Banks.
29. Kevin Merida, "Cos and Effect," *Washington Post*, February 20, 2005, D01.
30. Tracy Hunter, "To Today's Black Leaders Part I: You're Misleading My People,"
    Faces & Voices 5: An Anthology of Verse and Prose, Howard University,
    2000-2001. www.howard.edu/library/FacesVoices5/HunterT_Today's.htm.
31. www.cnn.com/2005/LAW/12/13/williams.execution/index.html.
32. *Washington Post*/ABC Poll June 2006.
33. Ibid.
34. Ibid.
35. www.ojp.usdoj.gov/bjs/homicide/race.htm.
36. McGlowan, Brown interview.
37. "XZIBIT Understands Black Crime," WENN Entertainment News Wire Service,
    September 16, 2006.
38. Orlando Patterson, "A Poverty of the Mind," *New York Times*, March 26, 2006.
39. Stanley Crouch, "Memo to Young Black Men: Please Grow Up," *New York
    Daily News*, November 20, 2006, www.nydailynews.com/front/story/
    473178p-397971c.html.
40. Angela McGlowan interview with Hallerin Hill.

41. Ibid.
42. Angela McGlowan interview with Kay Hymowitz.

Chapter Five

1. Stephen Armstrong, "'I Got Latinos to Vote . . . But They Voted Religion," *New Statesman*, November 6, 2006, 36–37.
2. Michael Lerner, *The Left Hand of God* (HarperSanFrancisco, 2006) 127–128.
3. Steven Waldman, "The Religious Left," *Slate Magazine*, April 5, 2006.
4. Angela McGlowan interview with John Gibson.
5. "Church Leaders Look for Ways to Stem Hispanic Exodus," Associated Press State & Local Wire, June 9, 2006.
6. pewforum.org/publications/surveys/postelection.pdf.
7. Bob Abernathy and Kim Lawton, "Vigorous Organizing Inside Latino Churches," Religion & Ethics NewsWeekly, October 6, 2006.
8. Farai Chideya, "Some Evangelicals Losing Faith in GOP," National Public Radio (NPR) *News & Notes*, November 3, 2006.
9. Amber Nasrulla, "God's Entourage: How Private Faith is Going Public Among the African American Elite in Hollywood," *L.A. Times Magazine*, October 22, 2006, Part I, 26.
10. Angela McGlowan interview with Congressman Jesse Jackson, Jr.
11. Angela McGlowan interview with Frances Rice.
12. Angela McGlowan interview with Lloyd Williams.
13. D.F. Oliveria, "Numbers Game," *Spokesman Review*, March 30, 2006, B4.
14. Naseem Sowti, "Abortion: Just the Data," *Washington Post*, July 19, 2005, HE01.
15. www.guttmacher.org/pubs/fb_induced_abortion.html#7.
16. Randy Hall, "Abortion Causing 'Black Genocide,' Activists Say," CNSNews, February 7, 2005 www.cnsnews.com/ViewSpecialReports.asp?Page=%5CSpecialReports%5Carchive%5C200502%5CSPE20050207a.html.
17. Joe Garofoli, "Abortion Foes Seek Allies in Black Clergy," *San Francisco Chronicle*, January 15, 2006, A1.
18. Ibid.
19. Ann Coulter, *Godless* (Crown Forum, 2006), 78.
20. www.feminist.org/calendar/cal_details.asp?idSchedule=5589.
21. www.prochoicemaryland.org/takeaction/200611151.shtml
22. In 2004, Matt Drudge of the Drudge Report unleashed a media firestorm when he posted a link to a Planned Parenthood portal where women could buy t-shirts that proudly declared "I had an abortion." Jennifer Baumgardner, New York writer who designed the t-shirts, was merely part of a larger effort to "recast the anniversary of the abortion-legalizing *Roe v. Wade* Supreme Court decision as "I'm Not Sorry Day," www.ppaction.org/plannedparenthoodlam/notice-description.tcl?newsletter_id=2902061.
23. Ibid.
24. Hall, "Abortion Causing 'Black Genocide.'"
25. www.nrlc.org/news_and_views/July06/nv071106.html.
26. www.lifenews.com/nat431.html.
27. Angela McGlowan interview with Reverend Al Sharpton.
28. pewforum.org/docs/index.php?DocID=150#1.
29. Sheryl McCarthy, "Same-Sex Marriage is Surely a Civil Right," *USA Today*, August 22, 2006, 11A and Eunice Moscoco, "Most Latinos Back Gay Marriage Bans" *Atlanta Journal Constitution,* March 27, 2005.

30. Allison Samuels, "A Battle for Black Souls and Votes," *Newsweek*, November 6, 2006. www.msnbc.msn.com/id/15594718/site/newsweek/.
31. Ibid.
32. Ibid.
33. Ibid.
34. Armando Solorzano, "For Latinos, Spirituality at Core of Being," *Salt Lake Tribune*, September 7, 2006.
35. www.whitehouse.gov/government/fbci/final_report_2005.pdf
36. www.jointcenter.org/pressroom1/PressReleasesDetail.php?recordID=113
37. Michael A. Fletcher, "Few Black Churches Get Funds," *Washington Post*, September 19, 2006, A19.
38. Chideya, "Some Evangelicals Losing Faith in GOP."
39. Ibid.

Chapter Six

1. www.democrats.org/a/national/civil_rights/.
2. Angela McGlowan interview Congressman Jesse Jackson Jr.
3. Angela McGlowan interview with Niger Ennis.
4. Angela McGlowan interview with Michael Zak.
5. Angela McGlowan interview with James A. McPherson.
6. For more on the subject see: www.wayneperryman.com.
7. McGlowan, McPherson.
8. McGlowan Zak interview.
9. Ibid.
10. WorldNetDaily, "NAACP Chairman Compares GOP to Nazis," February 2, 2006, www.worldnetdaily.com/news/article.asp?ARTICLE_ID=48635.
11. Larry Elder, "The Borking of Bill Bennett," Townhall.com, October 6, 2005. www.townhall.com/opinion/columns/larryelder/2005/10/06/159562.html.
12. Rod Thomson, "Woman Tries to Persuade Fellow Blacks to Switch, Vote Republican," *Sarasota Herald-Tribune*, June 7, 2004.
13. Tony Brown, *Black Lies, White Lies* (Quill William Morrow, 1995), 235.
14. U.S. Senate, www.senate.gov/artandhistory/history/minute/The_Caning_of_Senator_Charles_Sumner.htm.
15. Allen W. Trelease, *White Terror*, xlvii.
16. Michael Zak, *Back to Basics for the Republican Party* (Signature Book Printing, 2003).
17. Eric Foner, *A Short History of Reconstruction* (Harper & Row, 1990), 146.
18. Ibid, 184.
19. William Peirce Randel, *The Ku Klux Klan: A Century of Infamy* (Chilton Book Company, 1971).
20. Trelease, 227.
21. Ibid., 228-230; *New York Times*, March 24, 1870.
22. Allen W. Trelease, *Reconstruction: The Great Experiment* (Harper & Row Publishers, 1971).
23. James McPherson, *Ordeal by Fire: The Civil War and Reconstruction* (Knopf, 1982), 467.
24. McGlowan, Zak interview.
25. McPherson, *Ordeal by Fire*, 498.
26. Michael Zak, *Back to Basics for the Republican Party* (Signature Book Printing, 2003), 100.
27. Ibid., 99.

28. Trelease, *Reconstruction*, 162.
29. Ibid.
30. *Raleigh Sentinel*, May 27, 1870.
31. Randel, *The Ku Klux Klan*, 82.
32. Trelease, *White Terror*, 197–200.
33. Ibid., 204.
34. Ibid., 207.
35. Ibid.
36. Article about the *Raleigh Sentinel*, April 29, November 2, 1869.
37. William Peirce Randel, *The Ku Klux Klan*, 134.
38. Harry A. Ploski, Otto J. Lindenmeyer, and Ernest Kaiser, editors, *Reference Library of Black America: Book I* (Bellwether Publishing Company, Inc., 1971), 34.
39. Randel, *The Ku Klux Klan*, 134.
40. Trelease, *White Terror*, 197.
41. McPherson, *Ordeal by Fire*, 544.
42. *Washington Post*, www.washingtonpost.com/wp-dyn/politics/elections/2000/states/la/.
43. Lewis L. Gould, *Grand Old Party: A History of Republicans* (Random House, 2003), 48; see also Zak, *Back to Basics*, 104.
44. Ibid.
45. Michael Zak, *Back to Basics*, 113.
46. David Herbert Donald, *Charles Sumner* (Da Capo Press, 1996).
47. Wayne Perryman, *Unfounded Loyalty* (Pneuma Life Publishing, 2003).

Chapter Seven
1. Nicholas Lehmann, "On the Way with L.B.J," *New York Times*, July 21, 1991.
2. Former Ku Klux Klan member Senator Robert Byrd, President Pro Tempore-elect Speaking to Fox Cable News in 2001.
3. Angela McGlowan interview with John McWhorter.
4. Angela McGlowan interview with Michael Zak.
5. Angela McGlowan interview with James McPherson.
6. Richard Wormser, *The Rise and Fall of Jim Crow* (St. Martin's Press, 2003), 118–119.
7. Ibid.
8. Ibid.
9. Ibid, 120.
10. Ibid, 121.
11. McGlowan, McPherson interview.
12. W. E. B. duBois, "President Harding and Social Equality," 1921, see also www.teachingamericanhistory.org/library/index.asp?document=1129.
13. www.hooverassociation.org/republicanconvention.htm.
14. McGlowan, McPherson interview.
15. Jim Powell, "Why Did FDR'S New Deal Harm Blacks?" CATO Institute, December 3, 2003, www.cato.org/pub_display.php?pub_id=3329; Also see Jim Powell, *FDR'S Folly* (Crown Forum, 2003).
16. Angela McGlowan interview with Reverend Al Sharpton.
17. Nick Bryant, *The Bystander* (Basic Books, 2006), 469.
18. Robert A. Caro, *Master of the Senate: The Years of Lyndon Johnson* (Alfred A. Knopf, 2002), xv.
19. Robert Parker, *Capitol Hill in Black and White* (Dodd Mead, 1986), v, vi, 16, 23.
20. Ibid.

21. Michelle Malkin, "Democratic Sen. Robert Byrd, Ex-Klansman," *Capitalism Magazine*, March 8, 2001.
22. Eric Pianin, "A Senator's Shame," *Washington Post*, June 19, 2005, A01.
23. www.senate.gov/artandhistory/history/minute/Civil_Rights_ Filibuster_Ended.htm. "U.S. Senate, June 10, 1964: Civil Rights Filibuster Ended."
24. Malkin, "Democratic Sen. Robert Byrd, Ex-Klansman," www.capmag.com/article.asp?ID=383.
25. The Dirksen Center, "E. Dirksen Notebook, n.d.": www.congresslink.org/print_basics_histmats-civilrights64_doc3.htm.
26. Robert Mann, *The Walls of Jericho*, 395.
27. Angela McGlowan interview with Frances Rice.
28. Wynton C. Hall, *The Right Words: Great Republican Speeches That Shaped History* (Wiley, 2007).
29. McGlowan, McPherson interview.
30. Caro, *Master of the Senate*.
31. Ibid.
32. www.jewishworldreview.com/cols/coulter121902.asp.
33. Mike Allen, "RNC Chief to Say It Was 'Wrong' to Exploit Racial Conflict," *Washington Post*, July 14, 2005, A04.
34. Angela McGlowan interview with Secretary Alphonso Jackson.
35. Ibid.
36. Jon Ward, "Democrats Hit for Lack of Black Candidates," *Washington Times*, October 6, 2006.

Chapter Eight
1. today.reuters.com/news/articlenews.aspx?type=domesticNews&storyid= 2006-12-06T202410Z_01_N06412806_RTRUKOC_0_US-USA-HURRICANESWASTE.xml&src=rss&rpc=22.
2. www.newsmax.com/archives/ic/2005/9/26/121533.shtml.
3. www.foxnews.com/story/0,2933,172276,00.html.
4. David Asman interview with John Barry, FOX News, October 13, 2005.
5. Angela McGlowan interview with John McWhorter.
6. www.usatoday.com/news/nation/2005-09-09-katrinacharities_x.htm.
7. www.msnbc.msn.com/id/10370145/.
8. Ibid.
9. Angela McGlowan interview with Secretary Alphonso Jackson.
10. Angela McGlowan interview with Secretary of State Ken Blackwell.
11. Angela McGlowan interview with Reverend Al Sharpton.
12. Angela McGlowan interview with Secretary Alphonso Jackson.
13. www.cnsnews.com/newnation.asp?page=nationarchive/200220/ NAT201100ie.html.
14. www.thenation.com/blogs/capitalgames?pid=1353.
15. www.theatlantic.com/doc/200109/power-genocide.
16. www.cnn.com/SPECIALS/views/y/9804/hanna.africa/.
17. Armstrong Williams, "Bush Discovers Africa," TownHall.com, July 16, 2003, www.townhall.com/columnists/ArmstrongWilliams/2003/07/16/bush_ discovers_africa.
18. Bill Salmon, "Bush Praised for Efforts to Help Blacks in Africa," *Washington Times*, July 7, 2003.
19. Ibid.
20. Ibid.

21. Jill Nelson, "We've Been Bill-Boozled," *Savoy*, May 2001.
22. Angela McGlowan interview with Frances Rice.
23. Kenneth R. Timmerman, *Shakedown: Exposing the Real Jesse Jackson* (Regnery, 2002); Jesse Lee Peterson, *Scam: How the Black Leadership Exploits America* (Nelson Current, 2003).
24. Angela McGlowan interview with Lloyd Williams.
25. Angela McGlowan interview with Bill O'Reilly.
26. J.C. Watts, Jr., *What Color is a Conservative?* (HarperCollins, 2002), 199.
27. McGlowan, Jackson interview.
28. McGlowan, McWhorter interview.
29. Steve Miller, "Mfume Calls Black Conservatives Puppets," *Washington Times*, July 13, 2004. washingtontimes.com/national/20040712-103848-4561r.htm.
30. Ibid.
31. Jeff Jacoby, "Slurs Fly from the Left," *Boston Globe*, December 28, 2005.
32. Angela McGlowan interview with Lt. Governor Michael Steele.
33. Ruben Navarrette, Jr., "Racism, Democrat-Style," *San Francisco Chronicle*, November 24, 2004, www.sfgate.com/cgi-bin/article.cgi?file=/chronicle/archive/2004/11/24/EDG029VV011.DTL.
34. "Cartoon and Calumny," *Wall Street Journal*, October 22, 2004, www.opinionjournal.com/taste/?id=110005788.
35. Angela McGlowan interview with Hallerin Hill.
36. Ibid.
37. Angela McGlowan interview with Bill O'Reilly.
38. Stanley Crouch, "To Move Up, Kids Must Stop Being Slaves to Fashion," *New York Daily News*, December 11, 2006.
39. Juan Williams, *Enough* (Crown Forum, 2006), 142–143.
40. Crouch, "To Move Up, Kids Must Stop Being Slaves to Fashion."

Chapter Nine

1. Charles Hurt, "Reid Calls Language Proposal Racist," *Washington Times*, May 19, 2006.
2. Ibid.
3. Ibid.
4. Ibid.
5. John B. Judis and Ruy Teixeira, *The Emerging Democratic Majority* (Scribner, 2002), 59.
6. Tamar Jacoby, "'Getting' Latinos," *Los Angeles Times*, November 17, 2006, A35.
7. Ibid.
8. www.census.gov/Press-Release/www/releases/archives/population/001720.html.
9. James G. Muhammad, "Not All Blacks Are Liberal," *N'DIGO*, August 5–11, 2004, pg. 6-7.
10. Stanley B. Greenberg, *The Two Americas* (Thomas Dunne Books, 2004), 123.
11. Michelle Mittelstadt, "Immigration Alone Didn't Sway Hispanics from GOP," *Houston Chronicle*, November 28, 2006, A1.
12. Darryl Fears, "Republicans Lost Ground with Latinos in Midterms," *The Washington Post*, November 18, 2006, A03.
13. "4 Hispanic Lawmakers, 4 Differing Views, 1 Point," *USA Today*, April 3, 2006, 8A.
14. Tamar Jacoby, "GOP Can't Lose Latinos," *Los Angeles Times*, November 17, 2006.
15. www.vdare.us/sailer/041209_myth.htm.
16. "2005 National Latino Survey Topline," The Latino Coalition, January 5, 2006.

17. Farai Chideya, "Some Evangelicals Losing Faith in GOP," *National Public Radio News & Notes*, November 3, 2006.
18. Elizabeth Aguilera, "Dems Won Over Latino Voters," *Denver Post*, November 28, 2006, A-01.
19. Fears, "Republicans Lost Ground."
20. Angela McGlowan interview with Edward Juarez.
21. Angela McGlowan interview with Ed Clancy.
22. www.humanevents.com/article.php?id=18399.
23. Nick Bryant, *The Bystander: John F. Kennedy and the Struggle for Black Equality* (Basic Books, 2006), 472.
24. Patrick J. Buchanan, *State of Emergency* (Thomas Dunne Books, 2006); Tom Tancredo, *In Mortal Danger* (Cumberland House Publishing, 2006); J.D. Hayworth, *Whatever It Takes* (Regnery, 2006).
25. Angela McGlowan interview with Bill Kristol.
26. Angela McGlowan interview with Frank Gomez.
27. Angela McGlowan interview with John Gibson.
28. Ben Johnson, "Who's Behind the Immigration Rallies?" FrontPageMag.com, March 29, 2006, www.frontpagemag.com/Articles/ReadArticle.asp?ID=21841.
29. Angela McGlowan interview with Robert de Posoda.
30. McGlowan, Gomez interview.
31. McGlowan, de Posada interview.
32. Edwin J. Feulner and Doug Wilson, *Getting America Right* (Crown Forum, 2006), 203.
33. Ibid.
34. Ibid.
35. Tyche Hendricks and Jill Tucker, "Influx of English Learners a Challenge for California," *San Francisco Chronicle*, November 29, 2006, A1.
36. Miguel Perez, "Need for English Divides Immigrants," *The Record*, August 13, 2006, A01.
37. Ibid.
38. John Moreno Gonzales, "English, Please," *Newsday*, July 9, 2006, A04.
39. Don Soifer, "The Importance of Learning English," *New York Sun*, September 6, 2006, 9.
40. Hendricks and Tucker, "Influx of English Learners."
41. www.washtimes.com/national/20061204-112837-6992r.htm.
42. David McGrath, "English as Official Language Insulting," *Birmingham News*, June 18, 2006, 1C.
43. Ibid.
44. www.opinionjournal.com/best/?id=110006106.
45. www.newsmax.com/archives/ic/2004/12/30/150934.shtml.
46. www.opinionjournal.com/best/?id=110006106.
47. McGlowan, de Posada interview.
48. Elaine L. Chao, "Remarks Delivered by U.S. Secretary of Labor Elaine L. Chao at the *LATINA Style* 50 Event," Washington, D.C., February 9, 2006.
49. Angela McGlowan, interview with Ed Clancy.

Chapter 10
1. Angela McGlowan, interview with Kim Gandy.
2. Jessica Valenti, "'Strident' and Proud," *Salon.com*, July 12, 2006.
3. Naomi Schaefer Riley, "'Post-Neanderthal Equality': Where is the Next Feminist Revolution?" *Wall Street Journal Online*, December 15, 2006.
4. Kay S. Hymowitz, *Marriage and Caste in America* (Ivan R. Dee, 2006), 127–128.

5. www.census.gov/Press-Release/www/releases/archives/facts_for_features_ special_editions/006232.html.

6. Michelle Locke, "Gender Gap Growing in California College Enrollment," *Associated Press State and Local Wire,* June 27, 2006.

7. www.census.gov/Press-Release/www/releases/archives/facts_for_features_ special_editions/006232.html.

8. Angela McGlowan interview with U.S. Secretary of Labor Elaine L. Chao. See also "Remarks Delivered by U.S. Secretary of Labor Elaine L. Chao at the Agnes Scott College Commencement, Decatur, Georgia," May 13, 2006.

9. Cheryl L. Reed, "Couples Adjusting as 25% of Women Outearn Husbands," *Chicago-Sun Times,* May 15, 2005.

10. Angela McGlowan interview with Robin Read.

11. McGlowan, Gandy interview.

12. Angela McGlowan interview with Bonnie Erbe.

13. Angela McGlowan interview with Kelly Anne Conway.

14. Stanley B. Greenberg, *The Two Americas* (Thomas Dunne Books, 2004), 126.

15. Daniel J. Flynn, *Why the Left Hates America* (Forum Prima, 2002), 116–117; quoted in Paul Hollander, *Anti-Americanism: Critiques at Home and Abroad, 1965-1990* (Oxford University Press, 1992), 70–71.

16. Kathryn Jean Lopez, "Women Who Make the World Worse: Q&A with Kate O'Beirne," *National Review Online,* December 29, 2005, www.nationalreview. com/interrogatory/obeirne200512290819.asp.

17. Cheryl L. Reed, "Feminism Shaken, Not Stirred," *Chicago Sun Times,* June 18, 2006, B8.

18. Caitlin Flanagan, *To Hell With All That: Loving and Loathing Our Inner Housewife* (Little, Brown and Company, 2006).

19. Angela McGlowan interview with Irene Natividad.

20. Christina Hoff Sommers, *The War Against Boys* (Simon & Schuster, 2000), 48–49.

21. www.wageproject.org/content/wage/advisors.php.

22. www.wageproject.org/content/wage/donors.php.

23. Bonnie Erbe, "There's a Way to End the Wage Gap," *The Seattle Post-Intelligencer,* August 15, 2006, B6.

24. clinton.senate.gov/issues/women/.

25. Arrah Nielsen, "Working Girl," Independent Women's Forum Issue Paper, July 15, 2005, www.iwf.org/issues/issues_detail.asp?ArticleID=785.

26. Kathryn Jean Lopez, "Women Who Make the World Worse: Q&A with Kate O'Beirne," *National Review Online.*

27. Arrah Nielsen, "Gender Wage Gap is Feminist Fiction," Independent Women's Forum Position Paper, April 15, 2005, www.iwf.org/issues/issues_detail.asp?ArticleID=749.

28. Warren Farrell, *Why Men Earn More: The Startling Truth Behind the Pay Gap* (AMACOM, 2005), 19.

29. Flanagan, *To Hell With All That: Loving and Loathing Our Inner Housewife* (Little, Brown and Company, 2006) XYZ.

30. Angela McGlowan interview with Robin Read.

31. Angela McGlowan interview with Irene Natividad.

32. Angela McGlowan interview with Robin Read.